UNCOVERING and DISCOVERING THE KEY TO SPIRITUAL GROWTH

PERSONAL PEACE, LOVE and THE SURVIVAL of the PLANET

BY

RICH KAE

This book is a work of non-fiction. Names and places have been changed to protect the privacy of all individuals. The events and situations are true.

First published by AuthorHouse 10/15/04

ISBN: 1-4184-0673-2 (e-book)
ISBN: 1-4184-0674-0 (Paperback)

Printed in the United States of America
Bloomington, Indiana

This book is printed on acid free paper.

DEDICATION

WE DEDICATE THIS BOOK

To our Children

LA DONNA, LAUREN, JOHN, LEAH AND LOWELL

to
Their spouses and significant others
To their children
And their children's children
and
To all the children of the world

CONTENTS

ACKNOWLEDGEMENTS

I acknowledge from the outset the two knowledge platforms from which this book was written. In the final analysis it is quite probable that these two platforms are but one. However, I do not wish to get too esoteric in the acknowledgements but it <u>is</u> a good place to point out that in the area of mysticism there is both the <u>experience</u> of the mystic and there is the attempt of the mystic to <u>relate</u> his/her experience in books, poetry, music etc.

Therefore, I wish to thank the great mystery of the universe for communicating to me and for leading me to others who have shared their experience through books and the arts.

I wish to acknowledge that my own experience has been enriched and confirmed by those who have for centuries attempted to share their own mystical experiences. The names of these individuals appear throughout the book.

I acknowledge and thank those who have encouraged the writing of this book, especially my Niece, Tana Hart and Terry and Edward Rosen. I also wish to acknowledge and thank those who have read the manuscript and made comments and suggestions. This list includes: Carl Peacock, Dave Kingsley, Renee D., Jim and Joy B., Kenny H., Marion, Carol McCoy, Susie, Fred W., Bob Rhine, Mike Hand, Joe Salgo, Carolyn Salgo, Janet Darr, Marion Land and Jerry.

A special thanks goes out to: Rev. O.B. Fjelstad who has been my main sounding board for many years. Also to Dr. Robert

Lookabaugh, Rev. Donald Tastad, Ronda Skinner and Fred Foley. Each read the manuscript numerous times, offered suggestions, entered into dialogue and gave encouragement. Their individual and combined contributions have been huge!

Finally, I would like to acknowledge and express my appreciation for all those who in any way, for thousands of years, have contributed to what we now call, "The Perennial Philosophy."

FORWARD

This book is about spirituality, not religion. However, we believe that what we call the **key** is at the heart of almost all religions. We seek to illustrate this fact by appealing to your intellect, emotions and spirit. In order to reach these various levels we use history, science, personal stories, myth, biography and poetry.

While we use the twelve-step programs as an example of a spiritual rather than a religious program, we are not just trying to appeal to people that are members of, or candidates for, these programs. Rather, we are trying to reach out to <u>all</u> people who are searching for, or hoping for, more meaning, purpose and serenity in life.

The title to this book emphasizes three words. We have already mentioned two of them – <u>key</u> and <u>spiritual</u>. The third word is <u>growth</u>. We believe that <u>spiritual growth </u>is the key to true success in life. However, growth alone is not the <u>key</u> that opens the lock to a <u>spiritual life.</u>

One story that you will read in the body of the book illustrates this distinction. It is the story of a successful man who lost everything due to drink. He didn't start drinking until he was thirty-five years old but within a few years he ended up in an asylum because, when he drank, he became very violent.

After he left the asylum he started going to A.A. He temporarily met with success but later ended up back in the asylum. The explanation given in the *BIG BOOK OF ALCOHOLICS ANONYMOUS* says, "All went well for a time, but he failed to enlarge his spiritual life." People who attend twelve-step programs often express this thought by saying, "If I don't continue to grow spiritually, I will soon be dead, in jail, or insane."

We believe candidates for twelve-step programs as well as prison and asylums, are only different from the mass of society in the degree of their dis-ease. We believe that <u>spiritual</u> <u>growth</u> is the purpose of life and that there is a <u>key</u> that opens the lock to this <u>spiritual growth</u>. Read on with an open mind and you are sure to discover THE KEY TO THIS IMPORTANT JOURNEY.

Rich Kae January 2004

INTRODUCTION

The stuff of this book is the result of pursuing a question. In a perverse way there have been times when I felt that the question was following me. During these times the picture of Robert Redford and Paul Newman often comes into my mind. The picture comes from the movie, "Butch Cassidy and the Sundance Kid." The question asked throughout the movie concerning the men following them was, "Who are these guys?" The question that pursues me is this: "What was that experience and what does it mean?" The experience I refer to will be discussed in detail later.

Some have suggested that the material in this book would have been better served had I started with the details of this experience. But I have not done so. Rather, I have danced around it, attempting to build a context in which the experience might be shared. I have chosen to do this because I believe that pursuing the questions raised by my experience are far more important for the reader than my personal experience. However, concerning this experience I will not keep you completely in the dark. It was a transformation, a breakthrough (maybe psychological, spiritual, or both). In the future I will often refer to this breakthrough as my healing.

This book is a product of intuition, trial and error, living, synchronicity, and casual reading. To some degree it is the product of premeditated research. This research, although planned, has always been fragmented and never systematic. The research was motivated by a desire to fill in a gap or to answer a question that had arisen in the course of my unsystematic or intuitive quest. However, I have been surprised to find that some of the ideas that I have written about have been the focus of scholars for many years. Some of these concepts have slowly evolved for more than a century.

I will illustrate this with one recent and I believe striking example. I have a daughter-in-law, although already in her forties, just recently graduated from college. She read the pre-publication manuscript of this book. Her reaction was positive and her criticism was constructive.

Near the end of our discussion she handed me a couple of books that she thought might interest me. One, *THE WEB OF LIFE* by physicist Fritjof Capra, was obviously a book with which she had spent considerable time. It was underlined with several different colors of ink, many words were circled, and there were notations in the margin. Her comment to me concerning this book was, "The Author seems to have the same concern about modern-fragmented thinking as you do." I was pleased that she was able to glean this information from my manuscript.

Capra's book is an overview of a revolution that he says has taken place in both physics and biology in the last one hundred years. In order to stress its importance he states that it is of greater importance than the Copernican revolution (the revolution that followed the discovery that the earth revolves around the sun). The Author says that this revolution in science has significant implications for society, one that has not yet impacted most people or their politicians. He goes on to say that this is a tragedy and if our politicians do not adopt and apply this new paradigm to society's ills, our planet will continue to be in big trouble.

My appreciation for Capra's book was immediate and can be illustrated by my reaction to his discussion about a school of thought called "Deep Ecology." "Deep Ecology" was founded in the early 1970's by the Norwegian Philosopher, Arne Naess. I consider the following quote by Arne Naess to be an excellent summary of much of what I am trying to convey in this book.

"Shallow ecology is anthropocentric or human-centered. It views humans as above or outside of nature, as the source of all value, and ascribes only instrumental or 'use' value to nature. Deep ecology does not separate humans—or anything else—from the natural environment. It sees the world not as a collection of isolated objects but as a network of phenomena fundamentally interconnected and interdependent. Deep ecology recognizes the intrinsic value of all living beings and views humans as just one particular strand in the web of life."

"Ultimately, deep ecological awareness is spiritual or religious awareness. When the concept of the human spirit is understood as the mode of consciousness in which the individual feels a sense of belonging, of connectedness, to the cosmos as a whole, it becomes clear that ecological awareness is spiritual in its deepest essence. It is, therefore, not surprising that the emerging new vision of reality based on deep ecological awareness is consistent with the so-called perennial philosophy of spiritual traditions, whether we talk about the spirituality of Christian mystics, of Buddhists, or of the philosophy and cosmology underlying the Native American traditions."

The reference to the traditions of the American Indian brings me to another issue that I want to mention at the outset. Years ago when the buffalo still freely roamed the range it was the practice of the Indian tribes to gather around their elders. The tribe would listen to its' elders because the younger people knew that the elders had lived many snows and had gained much wisdom and consequently they could take the LONG VIEW.

Both in my casual reading and my times of serious research, I started to realize that I was gravitating toward books written by prominent twentieth-century scholars and personalities, often written at the end of their lives. These books were not necessarily their breakthrough works, but they were the ones in which they took the LONG VIEW. Most of the people I studied were well versed in the written history of Western society. Thus, it was their perspective, not just their age, that enabled them to take this view.

Even though the Plains Indians did not have a written history, they did have an oral tradition; and it seems clear that it was in the elder years that Indians grew in appreciation for the teachings of their traditions and they were the ones who could make these stories and traditions come alive. The stories came alive not just because the storytellers themselves had lived many snows but because they had learned to appreciate the generations of storytellers before them. Because of this, they too could take the LONG VIEW. Their experiences of life itself had <u>informed</u> the stories (their traditions). This being <u>informed</u> (not just by life, but by the mystery) is the stuff of deep ecology, which enables one to take the LONG VIEW. For ultimately deep ecology is not a philosophy but as Capra suggests, it is an experience.

Although I was quite young, I remember where I was and how I felt the day that the Japanese bombed Pearl Harbor (December 7, 1941). I have now lived long enough to see the day that some are calling "The Second Pearl Harbor." I would have had ample time to change the text of the book to reflect these events but decided not to as I did not want to give the idea that anything that was said here was in any way a knee-jerk reaction. The events of September 11, 2001, however, have underlined for me two things: first, that the solution to mankind's dilemma that we point to in this book is valid, and second, only by taking the long view will we be able to bring it to fruition. Things take time (especially on the global level) and this one may take generations if not centuries, but we must become awake enough to work at it. This need not discourage you because on the personal level we can enjoy the fruits of this truth now, and with a long view you can share in a hopeful vision of the future.

Before we begin with the subject (practical spirituality), we need to take care of a few housekeeping matters. The author of this book is Rich Kae. For reasons that will become clear, Rich Kae is a pseudonym. Further, Rich Kae is not one person but two. Rich and Kae are husband and wife. The majority of the writing was done by Rich but just as there would be no book without what I call "my healing experience," likewise there would be no book without Kae's help, encouragement, and poetry. Because this is the case, sometimes I (Rich) feel comfortable using the pronoun we and at other times, the pronoun I. Often, the use of the pronoun <u>we</u> will be an attempt to include <u>you</u> the reader.

In this book I use terminology that needs some explanation. Throughout the book, I talk about two differing selves. One is the small self that is closely tied to the twin masters, heredity and environment. The other is the larger self, an "ideal self," a self that has not been conditioned by heredity and environment. I say "ideal self" because, for most of us, it is only a glimmer, a goal, and a direction toward our evolutionary future. Even so I believe that this "ideal self" is capable of considerable realization in the present; it is this realization of SELF in the present that makes spirituality practical.

Our notion of the ego-self, being tied to heredity and environment (genetics and culture), may well be modified over the next twenty-five years due to the rapid progress being made in genetics. This progress is already evident in the human genome projects that will answer many questions regarding diseases, mental disorders, and the human personality. Some questions posed will be addressed such as these: Are mental disorders cultural or genetic? Is personality a product of genetics or culture or is it a blend of both? These and the answers to other such questions could become clear in the 21st century.

This book is a distillation of a lifetime of self-analysis and reflection. Sometimes this has demanded the pursuit of further study. Sometimes it has demanded the pursuit of a knowledge that comes not from books but only from the INNER SILENCE.

This book is divided into five sections. The first includes post-healing glimpses of my SELF-understanding. The second section includes history that will help you take the long view and give you an appreciation for how much the planet yearns for an understanding of deep ecology. This background material will help you as an individual recognize the symptoms of "shallow ecology" – reasons why you sometimes feel disconnected; yes, even discontent.

The third is a study of the pursuit of SELF in the light of one of Carl Jung's archetypes (the inner hero). The discovery of the inner hero (the Divinity Within) is truly the key to the experience of what Arne Naess calls "deep ecology." The fourth lays out the basics of practical spirituality. In this section we present some of the actual practices and attitudes that, if practiced, can lead to a life of freedom, love (connectedness), and joy – to a life we never thought possible. The fifth is a vision of the future—a vision that can only be appreciated by those who have been thrust into the realm (experience) of DEEP ECOLOGY. This section illustrates how our individual experience of peace, freedom and joy can become the building blocks of a more peaceful and connected planet. The Appendix adds detail and insight not covered in the body of the book. The index for the Appendix is found at the beginning of the appendix, on page 349.

GLIMPSES OF GOLD

SECTION I

INTRODUCTION

GLIMPSES OF GOLD

"Now and then we may be granted a glimpse of that ultimate reality which is God's kingdom." (*TWELVE STEPS AND TWELVE TRADITIONS,* page 98)

In the first chapter of this section we define the problem. As we see it the problem is specific but far-reaching. After defining the problem we state our thesis. Stating the thesis will give you an overview of our purpose and will help you stay on target as you read the text. Following the thesis, the subsequent chapters of this section are stories that have been written at various times over the past fifteen years. These stories are intended to give one a hint, a glimpse of the solution. They were written with a reader in mind. What reader? I had no idea. Today, that reader is <u>you</u> and I believe in this life there are no coincidences. You are the reader and if you are willing to devote a modest amount of time, thought and action to the message of this book, your efforts will be rewarded.

In these stories I am sharing with you a phenomena. I am virtually shouting with joy, "See how I see things <u>now</u>!" What I am saying is that there has been a change in me, a change so dramatic and so beautiful I can hardly believe it.

3

In one sense I am asking you to rejoice with me, to be glad for my good fortune. I now see with new eyes and hear with new ears. In another sense I am asking you to recognize (with new clarity) your own INNER REALITY, an INNER REALITY that has the potential to inform you about another dimension of life. You may or may not have had a clear experience of this dimension (realm). If you haven't, I'm not asking you to accept that there is such a reality. I simply ask you to read on with a mind open to the possibility of such an experience. However, I do hope that these stories in some way will either put you in touch with your own INNER REALITY or remind you of times when you were in touch.

If you are anything like I was before my breakthrough, it is quite possible that you have no idea what I am talking about. On the other hand you may be one of those who has had frequent glimpses of this INNER REALITY but does not know how to sustain the contact. Regardless of where you stand, these stories should remind you of something within yourself that can serve as a foundation from which you will grow.

For example, when Kae read these stories she was reminded of childhood experiences, especially the times when she would go fishing with her dad. She wouldn't fish; she would just sit or lie in the sun, recognizing a wonderfully warm feeling exuding from within, a feeling she says, seemed to connect her to the very core of her being. She now feels, except for one short period in her adult life, she has always been more or less in touch with this INNER ESSENCE.

I feel in this regard, Kae and those with similar experiences are a minority. Sadly, it seems that most of us are essentially blocked off from our INNER REALITY. This is sad because this inner world can inform our lives about the true purpose and meaning of existence as well as our conscience. Newspaper headlines in these early days of the new millennium repeatedly speak to us about leaders in business, government, and the church, who have brought shame to themselves and to those they represent. I believe that it is fair to say these are individuals who have lost touch with that which informs both life and conscience.

In the Introduction, a reference was made to the tragedy of our politicians not being influenced by the new holistic paradigm of physics and biology. I think if the author of these words had written them in 2003 rather than 1996, he would have used a broader term like leaders rather than politicians. At this point it may be proper to remind ourselves of the often-used phrase, "the people usually get the leaders they deserve."

Chapter 1

THE PROBLEM

The practical spirituality I will spell out in the ensuing pages is a solution that has worked for me for over thirty years. I started to discover this solution in the midst of the most devastating crisis of my life. It might even be more appropriate to say that the solution found me, rather than me finding it. Some, more religious than I, have called such a phenomena "being surprised by Grace."

Be it Grace, peak experience, or dumb luck, there would be no book if it had not been for this experience and what was to follow. This portion of my life will be specifically detailed in the third section, "The Vision Quest Hero." First, I invite you to explore with me the nature of the problem that faces civilization. After that we will move in the direction of the solution or prescription. I am confident if this prescription is pursued, it will enable you to experience a life filled with peace, meaning and purpose.

During a rewrite of this book, a friend of mine encouraged me to read *THE EVOLVING SELF* by Mihaly Csikszentmihalyi. (Pronounced - Chick-sent-mahi). The author is a Professor of Research Psychology at the University of Chicago and has written ten books including *FLOW: THE PSYCHOLOGY OF OPTIMAL EXPERIENCE*. "*FLOW*" caught the public's attention when it was mentioned on the 1993 Super Bowl broadcast as the book that had inspired Jimmy Johnson, Coach of the Dallas Cowboys. When Michael Jordan and other athletes talk about being in the zone, they are describing an aspect of what Csikszentmihalyi calls, "flow."

THE EVOLVING SELF is a sequel to *FLOW*. The author says, these books are a result of twenty-five years of systematic research on happiness. In *THE EVOLVING SELF* he makes a strong case for the idea that the present day self-concept is inadequate for the coming millennium. He says it is so inadequate that our very survival and the survival of our environment may depend on the development of a more viable concept of self. With anguish he says that to wait for evolution by itself to produce such a self-concept could take a very long time—maybe too long for our species to survive. "Time," he says, "seems short, and perhaps there are ways to accelerate this process. Selflessness, conformity, and even development of unique individuality are no longer sufficient to give life meaningful purpose at a time when we are capable of destroying ourselves and our environment with increasing ease."

I, too, have spent many years exploring the realm of "SELF." Although I studied psychology, did some clinical work, and had a brief counseling practice, I have not attempted to stay current in the field of psychology. My research, as you will see, has been along different lines. However, I was literally amazed at how much my own thinking was detailed in Csikszentmihalyi's book. I was also re-energized by the conviction that my insights, experience and observations are not only valid, but may constitute a significant contribution to the development of a self-concept appropriate for the third millennium.

In his book, *CREATIVITY*, Csikszentmihalyi, with the assistance of his graduate students, seemingly is seeking to find the key that will unlock the door to this new template for humanity. He interviewed more than ninety of the most successful people of our day. Those interviews included people like Linus Pauling (the recipient of two Nobel Prizes—one for physics and one for peace); Dr. Salk, who discovered the Polio Vaccine; Ed Asner of television fame; Senator Eugene McCarthy; Pianist Oscar Peterson; Sitar player and composer Ravi Shankar, and Dr. Benjamin Spock, the noted baby doctor.

According to Csikszentmihalyi, each of these individuals exhibited their own brand of "flow." However, according to Csikszentmihalyi, Dr. Spock is the only one who had anything like a spiritual conversion.

Most, if not all, of the people who Csikszentmihalyi interviewed, exhibited qualities that we would deem admirable. However, one must ask if these qualities form the template upon which a viable self-concept should be built. My answer in part is "yes" and in total, "no!" I say no because there is something lacking, and I think Csikszentmihalyi comes close to identifying this when he says that Dr. Spock was one of the few who spoke of spirituality and explains that even "his understanding of spirituality is a far cry from that of institutionalized religions." He quotes from Dr. Spock's book:

"Spirituality, unfortunately, is not a stylish word. It's not a word that gets used, that's because we're such an unspiritual country that we think of it as somewhat corny to talk about spirituality. 'What is that?' people say. Spirituality, to me, means the non-material things. I don't want to give the idea that it's something mystical; I want it to apply to ordinary people's lives; things like love, helpfulness, tolerance, and enjoyment of the arts, or even creativity in the arts. I think that creativity in the arts is very special. It takes a high degree and a high type of spirituality to want to express things in terms of literature or poetry, plays, architecture, gardens, creating beauty any way. And if you don't create beauty, at least it's good to appreciate beauty and get some enjoyment and inspiration out of it. So it's just things that aren't totally materialistic. And that would include religion."

I appreciate Dr. Spock's definition, but I would take umbrage with the statement, "I don't want to give the idea that it's something mystical;" because it is my contention that what underlies the mystical experience is precisely what is missing in the ordinary lives of people. It is the awareness of mystery that is missing, a mystery that is missing in love, in the enjoyment of the arts, gardening, and religion.

9

I also have selected some 20th century figures (most are deceased) who I believe manifested the human attributes that must be our model as we forge into the new millennium. Most of these people also have not associated themselves with institutional religion, but they did retain a wonderful sense of mystery. It is my belief that for most mystics, there is little difference between being a mystic and being in touch with love and having awe for the mystery of life.

One of these 20th century figures who I point to in this regard is the great scientist, Albert Einstein. In 1932 he delivered an address to the German League of Human Rights called "MY CREDO." This short speech concluded with the following paragraph:

"The most beautiful and deepest experience a man can have is the sense of the mysterious. It is the underlying principle of religion as well as all serious endeavors in art and science. He who never had this experience seems to me, if not dead, then at least blind. To sense that behind anything that can be experienced, there is something that our mind cannot grasp and whose beauty and sublimity reaches us only indirectly and as a feeble reflection; this is religiousness. In this sense I am religious. To me it suffices to wonder at these secrets and to attempt humbly to grasp a mere image of the lofty structure of all that there is."

You can see in these words, along with his uncanny intuition and humanitarian concerns, why some have called him a mystic. In the best sense of the word, that is exactly what he was. We will look at others who reflect similar attitudes that I believe can help us form our vision of mankind in the next millennium. Among others, we will look at the mythologist Joseph Campbell, psychotherapist Carl Gustaf Jung, writer-philosopher Aldus Huxley, and priest mystic and scientist Teilhard de Chardin.

Huxley, who died in 1963, wrote and published his novel, *ISLAND*, shortly before his death. In the flyleaf of *ISLAND*, the following quote from Aristotle appears: "In framing an ideal we may assume what we wish but should avoid impossibilities." In writing his book, Huxley adhered to the premise of this quote producing ideas in this novel that are not just fantasy, but possibilities.

The story is about an island community in Southeast Asia that had cut itself off from modern society for more than two hundred years carefully letting in only that which they felt would be beneficial. The novel is, to be sure, an indictment of the human condition and much of modern culture. It is, in part, Huxley's answer to what the man of the third millennium must be in order to survive. Huxley's answer in brief was that humankind must subscribe to the perennial philosophy and move towards expanded consciousness. He saw it as the bedrock of truth and the way toward the expansion of human consciousness— the path to this truth. For those who are not familiar with the concept "perennial philosophy," we will spend some time with this later.

I echo Aldus Huxley's insights and prescription as the answer to humankind's problems, the key that will enable us to participate in our own successful evolution into the third millennium and beyond. I regard Huxley as one of the most skillful and successful analysts of the twentieth century. What follows is my attempt to endorse this idea and to explain it. I also will show why I embrace it and why I believe in the end it must be embraced, if not by all, at least by a substantial minority.

In addition, we will look at modern day examples like Buckminister Fuller, who, though quite critical of contemporary organized religion, was open about the transformational experience that changed his entire outlook on life, the world, and his place in it. I see in these transformational experiences, whether ancient or modern, a template for the new self-concept that Csikszentmihalyi cites as needed for the third millennium. In the transformation, we discover the truth about humanity that lies beyond genetics and culture.

Above I used the phrase "transformational experience." Let me be clear from the beginning that this can refer to a gentle, slow displacement of old ideas and conditioning, as well as to a more immediate or sudden displacement. When I use the term transformation, whether the experience is slow or sudden it connotes an expansion of the self toward the SELF.

THE THESIS

Nature (including mankind) is endowed with an INNER REALITY. When we (as individuals or collectively) are cut off from this reality, we become empty, anxious, angry, fearful and unhappy. Emptiness, anxiety, anger and fear can and often do lead to violence. When we are in touch with this INNER REALITY, this reality is able to <u>inform</u> us as to the true meaning of life; and thus, we become less empty, less anxious, less angry, less fearful and less violent. This we believe to be true both for society and the individuals who are its members.

This reality, although hidden, can be accessed. In order to be accessed, it usually takes techniques, desire, discipline, and attention.

The next thing to consider is that the nature of this reality cannot be taught; it can only be experienced. Therefore, we will not attempt to define it. We will only share with you our experience, strength, and hope. We will point to what we feel is the way to this INNER REALITY. We will be content to encourage you to seek this reality and let it <u>inform</u> you concerning its nature and if necessary (for you), its name.

Finally, the degree to which we become less empty, less anxious, less angry, less fearful, and less violent will be the degree to which we access the INNER REALITY. This then, is the key to mankind's survival.

(Note) I suggest that each time you pick up this book you may find it helpful to reread this thesis.

Chapter 2

WHAT IS MAN?

When I was about twelve years old, my father, who worked for the federal government, was transferred from Custer, a small town in eastern Montana, to Coeur d' Alene, Idaho. No one in my family had ever been to Coeur d' Alene, but friends who had visited there, told us that it was very nice. We had no idea what to expect, except by looking at a map we knew that the town was situated on the shore of a large lake. I lived in the dry prairie and plains area of Montana most of my life and just visiting a wilderness lake was all but a dream. Now I was going to live near one!

Coming from the east you arrive at the edge of Coeur d' Alene Lake about thirteen miles before you reach the actual city. In those days the highway coming into town was up on the hills overlooking the lake. As the narrow road twisted and turned through the trees we would, from time to time, get a brief glimpse of the Lake. Every member of our family was filled with excitement and anticipation; and each time we caught a glimpse of the lake, we would call out, "There it is!" For many minutes the car was filled with oohs and ahs!

At one point we came to a turnout on the narrow road, and my father stopped so we could all have an extended look at the beautiful lake. We got out of the car; and even though we still couldn't see

13

much of the lake, we were thrilled with this limited view. We started to realize that the lake was quite large and was surrounded by hills lush with pine trees. The water was a beautiful blue, and there were boats—even sailboats! We got back in the car and to this day I remember saying, "Man, I had no idea there was any place in this world so beautiful!"

We were in for a greater surprise as the scenery just kept getting better and better. Anticipation grew as we came down out of the hills and started traveling along the lakeshore itself. When we reached the town we could see the main basin of the lake. We later learned that it was thirty-three miles long with many coves and bays. We also learned that besides Coeur d' Alene, there were other small communities nestled along its shores.

It was the first of July when we moved there. The rest of the summer I spent every minute possible at the city park that is located on the lakeshore. The park has a magnificent sandy beach, which provided an opportunity for great swimming and sunbathing! By late August, I was finally beginning to accept reality—that this wasn't a dream, this was my home. I felt like the luckiest kid alive!

This experience from my childhood is not unlike discovering your true SELF. Having spent all of my life in the arid prairies of Montana, I had no idea how beautiful a mountain lake in northern Idaho could be. Likewise, many of us who have lived much of our lives substantially cut off from our true nature have no idea what our true nature is like, how truly beautiful and serene it is. On a day when there is no breeze, Coeur d' Alene Lake can be as smooth as glass and absolutely serene. Our true nature is also like that.

When we first start down the path of discovery, we catch only glimpses of our true nature, like a glimpse of lake through the trees. As we continue, the glimpses become larger and more frequent. In time, we will find ourselves with a fairly clear sense of this higher SELF. At some point, maybe soon, maybe later, the time will come when we will start to feel at home with our true nature and will likely say, "I had no idea; I had no idea how beautiful I am!"

I lived in Coeur d' Alene for ten years and have been back many times since. I still call Coeur d' Alene my home, but many coves and bays I have yet to explore. Likewise, I continue to explore my true nature below the surface and beyond the ego; and in so doing, I realize that I have just begun the journey! Now I am aware that indeed, "still water runs deep."

Just as that trip years ago on that narrow road in the hills high above Coeur d' Alene Lake afforded me glimpses of a place that I would later call home, so I hope this book will somehow encourage you to seek glimpses of your true SELF.

****

I was seventeen years old, a Coeur d' Alene high school student with a date for the prom. I had a part-time job, played in the band and orchestra, participated in some sports, and excelled in public speaking. However, I wouldn't be going to the prom, and I wasn't sure I would ever do any of those other things again. For three weeks I had been lying in bed with a very serious strep throat infection, and I wasn't getting any better.

My mother was a nurse working in a doctor's office, but she couldn't do much for me other than watch me get worse. My father was a Christian Scientist so he believed that sickness is not real, that it is the product of human error or wrong thinking. Up until the time of this illness I too had chosen to practice Christian Science. I had experienced physical crisis before. I thought I lived through it with the help of Christian Science. I had been asthmatic all my life and over the years had experienced many serious asthma attacks. In the midst of those attacks I would repeat to myself, repeatedly, the Scientific Statement of Being written by Mary Baker Eddy, the founder of Christian Science. It reads as follows:

SCIENTIFIC STATEMENT OF BEING—There is no life, truth, intelligence, nor substance in matter. All is infinite manifestation, for God is All-in-all. Spirit is immortal Truth; matter is mortal error. Spirit is the real and eternal; matter is the unreal and temporal. Spirit is God, and man is His image and likeness. Therefore, man is not material; he is spiritual (*SCIENCE AND HEALTH WITH KEY TO THE SCRIPTURES*, p. 468-9).

This time it didn't seem to be working. I could see the concern in my mother's eyes and growing concern on my father's face. One day when my mother, a non-active Lutheran, came home from work she told me that she needed to talk with me. She told me that I didn't need to die because they had something at the doctor's office that would make me better. I asked her what it was. She replied, "penicillin."

We are all familiar with penicillin today, but we may not realize just how recently it was discovered. Its effectiveness on bacteria was first observed in 1929 by the Scottish biologist, Alexander Fleming but was not widely used until 1941 after it was purified and tested. This discovery is considered one of the greatest of the 20th century. Before its discovery, there was no effective treatment for bacterial infections like streptococcus. It was responsible for saving thousands of lives during the Second World War because it allowed physicians to perform many surgeries they would have otherwise not attempted.

I was faced with a choice. The choice to me seemed like a choice between my mother and father, God and science, life and death. At first I reminded her that I was a Christian Scientist. However, within a day or two I became very frightened for my life, and I choose to start taking the penicillin shots. Slowly I started to recover. I didn't go to my junior prom, but I was back in school in time to garner a first place in dramatic readings at the Regional Declamatory Contest. I had made a choice, and I never went back to the Christian Science Church. The question as to whether man was material or spiritual was not given serious consideration for many years.

Some years later I joined the Lutheran Church. Its doctrine was that man is both material and spiritual. For the time being that must have been a satisfactory answer because I do not remember ever questioning it. I never looked for any healings or any miracles in the church. I just looked for hope and meaning. I was assured that I could have that by believing in Jesus.

Before I was forty a time came when I needed a healing, and I got one. With that particular healing the old questions came back, "Is man material or is he essentially spiritual? Are we both? Could it be that we are neither? What are we really? Are we, as Al Gore said when he was running for President in 2000, 'spiritual beings on a human quest or are we on some kind of a spiritual quest?'" NOTE: His exact quote was, "I don't believe we are human beings on a spiritual quest but spiritual beings on a human quest." Considering the closeness of this election, this idea alone might account for his defeat as this idea is associated more with new age thinking then with mainstream American religion.

When I was about thirty I went into a bar in a Chicago suburb and ordered a drink. The bar was not busy, and I struck up a conversation with the bartender. I soon learned that he was a famous ex-major league baseball player having pitched in the 1948 World Series.

We started telling stories and jokes to each other; and from time to time he would say, spoken with a country drawl, "You gotta be something else!" I had never heard this expression before, and my ego got rather inflated and I thought, "This famous guy really likes me." I later learned that this was a new expression being used by the "hip," and he said it frequently to everybody—I was no exception. However, today that is <u>exactly what I believe</u>, I AM SOMETHING ELSE! The noted late 20th century astronomer, Carl Sagan, in his popular public television series about the universe referred to us as "star stuff." Well, my body might be star stuff, but I AM SOMETHING ELSE.

Today I don't believe that I am my body, my personality, my ego, my id, my super- ego, my past, my profession, my thoughts, my education. No! I AM SOMETHING ELSE! Now, just what that is I am not certain, but I know what I know, and that is I AM SOMETHING ELSE. The healing I received when I was almost forty years old, was the first real glimpse of the SOMETHING ELSE, and soon afterwards I realized that YOU TOO ARE SOMETHING ELSE!

NOTE: In contrast to Richard's background, which included thirteen relocations before the age of twelve, Kae experienced few childhood trials. The only move she made until she left home to attend college was from the family farm located in eastern Nebraska to a house in town. Her family life was very stable, and she was described by her mother as "such a happy child." Her parents were active in the Lutheran Church, and she attended a parochial grade school. The family was not financially affluent, but there was never a financial crunch. There always seemed to be plenty of money, and there was always lots of love.

Chapter 3

THE MIRACLE OF AWARENESS

For many years now, we have been best friends, lovers, partners, and helpmates. Our marriage has been and continues to be so meaningful and enriching that both of us at various times have expressed the fact that meeting each other, growing together, and supporting each other over a period of more than thirty years is nothing less than a miracle—truly, one of life's great mysteries.

However, the first six years of our marriage was a different story. To clarify something about those first six years, we will individually give some insight. This is Richard's story:

"I met Kae in the year following my divorce. At that time I pretty much made up my mind that I would never marry again. I had also decided that I would attempt to enjoy relationships with women without using them. When I met Kae, I was seeing several interesting women. I really was not looking for an additional relationship."

"After meeting Kae in a distant state and spending several nights dancing, I returned home. I did not really expect to see her again, and I was surprised when I received a letter from her that included a poem. (As you will see, Kae is a fine poet) In the letter Kae said she enjoyed my company and that she hoped that we would be able to see each other again. At that point, I realized that I had enjoyed her company, too. I loved the poem, and I subsequently realized that this woman was not only very bright but also warm and creative. Like so many people coming out of a divorce, I knew that she had been hurt and was on guard but that she really wanted to open up, love, and trust again. Something in me wanted that too."

Kae's story of the initial meeting:

"My mother always wanted me to marry a well-educated man and here he was swept into my life at a time when I was losing respect for most men except my father. Here was Richard, not only a well-educated man but also bearing the same birthday as my dad and wearing the same size shoes. And I didn't think anyone could walk in my dad's shoes. Not that my dad was perfect, not by any stretch of the imagination, but I respected and loved him. And this man could dance! All this went through my mind at our first and subsequent meetings. Three or four days with some contact and then we were off in different directions. Richard headed back to the State of Washington, and I headed home to Lincoln, Nebraska.

"When I returned home, I wrote a poem. Writing one was not unusual when something was stirring within me. What was unusual was that I sent the poem to Richard, and shortly thereafter I arranged to visit my best friend from my high school days. She, conveniently, was living in Washington. I have come to believe that if we are open, nature provides.

"I spent a good portion of that trip to Washington with Richard and became fascinated with many facets of the man. He was bright, deep thinking, attentive, and extremely interested in personal growth. He was also dealing with a personal trauma that made me feel needed. Within a few months, I sold my home, packed up my twelve-year-old son, and moved to Washington. Richard and I were married eight months after that move."

(Richard continues) "As we began to know each other better, we realized that we both saw something in the other that we wanted for ourselves. Kae wanted to be more of a free spirit; she was tired of having run through her mind, 'Is that all there is.' I was looking for more stability. I didn't want to lose my free spirit, but subsequently I knew it had to be anchored. Kae's maturity and stability could give me that.

These very things that brought us together then began to drive us apart. As the relationship evolved, these characteristics became a threat, not only to the marriage but also to each personally. I was moving too fast, and Kae dug in her heels too deep.

Prior to meeting Kae, I had worked at a Social Service Agency as a marriage counselor; and after some time recognized a dynamic in our relationship I had seen in many others. As a marriage counselor I had helped many couples recognize that what attracted the two people to each other on the deepest level to begin with had now become the biggest threat to the relationship's stability. What, at first, each person had seen as a strength in the other, and something that they wanted themselves; they now saw as a weakness. As a counselor I attempted to get the counselees to see that they really didn't want to become like the other person but they were both looking to the other as a catalyst for growth. When this is accepted, the marriage can be put back on a new footing, and they then begin to willingly grow towards each other rather than to pull apart.

I shared this with Kae, and little by little we recognized that this was a reality in our case as well. The history of our relationship contained the following indicators. We were together almost constantly, as we worked together and shared our social life with very few outsiders. Although she was eager for new experiences, some of the experiences I was leading her into frightened her after initial exposure; and she became a rope around my neck, tending to harness my free spirit. The very thing that drove Kae to me was now driving her away. There were too many new things to try, too expensive as our income was limited and too many unsettled days. Our relationship was operating as a pogo stick—big ups and big downs in close succession. An example of this shows up in two poems written by Kae. Note the difference in mode and the close proximity in time."

> When the willows wither
> and the saddened sun departs,
> leaves roses strewn in wretched ruin

and stenches rise above the earth
and worth is worthless in the gloom.
Oh, sol return.

(written December 20, 1973)

To Richard—

As Christmas dawns this lovely day,
thought transfers into much to say.—
I feel the love I give as real
and most of all, I know I feel
and knowing what I feel, I know
the beauty, the majesty adds to the glow
of the inner warmth I share with thee.
What's glowing there inside of me
is burning brighter, blessed from above
because I feel as real, your love.

(written December 25, 1973)

"The love was there, but we definitely had stumbling blocks. I dragged Kae, kicking and screaming, to a number of counselors attempting to help us understand the negative dynamics of this relationship. We somewhat numbed our relationship so that we remained together with lower highs and higher lows, but we hadn't resolved the stumbling blocks. Kae couldn't be exactly as I wanted her to be, and I tried to curtail certain aspects of my free spirit and suffered considerable deadening pain (depression).

In October, 1979, Kae attended a three-week seminar devoted to getting in direct contact with the better SELF. She returned home and said to me, 'This course may have saved our marriage.' Kae urged me to also take the course. I did, some months later. We both continued to practice the principles introduced in the course and slowly improvements in our relationship began to surface. I started to demonstrate some settling in my searches and seemed more content as my continuous need to try new and different things abated to some degree. Kae started to find some comfort in my growth, and at the same time became less afraid to join in some of my new interests.

We seemed no longer to need to protect our opposite poles and consequently moved toward meeting somewhere near the center. As this progression took place, we noticed less and less conflict and hostility in our relationship. That didn't mean that I was not still searching, and it didn't mean that Kae wasn't questioning every new adventure. It did mean that the underlying anxiety and anger were diminishing, and even in conflict we could usually quickly resolve and return to the centeredness of the love we felt for each other. It took time, however.

Today, as we look back at those early years of our marriage, it seems clear that those characteristics in the other that both attracted and frightened us were characteristics that spoke to our better nature. In the final analysis, it was getting in touch with this better nature through the techniques introduced at spiritual seminars that we started to see that our better nature wanted us both to grow and that our relationship could become the catalyst for that growth. Kae began to see that she didn't want my distorted value of freedom which was often self-destructive, and I could see that I didn't want Kae's rigid maturity that rejected change and was needlessly self-protective. What we both wanted was to moderate these extremes.

Somehow we had found in each other the weakness that could be the source of our growth. I wanted what Kae had but didn't want it in an unhealthy form. Likewise, she wanted what I had but didn't want it in an unhealthy form. We found if we were willing to give up our sick and distorted concept of what we valued as our strength and allowed our better natures (which we had made direct contact with in the seminars) to lead us, they would move us toward each other and toward health and wholeness.

Our attraction to each other had a sick or distorted side, but our better natures knew what they were doing. We began to feel what initially attracted us to each other could now lead to a miracle of health and love. For what initially attracted us to each other, we could now see as the stirring of our better selves.

Now that's our marriage "in a nutshell." This book is not about marriage, but we did want to introduce ourselves to you in the context of our marriage. Our miracle marriage is the result of our introduction to our better nature, and this book is about accessing and growing in that nature.

The term "in a nutshell" used above is frequently observed in Jewish literature. It is used to picture the full reality of creation, a reference to what is seen as well as what is not seen. In creation we see the shell, but we don't see what is inside the shell; and it is what is inside that is important. In some Jewish traditions it is believed that the "Divine Spark" resides hidden in every particle of the material world just as the nut lays hidden inside the shell.

Above we have referred to our better nature. We have come to believe through experience that it is indeed this hidden Divinity. What we share here is our effort to see beyond the shell of bodies, our personalities, and our beliefs to the reality who lies hidden within. Our experience leads us to believe that when Jesus spoke of the "Kingdom of God" that he was continually urging His followers to seek and see the Divine within everything, within themselves and within their neighbors. He said the "Kingdom of God is at hand." They seem to ask, "Where? We can't see it!" Jesus said. "It's within." It's in the nutshell.

Our marriage experience is an example of a number of experiences that we have had in the past thirty years that have led us to believe that there is a powerful force for good in the universe, that this force can be found deep within the psyche of humankind. Various ideas and techniques help us to tap or grow closer to this force within. This force probably exists in all things, yet it is incomprehensible and remains a mystery. Some people in the history of mankind have manifested this force in their lives in a most significant manner.

We have concluded that all great religions have at their source this great power, but in an attempt to lay exclusive claim to it and make it comprehensible, they have diluted its majesty. There are not two powers (i.e. good and evil), but one power (good) and the appearance of evil that is but the blocking, masking, and distorting of this power.

Down through history many philosophers and spiritual teachers have implied that humankind is basically ignorant in regard to the powerful force for good in the universe. Some versions of the Christian doctrine of "original sin" fall into this category. The Garden of Eden story referred to as "the fall" is seen by many as the birth of this state of ignorance.

With this idea as a background, many techniques have been developed to help individuals break through their ignorance to the TRUTH. Shocking the student in various ways has been one technique used for this purpose. Shock was often the basis of rites performed by ancients who practiced what we call "nature religions." One 20th century teacher and writer (Vernon Howard) often used shock in his seminars, demeaning students and calling them utterly stupid and ignorant. Ignorance may sound like a harsh term because we do not like to think of ourselves in this way. Still without watering the term down I would like to make it more palatable by sharing a personal incident from my past, an incident that I feel, in a simple way, illustrates the definition of ignorance as being unaware. The state of unawareness properly describes humankind and its relationship to the powerful force for good in the universe.

(Written February 5, 1990)

A few weeks ago while playing golf with a good friend, I observed something that in a small but significant way changed my view of the world. We were sitting on a golf cart waiting for a foursome ahead of us to clear the green. I was looking beyond the fairway into the open desert when I saw something that literally made me rub my eyes. It was a bird, and I couldn't take my eyes off of it. Just as the bird disappeared behind a piece of bush, my partner informed me that we could shoot. I didn't pay any attention to him, and he became annoyed. He said with irritation in his voice, "What are you looking at?" The bird came from behind some brush, and I said, "Look over there, what is that?" He said, "A roadrunner!" exclaiming in a manner that implied I must be stupid. (ignorant) I replied, "I thought so," but by then I was too embarrassed to tell him what I was really thinking.

25

I had seen the roadrunner before in cartoons and comics and that is what I believed it to be, a cartoon character and that's all! I hadn't lived in the Southwest very long and that's my only excuse for not knowing that real live roadrunners exist. I was shocked! For me it was almost like running into an elephant that could really fly.

I said this was a significant event for me, and it really was! It was one of those pictures that is worth a thousand words. Now, I am not trying to say that finding out that roadrunners really live was for me a Copernican revelation, but it did remind me once again that what I think is not necessarily what is. What I have believed to be myth may be the expression of reality and truth that goes far beyond my human comprehension.

This book is the record of how the powerful force for good in the universe became a conscious reality and guiding power in our lives. It is also our attempt to add materials and information so that others might have a "roadrunner experience."

Chapter 4

WAITING FOR GODOT

We were sitting in a theater at the Utah Shakespearean Festival at Cedar City, Utah. The play had not started, and I was thinking about Herb Z. Herb was a cabinet maker by trade. He was a real man's man, a fisherman and hunter, yet sensitive and big-hearted. He had a passion for the outdoors, and his sensitivity showed through in his landscape oil paintings. I had not seen Herb for more than twenty years. Herb and I had both lived in a small town in eastern Washington. I was the pastor of a church there, and he was a member. It was uniquely appropriate that I should be thinking about him on this occasion because the play we were about to see was Samuel Becket's, "*WAITING FOR GODOT.*"

Herb was also a member of the local Junior Chamber of Commerce; and one Sunday after the service, he asked to speak with me. He told me he was going to enter the Chamber area "Speak Up" contest, and he would like to use an idea from one of my sermons, the one referred to was one in which I had used *WAITING FOR GODOT* as an extended illustration.

In that sermon I mentioned that the play had been performed before packed houses in the capitols of Europe following World War II. It was a time of reconstruction, not only a physical one of buildings and infrastructures but of the lives, families, and belief systems. It was a time of soul searching. I also explained that the play was about two men (hobos) sitting on a dusty road passing the time talking. As they talked, you could sense their loneliness and the meaninglessness of their lives. Only at times did there seem to be a small ray of hope. That hope was centered on their reason for sitting there, which was "waiting for Godot." They frequently seemed to forget their reason for sitting there, and from time to time one would remind the other that they were "waiting for Godot." The play is interpreted as waiting for that someone, something or some event that will bring meaning into their lives. The entire play is based on this meaningless waiting.

In my sermon, I tried to make the point that as Christians, we did not have to wait for meaning, that the biblical message is—in faith we believe that God brings meaning into our lives. I used the Bible verse from the Psalms that says, "This is the day that the Lord has made. Let us rejoice and be glad in it." I went on to say that in faith we not only believe that God creates the day for us, but also that He comes to us in spirit to bring meaning.

Herb apparently saw something in this that he could use for his speech. After talking about this with him for a few moments, we went to my library where we found a copy of the play, and I loaned it to him. A few days later Herb called and wanted to know how to pronounce the names of the main characters in the play, Vladimir and Estragon.

A couple of weeks later, Herb approached me again after church. When I finished greeting the congregation, we found a place to chat. I could see that Herb was excited. He said, "I won the Speak Up contest!" I congratulated him and told him I was curious about how he had developed his speech. He said, his speech was pretty much like my sermon except for one thing; he told his audience that you don't have to wait for meaning or for God like Vladimir and Estragon; all you need to do is to look deep within yourself, and you will find God and the meaning that brings.

As I remember it, I was somewhat stunned and did not have much to say. I thought to myself, that wasn't a very orthodox Lutheran teaching; but I made no effort to correct him. I did wonder where he got that idea. On one other occasion when I was teaching a Bible

28

study, Herb mentioned the same thing. He was very personal, simply saying, "I believe God is found within." Again, I ignored or passed over what he was saying.

My thoughts of Herb were interrupted as the curtain rose, and there were Vladimir and Estragon still on the dusty road waiting for Godot, for meaning and for God. As I sat there watching some magnificent acting, I smiled to myself knowing that Herb had been right and that which Godot represents need not be waited for but can be found deep within.

On that day long ago I was the preacher. I was the one with the college and seminary education. I was the one who knew the Bible, the doctrines of the church and the history of Christianity. But Herb was the one who had a conscious contact with the Kingdom within. I had beliefs and Herb had a knowing. I could talk about a God who had all power, but Herb had access to the Kingdom, its power, integrity, and its truth.

When I look back, I now realize that my fascination with the play was not just to produce a clever homily but said something very important about my subconscious. I, like the two hobos on the dusty road, had a soul sickness. I was still waiting for a sense of profound meaning in my life. I was still waiting for Godot. In the years that were to follow I would not only wait but search and research in every way I knew how to find that meaning.

Chapter 5

CANYON CALL

In these years since my healing I have asked of every person I have met, every song I have heard (whether it be from bird or man), every place that I have been, every book that I have read, every breeze that I have felt, "What can you teach me about my nature, about the nature of life, of love, of God?" (This sentence contains some hyperbole or as they say, poetic license, but it is essentially true.)

Those who knew me as a child and as a young man tell me that these questions have always been a part of my character, but only after my healing did I become conscious of this character. Only in finding did I seek to understand. Only in experiencing did I yearn to experience more.

Some time before the healing, I read Loren Eiseley's book, *UNEXPECTED UNIVERSE.* It moved me then, and it moves me yet today. Eiseley may not have been the first to show me the mustard seed (Matt. 13:31), but he certainly watered it, cultivated it, and just as certainly did it spring forth a few years later. I will share more about Eiseley and his influence on me in the third section of this book.

In the last autumn before the new millennium I went to the Grand Canyon to ask it these questions. While there I heard the plaintive sounds of the native flute. I saw the eagle soar high above the canyon walls. I heard the words "beautiful! peaceful! and awesome!" uttered by a thousand tongues in the language of people from the four corners of the globe. I heard the stories about forgotten people who lived in the canyon walls centuries ago; people who left behind a few relics and wall art. I heard stories of adventure, of daring feats by those early settlers, explorers, and scientists; those who, in the latter half of the nineteenth century ran the rapids, explored the caves, discovered hidden valleys, and climbed the ancient walls.

I heard about the five million who come to visit each year, most with camera in hand who look with awe from the rim to the canyon below. Many (over twenty thousand a year) do more then just look. They go within to explore, to seek knowledge about out earth, to ride the rapids, and to enjoy the silence.

This was my third trip to the canyon. Each trip has been different. The first trip was one of awe. The second was one of enjoyment and the third of inspiration. On the second trip I was privileged to witness a wedding being conducted near the canyon's wall. The classical music for the occasion was played by a string quartet. The time of the wedding was sunset that is one of the most beautiful moments of the day. Everything, including the weather, seemed perfect.

On this third trip I sat and listened to the silence of the canyon. I saw its shadows and its changing hues. I felt its gentle breeze and I said, "What can you tell me about my nature, about the nature of life, of love and of God."

The canyon replied, "I am ten thousand tabernacles in one. I am a lesson in earth's long history. I am a place of life—see the squirrel, the worms, the birds, the trees, the brush, and the grass. I am a place of continual change. Like life itself, I will not be the same tomorrow or even a minute from now. I am the source of inspiration—go, bend your ear, and hear the music I have inspired; go, open your eyes, and see the art I have engendered; go, listen to the people, and hear what joy I bring; notice the diversity I attract.

"Now, notice the sun and realize without the sun I have no shadows; I produce no life; I attract no throngs of people; I have no beauty, only darkness. Without the sun, I inspire no music and engender no art. For more than a million years, each evening the sun and I have put together a spectacular show, certainly one of the longest running shows in the history of earth. But, without the sun, there is no show.

"Like me," the canyon whispered, "you are nothing without the light. But the light of which I speak is not the sun. Unlike me, your light is not without but within. I am everything I can be because of the sun. Your earthly life, too, is dependent on the sun; but the true light of man is not the sun; it is the light of pure consciousness; it is the light referred to in the Gospel of John (John 1:9). It is that mystical sense referred to by Albert Einstein. It is the essence of man."

And then, like a gentle but stern master, the canyon said, "Look deep into my bowels, into the canyons within the canyons and see my beauty." After a long silence it said, "Go now, look into yourself; see your beauty and become conscious of your consciousness. For what you are looking for is what is looking." As I walked away the words repeated themselves like a mantra:

"Go now and become conscious of your consciousness for what you are looking for is what is looking."

CANYON SUNSET

Autumn gathers dusk in the light of day.
Wealthy waves of sunlight maintain their stay.
Lingering and languished they ignite the sky,
Seceding to darkness as dusk passes by.
What beauty these journeys to darkness share
With shoulders so broad, the rays that they bear
Ushering out the last light of the day
in a splendid, magnificent, heavenly array.
by Kae

Chapter 6

GOLD AS METAPHOR

I grew up in an all white culture. There was one exception. When I was in the second grade, I rode the bus five miles to school every day. My seat companion was often a boy of Japanese heritage. The day after the bombing of Pearl Harbor I asked him what he thought about the war. He said he didn't know what to think. A few weeks latter he was gone. I never saw him again. Now I know that in all probability he spent the next four years in a Japanese relocation camp.

For ten years Kae worked in a large business with a multicultural and multiethnic environment. She found this setting to be very gratifying. Often she would come home and say, she had spent her lunch break with some people from China, Mexico, or the Philippines. Over the years, she spent her lunch break with people from every continent except Antarctica, every race, almost every state in the Union and many, many countries.

Kae grew up in Nebraska and spent most of her life in the context of white, Protestant midwesternism. Those in both her church and home life cautioned her about association with others of different backgrounds. She, however, found cultural diversity to be a very rich and stimulating experience. The following poem expresses her gratitude for such exposure:

> I suppose I could propose
> What I am thankful for—
> A deep sense of appreciation
> For fellow employees from every nation
> And some you will find
> Of almost every kind of personality trait
> Wait—all of one spirit, each uniquely defined.
> Thank you for each and all of mankind.

Once she said to me, "Exploring unity in the midst of diversity is better than striking gold!"

One of Kae's friends at work was a woman from Thailand. Besides working at the hotel, she and her husband established a local Thai restaurant. One day Kae came home a little disconsolate. She said her Thai friend was moving back to Bangkok to start a restaurant there. Her friend told her there would always be a place for her in their home, and she hoped that we could visit them soon.

Shortly after her friend moved back to Thailand, I read about a Buddhist statue in Bangkok that intrigued me. I wanted to see it for myself. Now we had two good reasons for taking a trip to Southeast Asia. Jack Canfield wrote the story of the Buddha statue. Jack is one of the authors and compilers of the popular *CHICKEN SOUP FOR THE SOUL* series. In this story Jack tells about a particular day in Bangkok when he and his wife visited several Buddhist Temples. At the end of that day he said that one visit stood out in his mind, the Temple of the Golden Buddha.

He describes it as a small temple housing a solid gold Buddha weighing over two and one-half tons and standing over ten feet tall. You can imagine that the Buddha has tremendous value, but what really intrigued me was the story that is about the Buddha's history. According to Jack, the history was displayed on a typewritten page alongside a piece of clay about eight inches thick. Here is that history in Jack's words:

"Back in 1957 a group of monks from a monastery had to relocate a clay Buddha from their temple to a new location. The monastery was to be moved to make room for the development of a highway through Bangkok. When the crane began to lift the giant idol, the weight of it was so tremendous that it began to crack. What's more, rain began to fall. The head monk, who was concerned about damage to the sacred Buddha, decided to lower the statue back to the ground and cover it with a large canvas tarp to protect it from the rain.

"Later that evening the head monk checked on the Buddha. He shined his flashlight under the tarp to see if it was staying dry. As the light reached the crack, he noticed a little gleam shining back and thought it strange. As he took a closer look at this gleam of light, he wondered if there might be something underneath the clay. He went to fetch a chisel and hammer from the monastery and began to chip away at the clay. As he knocked off shards of clay, the little gleam grew brighter and bigger. Many hours of labor went by before the monk stood face to face with the extraordinary solid-gold Buddha.

Historians believe that several hundred years before the head monk's discovery, the Burmese army was about to invade Thailand (then called Siam). The Siamese monks, realizing that their country would soon be attacked, covered their precious golden Buddha with an outer covering of clay in order to keep their treasure from being looted by the Burmese. Unfortunately, it appears that the Burmese slaughtered all the Siamese monks, and the well-kept secret of the golden Buddha remained intact until that fateful day in 1957."

"As we flew home on Cathay Pacific Airlines, I began to think to myself, 'We are all like the clay Buddha covered with a shell of hardness created out of fear, and yet underneath each of us is a golden Buddha, a golden Christ, or a golden essence which is our real self. Somewhere along the way between the ages of two and nine, we began to cover up our golden essence, our natural self. Much like the monk with the hammer and the chisel, our task now is to discover our true essence once again.' "

I believe Kae's ability to see beneath the clay of ego to the essence within her fellow employees is possible because she has been fortunate enough to have discovered that essence within herself. Secondly, her appreciation of individual differences, even when those differences are unrefined and crude, is because she knows the true value of the individual lies not in their humanity but in their divinity.

In the fall of 1999 Kae and I did have the opportunity to travel to Thailand. We rode the elephants in Chang Mai, and we did see the beautiful golden Buddha in Bangkok. On this trip that included Malaysia and Singapore, we saw many temples and shrines gilded in gold. On other travels we have seen golden treasures from the tombs of Egypt and beautifully gold decorated churches in both Europe and Mexico. We have seen the sixty-one pound gold nugget that was discovered in Australia and is now on display in Las Vegas. None of these treasures affected me nearly as much as the gold of St. Petersburg, Russia.

It was a beautiful summer evening near sunset. Kae and I were aboard a Norwegian Cruise Ship. We were still fifteen to twenty miles from the city, and the sun was at our backs. We strained to get our first glimpse of the city built by Tzar Peter the Great. All at once we started to see glitter—first one, and then another, and then many! The brilliant glitter of gold was from the many spires and domes of St. Petersburg's churches and palaces. It was truly awesome. In many ways I felt that I was seeing gold for the first time and that this was the way it was meant to be seen. I had a better understanding of the allure that gold has had throughout the centuries. I felt its uniqueness, its beauty, and its purity. I was seeing gold in its proper light—gold, at dusk, reflecting the light of the blazing sun.

When the golden Buddha was covered with clay it reflected no light. If Jack Canfield's conclusion is correct and we are like that clay-covered Buddha then we too reflect no light. Was Jesus referring to a similar idea when he cautioned us not to hide our light under a bushel? Is it possible that beneath all the humanity (clay), all the enculturation, all the bad advice, false ideas, fears and anxieties, there is within each of us a light, an essence, a purity? If so, can it be symbolized by something as pure as gold that reflects the brilliance of the setting sun? Could it be that gold's real attraction is not its rarity or value in dollars and cents but the reminder of something hidden? Could the message of gold's glitter be a hint, a reminder that deep down in each of us lies something hidden, something beautiful, something pure, something eternal.

When I was a child, I was fascinated by what appeared to me to be my father's most treasured possession, a small box of rocks and a balance scale. The balance scale, when taken apart, fit into the drawer of the small wooden box. The box of rocks included labeled glass vials containing sand-like materials. I was not to play with these items. However, from time to time at my urging, my father would bring the box down from the shelf and tell me its stories.

My father was a graduate metallurgist from the South Dakota School of Mines. The box of rocks and glass vials made up one of his school assignments that was to identify minerals in rock formations. He would show me specks of gold in quartz and then another rock with even more gold specks. He would ask me which of the two was the most valuable. Until I finally caught on, I would always point to the one with the most specks. At that response, my dad would usually chuckle and once again tell me about galena, fool's gold.

He would then set up the scale, open one of the vials, and pour gold filings onto one side of the balance. He would place small thin weights on the other side until it balanced. Knowing the price of gold, we would then calculate the value of the filings. I do not know what happened to the box of rocks. The scale, however, has a prominent place in my home and today symbolizes my own search for balance. Often, these sessions were concluded with my dad reminiscing about his grandfather from whom he had inherited this little scale. My great-grandfather was a prospector. He lived in Custer, South Dakota. Early each spring he would ride off (on horseback) with a few supplies, including this scale and head for the wilds of British Columbia, Canada where he would stay and prospect for gold.

This great-grandfather, who died before I was born, had two sons and a daughter. The daughter was my grandmother. All three children in one way or another seemed to carry on their father's quest. From the research I have been able to do, I have discovered that each was an embodiment of an interesting combination of spiritual and material values. At least two of them investigated spiritualism, and all three practiced Christian Science to some degree. Both great-uncles spent their early years pursuing gold. One of them turned to black gold and was successful at striking oil.

On a trip to Cut Bank, Montana in 1997, Kae and I visited the local museum that is largely an exhibit of Cut Bank's early history as an oil town.   In one write-up on exhibit my great-uncle was mentioned. The dateline was 1937. The article said, "R.C. Tarrant brought in a gusher on the Miller lease, and there was oil all over the prairie." To my knowledge that great-uncle never quite found what he was looking for. He could have been a very wealthy man, but the quest it seems was more important than the wealth. Perhaps in that drive to find more oil he was unknowingly seeking that inner purity. I am reminded of the quote from St. Augustine that was prominently placed in a hospital chapel that I used to frequent. It said, "Our hearts are restless until they rest in Thee."

The history of the gold pursuit often seems to shroud the quest for spiritual fulfillment. This mixing of spirituality with materialism is probably best exemplified by the quest for the Holy Grail. We know that Christ drank from this mythical cup at the Last Supper. Somehow, over the years, that cup took on a meaning and value that is difficult to explain. It is believed that the Crusades themselves were, at least in part, due to this quest. Ironically, even if the grail were to be found, it would be just another relic, a relic that symbolizes what can only be found "within." The search in reality makes less sense than looking for the actual pearl of which Jesus spoke when he compared the Kingdom to the pearl of great price. Somehow the human mind continually finds ways to externalize what can only be found inside us. That is our dilemma! Our minds in the normal waking state of consciousness are not equipped to grasp the spiritual so there seems to be no choice but to seek meaning in the external world.

A movement that made this connection between gold, the physical element, and the inner essence of man was the medieval science known as alchemy. Most moderns, if they know anything at all about the alchemists, probably think of them as misguided fools or Dark Age scientists who tried to turn base metals like lead into gold. To be sure, there was an aspect of the movement that was just that.

As Carl Jung discovered when he studied the movement, the alchemists were not only physicists and chemists but also metaphysicians.   They were looking for a way to penetrate the baseness (clay) of man and to reach his golden inner core. I believe if these alchemists influenced no one but Carl Jung and his devotees, they have made a significant contribution to the evolution of man's spirit.

Gold artifacts from virtually every culture give credence to the idea that it is treasured far beyond its value as the medium of wealth and power. Gold is the metal used by cultures, ancient and modern, for their most revered objects. The highest aim of the alchemists was not mere riches, but divinity itself. Alchemy's roots can be traced back to the ancient City of Alexandria. This city with its great public buildings, its university, and its library of more than 700,000 scrolls was known as the Queen City of the Mediterranean. It became for a time an intellectual and cultural hub and a crossroad between East and West. Some prominent scholars of the city turned their attention to metallurgy. This was an area of Egyptian expertise in Alexandria; it came under the influence of Greek philosophy, and a new discipline took shape. The traditional practice of the goldsmith thus gave birth to the art of alchemy.

Alchemy was to become a science, an art, and a philosophy. Over the years, it produced the beginnings of western medicine, pharmacology—the discovery of new elements and the beginning of modern chemistry. Of major interest to us is its philosophy of metaphysics (beyond the physical). The history of alchemy has had many facets that include frauds, famous con men and women, and famous scientists like Roger Bacon, Robert Boyle, and Isaac Newton. The physician Paracelsus and prominent religious figures like Albertus Magnus and Thomas Aquinas were involved with alchemy.

I want to leave you with these thoughts about alchemy. Sir Isaac Newton embraced alchemy because he hoped that in or through it, he might find the underlying truth of nature. It may sound strange but I believe that in alchemy, Newton may have come closer to these metaphysical truths than did Einstein. I am convinced that these truths can only be accessed by human consciousness; and the metaphysical aspect of alchemy was just that, an exploration into human consciousness. Carl Jung made this clear in his study and presentation on alchemy. (See Carl Jung – bibliography)

If, as we have been suggesting, there is purity, a beauty, a divinity at our very core, then how do we account for man's tragic history? How do we account for all the wars, murders, hatred, bigotry, and misery that have been so much a part of history? Many have explored this subject, and volumes have been written. A satisfactory answer still seems to elude humankind. Could the answer lie in the metaphor presented to us by the Golden Buddha that for more than two hundred years was hidden by a covering of clay. Could the confusing science of alchemy give us clues about the development of the Western mind. Could it also gives us insight into the truth previously stated that the solution to our problem is simple, but the Western mind is incredibly complicated. Is the quest for Gold (riches) but a metaphor for our quest for the Divine?

Chapter 7

SECRET GARDEN

Recently[*] I saw a movie entitled, *SECRET GARDEN,* based on a children's story by the same name. It is about a little girl who lived in India and because she lost both parents, she was forced to go to England and live with a rich, but reclusive uncle. The uncle paid little attention to his newly acquired responsibility.

The little girl, with an inquisitive mind and much time on her hands, spent time exploring the grounds at her new home. She had been aware of a wall on the grounds, but she hadn't found the gate. One day she found it behind a mass of vegetation. After much effort, she was able to open the gate. Behind the wall she found what looked like a garden that was totally taken over by weeds. She soon learned that it once was a beautiful garden that belonged to her deceased Aunt. On her first visit she found one small sprout that wasn't a weed. She worked to uncover this sprout so that it would receive sunlight. She didn't leave the garden until the sprout was free to grow.

On subsequent visits she found more sprouts and pulled more weeds until one day she had pulled all of them, and in their place were

---

* Chapter written in 1994

beautiful flowering plants. She then introduced her uncle's sickly son to the garden. He enjoyed it so much that he started to gain in health.

It also seemed for the little girl that the more she attended to the garden, the less difference there was between her world inside of the garden and out. In spirit, she took the garden with her wherever she went. It became apparent that she and her garden had a positive effect on everybody around her.

I enjoyed every minute of this movie; it was so positive and uplifting. But I enjoyed it most because almost everything in the movie reminded me of my secret garden, that secret place within that today is so beautiful and so nourishing. Like the little girl's garden, my internal garden had been cut off from the sunshine (of the spirit), my consciousness. In fact, my consciousness was so filled with weeds (old ideas and stress) that I didn't recognize that there was a beautiful garden within. I just saw that first sprout and knew I wanted to nourish and water it.

I started going to my secret garden within me on a daily basis; and as time went on there were less weeds, more light, and I could see more beauty. Over the years I have encouraged others to seek out their secret garden and some, like the little girl, have found it to be a source of transformation.

Now, as the months and years go by and as I continue to care for my secret place (garden), I find that just like the little girl in the movie, there is less difference between my secret place within and my world without. Somehow, today, a great deal of the garden goes with me wherever I go, and the world itself is starting to look a lot like the garden—peaceful, beautiful, and full of light. This is not to say that I am not aware of ignorance and darkness in the world. I am saying that I am less and less affected by the chaos around me. As one of the longtime and beloved members of Alcoholics Anonymous wrote, "I see with *A NEW PAIR OF GLASSES*."[++] (Chuck Chamberlain 1902-1984)

++ *A NEW PAIR OF GLASSES was published following his death. It was based on a series of lectures he gave at a retreat in 1975.*

Chapter 8

AIN'T NO SUNSHINE

No doubt you can identify with my experience when it comes to some piece of music, a song, or part of a song. What I'm talking about is not being able to get that music out of my head. It just keeps cropping up! Sometimes it's the words. Most of the time, however, it is the combination of words and music that keeps grabbing me. A song, which at times literally lives in me is, "Ain't No Sunshine When She's Gone." Over the years it has continued to surface in my mind. I know part of it is the bluesy plaintive minor key (I seem to like minor key stuff), but it is also the words.

I haven't quite pinned it down, but I have a feeling that this song turns up when I am experiencing some sense of loss. I think its related to old tapes, "old ideas" that I no longer accept. Nevertheless they are ideas that I let resurface from time to time. The basic idea I am referring to is the notion that something or someone can take away my sunshine. The reason I call this an old idea which I no longer accept, is that I have come to an understanding based on experience, that my sunshine does not come from the outside, but from within me. In fact, my current belief is that it is not just a part of me but the sunshine is the true me! (radical thought: I am the sunshine of my life! Hum—)

45

Now, before you write me off as a narcissistic fool, let me try to explain. Some years ago I read a book by Allan Watts called *THE MEANING OF HAPPINESS*. In this book Watts introduced the idea that happiness is an inside job. He makes it clear that happiness has little or nothing to do with what is taking place on the outside. Now for me, this was a very radical idea, but, because of what I have been referring to as my healing, I bought it—hook, line, and sinker.

Even though I say I bought this, I have found that it is easier to say, than to live. From that time until the present I have been trying to prove to myself that Allan Watts was right; and I have proven it repeatedly. This, by the way, is one of the keys to my program. If you missed it I'll give it to you in a little different form. You've heard the story about the little boy in New York City who stopped the man on the street and asked him, "How do you get to Carnegie Hall?" The man answered, "Practice, practice, practice." Once you buy the idea that happiness is not something you get by looking for it in the outside world (money, relationships, fame, accomplishments, sex, religion, or even God in the heavens above) and that, just possibly, it's something you already have. The trick then is to begin putting this idea to the test. If you are like me you'll have to do this over and over again.

My experience is that the idea has never failed the test. The problem for me is that I think it still needs to be tested. For my ego-mind fights this idea, because for the ego to accept this is to accept the end of its rule; the end of its destructive life. The result is: I'm like the man who wants to go across the ocean in a balloon and continues to test the balloon even after he has proven to himself that it will work. I realize more each day that I already have all the sunshine, all the happiness I need; but like the man with the balloon, I find it difficult to cut myself off from the familiar, from the dry land. Maybe the balloon needs to take even longer trips over the ocean until one day the ocean will become as familiar as the dry land. Yes, that's what I mean by testing and practicing. It means to continue to rely even more on the happiness, the sunlight within, until it becomes so familiar that we can cut ourselves off from every idea that the world outside of us can add anything to the sunlight which we already possess. I believe this practice, practice, practice is what is meant by the word devotion.

Let's look at a real live example of what I am talking about. In over ten years of being a Lutheran minister I conducted many funerals and saw a lot of people in grief. Funerals for children and young adults were always the toughest. My observation is that some people had belief systems that were a comfort to them. Others had a belief system that for whatever reason could not sustain them in these times—some left the church, some became bitter, and some found a new faith.

A few people reflected something beyond comprehension. For want of better words, I'll call it joy in the midst of tears. The most memorable example of this was a funeral I attended (did not conduct) for the son of Dr. Alvin and Mrs. Rogness. Dr. Rogness was President of the Lutheran Seminary from which I graduated. Their son was returning home after studying in England for a year. He was struck by a car and killed just a few miles before arriving home. From all reports, he was a son to be proud of, bright and mature, with a promising future ahead of him. He is buried in South Dakota in a small town near where I was serving my first parish. Dr. and Mrs. Rogness greeted everyone who came to the funeral and shook their hand with tears streaming down their cheeks, yet with a look of serenity and joy in their faces.

As Christians, Dr. and Mrs. Rogness may not have explained their serenity in the midst of loss in the same terms that I would, but I believe either explanation would not violate the universal reality of the experience.

Where does this kind of faith come from? My answer is, "It comes from being in touch with who we are." Physically their son was gone, but their sunshine was not gone. With this as the basis of our understanding, our belief system cannot be shattered. It is not founded on intellectual constructs, teachings, or doctrines. We don't cry out, "Why?" And, if we do, we quickly realize that this question comes from a part of us to which we no longer give credence.

When the inner sunshine becomes stabilized and more real than what goes on in the world around us, we can respond to problems with the phrase, "sh- happens." This phrase, crude as it is, does express the attitude about the vicissitudes of life by a person who is one with his/her TRUE SELF.

The other aspect of this is the meaning of suffering for the people who have not reached such a high degree of oneness with their inner sunshine and consequently cut themselves off even further from it when sh- does happen. I went to a doctor once, and I bent over sideways in a certain way and I said, "It hurts when I do this." The doctor replied, "Then, don't do that." That's the answer! That's the point of our practice, practice, and practice. Don't do that! Don't cut yourself off from your sunshine. When he or she dies, don't cut yourself off from your inner sunshine and the sun won't quit shining.

Just recently I met a beautiful, seventy-five year old lady who was separating from her husband after over fifty years of marriage. It was not her idea; it was not something she wanted. It was difficult, but her sun was still shining. Why was it shining? Because she had learned not to shut the sun off, no matter what happened.

I keep mentioning practice, practice, practice. Now, just what do we mean by practice? In the fourth section of this book I will present a number of spiritual principles and techniques. If these are practiced in the proper way, they <u>do</u> work! Some of these have become distorted and used in a way that causes them to be ineffective. To illustrate this outcome, when Kae and I were in Singapore we learned that prior to World War II the government of Singapore built a fortress around the entire shoreline. They did this because they were convinced that the Japanese would come by sea. The Japanese did come but not a cannon was fired; the cannons were all pointed in the wrong direction. The Japanese invaded but not by sea but from the small land passage that was unprotected. Their fortress was ineffective because they were looking in the wrong direction. This is the reason that I have made such a point about seeking the divinity within oneself. If this is indeed where the divinity is found, then our prayers and exhortations to a God in a far-off heaven are misdirected and thus, less effective.

Number one: among the techniques indicated in the fourth section is meditation. I say number one because I firmly believe that it is our best resource for accessing the inner sunshine. In order to know it, we must access it and become familiar with it.

Number two: we need to choose in favor of inner joy and inner sunshine rather than seeking temporary relief for our suffering and pain. Now this sounds so easy, but those of us who have tried it know that it just isn't easy. The choice between happiness and suffering would seem to be obvious, but it isn't. We often hold onto suffering for both conscious and unconscious reasons.

I cite an example from my life. The pain that sent me to the doctor was caused by an automobile accident. I expected to be awarded some compensation for this injury, and my mechanical ego-mind found it difficult to let go of the suffering until the extent of the injury was determined. All suffering has some real or imagined payoff. On some level, we like it! My monkey (ego) mind says, "Wait until you get the dough." When will my ego let go of this idea? Usually not until my misery becomes strong enough to shock me into some kind of sanity and says one more time, "I've had enough." Then, I surrender to the inner sunshine.

Thankfully, more and more frequently, I can think the process through. I can see that if I pursue the ego course, I will hit the same stupid brick wall of pain and suffering, therefore I might as well choose love and peace right now rather than go through the trauma of needless pain and suffering.

In the twelve-step programs, there is a saying—"Insanity is doing over and over again the same thing and expecting different results." We grow when we become aware of our insanity and move on. Section two of this book is intended to help us identify the causes and effects of our insanity and what we need to do in order to move on.

We now close this section with a few lines from the Upanishad. This philosophy of India dates back to about 1300 years before the birth of Jesus. These lines are very much in keeping with what Aldus Huxley called the "Perennial Philosophy."

> "Like oil in sesame seeds, like butter
> In cream, like water in springs, like fire
> In a firestick, so dwells the Lord of Love,
> The Self, in the very depths of consciousness.
> Realize him through truth and meditation."

"The Self is hidden in the hearts of all,
As butter lies hidden in cream. Realize
The Self in the depths of meditation,
The Lord of Love, supreme reality,
Who is the goal of all knowledge."

This is the highest mystical teaching;
This is the highest mystical teaching.
From the Shveteshvatara *Upanishad*

CLAY AND BEYOND

SECTION II

INTRODUCTION

CLAY AND BEYOND

In 1909 the French government ordered the Eiffel Tower to be torn down. Robert Peary was the first explorer to reach the North Pole. The XVI Amendment to the U.S. Constitution was passed imposing the Federal Income Tax. Two friends boarded a steamship to take them to America to celebrate the twentieth anniversary of a small but prominent private college. Today, Clark University is not only known for bringing these two friends to America, but also known for many of the researchers who have had positions at Clark; researchers like Robert Goddard, the father of space exploration, and A.A. Michelson, the first American Scientist to receive the Nobel Prize.

Now, almost one-hundred years later we all know the Eiffel Tower still stands tall and in the United States, the income tax effects us all. But what about those two friends who came to Clark University to share, for the first time on this Continent, the message of psychoanalysis? We do know both are more famous than Peary, Michelson or Goddard. They are even better known than Clark University where their first lectures were given. We know that when these two men boarded the steamship they were fast friends and colleagues even though they had known each other less than two years.

We also know that the older man, fifty-two year old Sigmund Freud, looked upon the younger man, thirty-three year old Carl Gustuf Jung, as his prodigy and successor. We know it would not be long until there would be a split between these two and they would no longer be colleagues or even friends. We know that the main obstacle (barrier) to their working together was the question that we asked early in this book – namely, "What is man?" Is he/she material or spiritual? Freud said material and Jung said spiritual. The atheist Freud said that Jung was not following science. Jung, a believer, said that Freud was blind to great truth. Soon there were two new schools of thought regarding man's psyche[*]: one from Zurich led by Carl Jung; the other in Vienna led by Sigmund Freud.

And thus, in the story of these two men who boarded a steamship for America as friends in 1909, we have a microcosm of the struggle that has continued in the Western World from the time of Isaac Newton to our present day.

In the introduction to this book we introduced the ideas of "Deep Ecology" and the "Web of Life." In Chapter Eleven, entitled, "Sickness of the Mind," we will take an imaginary trip into outer space and look back at our "Home," Planet Earth. We will look deeply into its interconnected ecology. We will also see the ever-increasing threat to the "Web;" we will see the ecosystem being destroyed. The reason for this destruction is clear – the fractured mind of mankind. In this Section we look more deeply into the broken web and the brokenness which lies behind this condition, the fractured consciousness of humankind.

Tragic as it may sound; it appears that many people, if not most, live their lives blocked. Before we look at the ways in which we can get through these blocks, we need to become more familiar with the blocks themselves (the clay). The fact that we are largely blocked is the tragedy of mankind. It is a tragedy alluded to in the myths of many cultures. The myth most familiar to us (in Western Society) is the story of Adam and Eve that ends with the couple being ushered

---

[*] "The human soul; also, the mind; the mental life" Websters Dictionary

out of paradise. Being ushered out of paradise is synonymous with being blocked from our INNER REALITY, our SELF, the KINGDOM OF GOD within.

"People travel to wonder at the height of the mountains, at the huge waves of the sea, at the long courses of the rivers, at the vast compass of the ocean, at the circular motion of the stars, and they pass themselves by without wondering at all." St. Augustine (354-430)

Because I referred to the Adam and Eve story, I think it is also appropriate to mention the words of Genesis 1, verse 27. "So God created man in his own image, in the image of God created he him; male and female he created he them." This is often referred to by using the Latin phrase, "IMAGO DEI" (the image of God). Metaphorically to be ushered from the Garden is to lose touch with the IMAGO DEI, to experience fractured consciousness. Thus, in the greater context, fractured consciousness is not just something that we have experienced since the onset of modern science, but apparently, an awareness that goes back to the beginnings of civilization.

Why do we pass ourselves by as St. Augustine suggests? A man who seemed to understand all this long before Freud and Jung was the medieval German Mystic, Meister Eckart. Regarding the INNER REALITY, he said it was the basis of conscience and of spiritual awareness. Now, think about that for a moment. If we are substantially blocked from our core, are we then substantially blocked off from our conscience and our awareness of spirituality? Could this, being blocked, be the reason that so many leaders in business, government and the Church lack integrity? In this regard Eckart also said:

"A man has many skins in himself covering the depths of his heart. Man knows so many things; he does not know himself. Thirty or forty skins or hides, just like an ox or a bear, so thick and hard, cover the soul. Go into your ground and learn to know yourself there."

55

As you read this section, you need not get overly involved with the names and places; but rather, pay attention to the skins which cover our core. Here are some that you might look for:

> Distraction—current events and living issues
> Biases and prejudices—mindsets
> Deep-seated fears, hurts, and anxieties—
> many based on past trauma
> Anger and hate
> The ego itself—identification with the skins, the clay

Chapter 9

CLAY

In the chapter on gold, I mentioned that my great-grandfather's gold scale had become a symbol of my search for balance. Let me explain. When you use a balance scale to weigh gold, you put the gold on one side and the weights on the other until the scale is balanced. The gold is obviously worth more than the weights. However, the weights are not worthless. Their value is in their function. Without them the gold could not be weighed. The same can be said for the clay that hid the Golden Buddha. The clay, having little intrinsic value, had great functional value because it protected the Buddha from destruction for over two hundred years.

In a similar way, the clay of our lives has significant value, but we must remember that the value is relative. The clay of our lives finds its value in relationship to those values, which are symbolized by gold. Clay symbolizes the temporal and changing aspects of life while gold symbolizes the ABSOLUTE, eternal, unchanging aspects of life. Both have value, but the changing values of life (such as material possessions, relationships and belief systems) should find their meaning relative to the ABSOLUTE and unchanging. This relationship must be reached for there to be any true balance. It appears that some people maintain this contact on an <u>unconscious</u>

level. However, it seems obvious that contact on a conscious level is preferred.

I became the owner of this scale after my father's death. My children, like me, enjoyed playing with this scale from time to time. Over the years some of the weights were lost. This loss was upsetting to me because in a real sense, the sentimental value of these items had become more precious than gold. In life the changing values can also take on emotional, sentimental, and even irrational value quite apart from the unchanging value. Before we go on, let me define ego. For the most part we will be using Carl Jung's concept of ego.

Jung defines ego as the organizing entity of emotions, sentiments, defenses, etc. and states that this entity is not related to the inner-core or essence of our being. In simple words, according to Jung, ego is the manager or little general organizing the relative values of life often without regard for the ABSOLUTE. In many of us this little general becomes so distorted that it essentially blocks out any conscious contact with the ABSOLUTE. Some in Twelve-Step Programs use an acronym of ego that is in keeping with Jung's understanding. The acronym is Easing God Out. (EGO)

Just as clay protected the Golden Buddha, ego defenses have their place in the development of the mature person. The tendency of the ego to manage without regard for the ABSOLUTE qualities of life causes it, in many cases, to hang on too long; and when it does, it stifles rather than nurtures growth.

History shows us that these little generals can sway whole societies and that much of humankind can be substantially cut off from the ABSOLUTE nature of life. Ideally the role of religion has been to remind man of his greater nature. But history tells us that religion, as an institution, has also often been swayed by the little general. In the history of Judaism, for example, it was often the lone prophet who reminded the leaders, both king and priest as well as the masses, that they had a higher calling and a higher nature.

One of the leading lights of the twentieth century was the mythologist Joseph Campbell. He spent his entire life becoming familiar with and seeking to understand the myths of humankind. I believe that he, as much as anyone, has uncovered the information that can help us right our course. In his taped series, "The

Transformation of Myth Through Time," Campbell makes it clear that although mythology has gone through a transformation over the past fifty thousand years, its purpose has never changed. He says that the purpose of myth has always been to introduce and reintroduce man to that which is transcendent. He says that the history of mythology shows that man has always perceived the two basic values of life, the changing and the unchanging.

Mythology, according to Campbell, has always been the vehicle which has helped man to adjust to change by reminding him of and introducing him to the realm of the ABSOLUTE. He also says that some of the earliest artifacts of man found in caves and graves indicate that man was indeed aware of both his temporal and transcendent natures—both the gold and the clay.

****

Now, I am going to throw you a curve ball. His name is modern man, often a scientist or a person with a scientific bent. This person believes that there is not now and never has been a Great Spirit who molded man out of clay and breathed into him the breath of life. Therefore the person believes there is no God, no design, and ultimately no meaning. Clay is all we are and clay is all we shall be! "From dust we came and to dust we shall return."

Such a man is George Klein, one of the subjects of Csikszentmihalyi's book, *CREATIVITY*. George is a noted cell biologist. He has made significant contributions to cancer research. He loves his work; when he speaks about a living cell, he uses terminology that is reminiscent of a poet describing a sunset. Indeed, George Klein is more than a scientist. He is a man who enjoys the arts. He plays the piano, reads poetry, and tries always to be open to the truth. Although Jewish, he believes there is no God and that life absolutely has no meaning. Yet, he is happy in his work along with his relationships, and refers to himself as a "sunshine-colored pessimist." I said that I was going to throw you a curve ball. Did you catch it? Maybe not!

I am not using George just as an example of an atheist who has contributed to society and who is happy. I am using him as a man from whom we can learn. The lesson that George teaches us is: "To what we are connected is by what we are directed." (Guy Finley, *THE SECRET OF LETTING GO*) Unlike George, I believe that we are both clay and spirit. I also believe that George is more connected to and directed by the spirit than many who claim to believe in it. I repeat, it is not what we believe that directs us but to what we are connected that directs us. I suspect that George is an example of one with an unconscious contact with the ABSOLUTE.

Kae understands this phenomenon better than I do. She often says that it is only in the contrast that we understand. She realizes that often things of the fourth state of consciousness are more apparent to me than they are to her because the degree of contrast is different. For me, it has been like coming out of the dark cave into the light. For Kae, because she has always been more or less in touch with this aspect of her being, it is like moving from one room to another, a room that is only relatively brighter than the first.

Although I have never met George, I am convinced that like Kae, he has always been in touch with the ABSOLUTE unchanging value of life. However, the scientific and agnostic environment in which he was raised has allowed him to interpret these qualities in an entirely different way than I do. Once again I say, "To what we are connected is by what we are directed." Later we will illustrate this statement by using electricity as an illustration.

Note: In the meantime, I am content to let George call himself a "sunshine-colored pessimist." I, however, believe his "sunshine" is due to what he is connected to, and his pessimism has everything to do with his belief system. <u>Remember, this book is not about belief systems</u>. It seems apparent to me that one can be cut off from the essence of their being and have all kinds of religious belief systems. Similarly, one can be in touch with their essence and because of the intellectual and cultural environment in which they were raised, can still be agnostic or even atheist. But we must ask the question, "Which is more important, the belief system or the connection?"

As you read keep two ideas in mind. One: The "little general" ego, for some reason, doesn't want us to get acquainted with our TRUE SELF. Two: Each of us born into the western world has a western mind-set that has, like the "little general," substantially walled us off from recognizing our ESSENCE. These essays are designed to help you recognize how both the little general and the western mind-set have been formed. Are we really the masters of our fate, or are we prisoners of the "little general" and his lieutenant the "Western Mind." These two components of our make-up comprise a great deal of what we are referring to as clay or if you prefer, skins.

Chapter 10

MISSING THE MARK

Back in my student days, long before I ever heard the term "perennial philosophy," the philosophers and philosophies of existentialism fascinated me. Names like Kafka, Camus, Marcel, Heidegger, Sartre, Kierkegaard, and Unamuno come to mind. I have always been fascinated with names. I often wake up in the morning with my first thought being some strange or obscure name. For a while it happened so often that I called it "the name of the morning." I have a feeling that part of my fascination with existentialism is these wonderfully strange names. When I read the writings of these philosophers, I was not always sure what I was reading. At times I even doubted that the authors themselves knew what they were trying to say. However, I did understand enough to draw some conclusions. I did determine that these authors disagree on many things, even the meaning of existentialism. I also determined that some of them did not wish to admit that they were existentialists. At one point (considering all of their variety and differences), it became clear to me that what marks a philosopher as an existentialist is his starting point—the human condition. There may well be as many existential philosophies as there are existential philosophers!

We have already looked briefly at one existential writing that has had influence on my life, that is Samuel Becket's, *WAITING FOR GODOT*. The human condition he wrote about was meaninglessness. Another existentialist writing that we will look at later is Franz Kafka's, *THE TRIAL*. The human condition he writes about is neurotic guilt, frustration, and meaninglessness.

As a student interested in theology, philosophy, and psychology I arrived at my own existential philosophy. This philosophy simply says, "Modern man is having a hell of a time finding meaning in a world where all the givens are gone." This grew out of a question that I formulated back in the 1960's when the validity of every teaching from the past and every institution in the present was being questioned. The question simply was, "What do you do when all the givens are gone?" In a fast-paced, rapidly changing world, we find that what is innovative one day can become passé within weeks or even days. In this kind of world, what can you trust and where do you find meaning? We know it is not only our tools that become obsolete, but also our ideas and the institutions based on those ideas.

I heard Bob Dylan sing, "The Times They Are A-Changin'" in an off-campus coffeehouse over thirty-five years ago. Not long ago I heard him singing the same song at a live concert in San Diego. After the concert I found myself reflecting on the past thirty-five years. I reflected not only on my personal life but also on the social unrest of the 1960s, the political chaos of the 1970s, the self-centered selfishness of the 1980s, "me too" generation, and the rapid technological expansion of the 1990s.

A poem written by Kae in the 1970s reflects her anxiety about this changing world, and I think it captures the uneasiness that many feel today.

> Nothing is certain;
> Assertions don't last.
> You can't hang your cap
> On a peg of the past.
>
> What you said yesterday
> Was lost in today.

The peg and the cap
Have been taken away.

Nothing is certain.
Time has no frame.
How do I respond
To this timeless game?

Kae ended the poem with the question, "Where do I set my center post for stability—not in a ploy!!" I interpret this as a crying out in the midst of chaos, of constant change for something other than superficial mind games that are designed to divert, cover up, and gloss over our angst, our pain, our deep sense of despair and meaninglessness.

This poem reflects a period when both of us had begun to throw off the shackles of old ideas. We questioned old ties, friendships, and illusions that no longer had power. This period also reflects the first glimpses of what the center post of stability might be.

It is not my purpose to delve deeply into the meaning of our relationship. We have already given you some insight into that. But, more importantly, the journey that I am about to outline is primarily a solitary one. It is as the Apostle Paul says, "Working out one's own salvation with fear and trembling." (Phil. 2:12) At the same time, it is not done in isolation. It is a work done in fellowship and in relationship. I cannot conceive of successfully making this solitary journey without the fellowship of other travelers and without significant love relationships.

In the past century, we literally went from the horse and buggy to moon rockets and from the pony express to the Internet. In the twentieth century we witnessed many wars, including two world wars. We became aware of man's inhumanity to man like no century before this. Tyrannical leaders killed millions just to gain and insure their power. Technology gave us a window to the world; and we saw ethnic cleansing, mass destruction of societies, and starvation from the comforts of our living rooms.

It is here in the midst of this social schizophrenia that I have found some of the writings on existentialism to be useful. It is here that we can ask the question, "What is humankind and his or her relationship to the ground of being?"

Let's spend just a moment with one of these philosophers. Gabriel Marcel was one of those who was not sure he wanted to be dubbed as an existentialist. At times he preferred to think of himself as a Christian Socrates. His book, *BEING AND HAVING*, includes what he calls a metaphysical diary and covers the years 1928 through 1933. Marcel's study of the human condition led him to see that there existed two orientations to life. One was a "having" orientation and the other a "being" orientation. It appears that his study led to a discontent with his own "having" orientation and a yearning for a transformation. He ultimately made this transformation in the context of his Roman Catholic Faith.

Following his conversion he started to feel that the time had come for a reuniting of philosophy and religion. (In a future chapter we will meet a man who has gone so far as to suggest that it is time for the uniting of theology and physics.) On March 5, 1929, shortly after his transformation, Marcel writes:

"I have no more doubts. This morning's happiness is miraculous. For the first time I have clearly experienced grace. A terrible thing to say, but so it is. I am hemmed in at last by Christianity fathoms deep. Happy to be so! But I will write no more. And yet I feel a kind of need to write. Feel I am stammering childishly…this is indeed a birth. Everything is different."

Reading on in his diary, it seemed obvious to me that it was not until after his conversion that he really began to struggle with the difference between having and being. During this time he was not just dealing with the implication of having things but even relationships concerned with the concept of having a body and having a mind. The questions arise, "Who is this who has a body, a mind?" "Where does having end and being begin and what is the difference?" We run into this kind of struggle again when in the next section of this book we look at the path of the "Vision Quest Hero."

When I read about these distinctions as a young man, I was intrigued. I even felt that I understood the difference. However, it was not until I was almost forty that I began to experience the difference. This new orientation and perspective can make a monumental positive change in the quality of life. The *NEW TESTAMENT* word that is translated "sin" (harmatia) is an archery term meaning "missing the mark." That is exactly the nature of a life lived solely in a having/doing orientation. It misses the mark. It misses the purpose of living. Angst underlies all our efforts because our very orientation is missing the mark. In this state and in an effort to remove the dread, we find ourselves sinking deeper into the having/doing orientation. This sinking deeper describes what we know to be compulsive behaviors and addictive life styles. In other words, we temporarily find something which masks the dread. That mask can be having things, experiences, or relationships. It can also be an obsession with work, food, drugs, and even religion. Having found the mask (something that works temporarily) we tend to run with it until we drive it into the ground.

Now, what is the mark? It is <u>Being</u>! Hitting the bull's eye is to know and experience pure Being. It appears, however, that being stuck in the having/doing mind-set often takes us further and further from the quality of Being. Alan Watts, in his book *THE MEANING OF HAPPINESS*, says that something causes man to move outside of himself into his environment searching for happiness when he should be looking inside. That something of which he speaks is the having/doing mind-set. What we call evil is this having/doing mind-set in full sway—wanting it all, doing it all, and finding ourselves moving farther and farther away from the bull's eye (Being).

Society (institutions, churches, and government) responding to the having/doing mind-set establishes laws and rules to keep the people in line. This ends up being a vicious cycle because the more laws we pass, the more laws we need. Consequently, the bureaucracies needed to enforce the laws become larger and more numerous. We have all heard the phrase, "you can't legislate morality," but we really do not understand what that means. In the final analysis, it means that we cannot legislate Being; there is no legislation capable of bringing forth an awareness of Being. Yet, that is the answer; it is the awareness of our Being that is necessary. We can only legislate having/doing that is missing the mark. Mankind's predicament is stated in the following poem thought to be Zen's oldest:

> "The perfect way (Tao) is without difficulty,
> Save that it avoids picking and choosing.
> Only when you stop liking and disliking
> Will all be clearly understood.
> A split hair's difference,
> And heaven and earth are set apart!
> If you want to get to the plain truth,
> Be not concerned with right and wrong.
> The conflict between right and wrong
> Is the sickness of the mind."

This poem contrasts the life with which we are familiar with one that is now unfamiliar to most of us. It contrasts the life of having/doing with a life centered in Being. Having/doing, as the poem suggests, is concerned with right and wrong, to live in the realm of opposites such as good and evil.

Man's orientation to life, with few exceptions has always been having/doing. (I believe this is the meaning of the Adam and Eve story. To eat of the tree of knowledge, then to become aware of good and evil is to enter the realm of having/doing. To be ushered from the Garden is to lose contact with Being.)

As previously suggested, like Gabriel Marcel, I had a healing experience that introduced me to this "perfect way." (Referring again to the poem above.) As you will see later, unlike Marcel, I did not interpret this experience specifically in Christian terms; however, I certainly identify with Marcel's use of the word "Grace." My purpose in this chapter is to suggest that there really is a way out. You may ask, "the way out of what?" Hang on, we'll get to that.

I have had a broad experience working with people. These experiences include working in schools, churches, government, prisons, youth centers, hospitals, retail outlets, and industry. I have held positions of authority and positions subject to authority. These experiences have shown me that most people have a vague feeling that there is a lot more to life than what they are experiencing. Some seem to search and not find while others would search if they just knew where to look.

Some people, of course, are in real trouble. I worked with troubled people at the McNeil Island Penitentiary, the Lutheran General Hospital near Chicago, and the Seattle Youth Detention Center and Drug and Alcohol Treatment Centers. It was my observation that many of these people did not know that they were in trouble. They were still in denial. Others knew that they were in trouble but took no responsibility, blaming their problems on something or someone else. Some had had enough and were ready for a new life, a new beginning. We should point out that Marcel had his conversion only after he started to realize that the "having" orientation to life was not just a human condition but it was his condition.

Each of us has our blind spots, our idiosyncrasies, and our abnormalities. On the surface, many of us appear to be successful with little outward turmoil in our lives, and yet inside we experience a deep sense of uneasiness, hollowness, and lack of fulfillment. This is the kind of person Henry Thoreau talked about when he said, "The mass of men lead lives of quiet desperation." In the solitude at Walden Pond, Thoreau felt that he discovered some truth, something that addressed the question asked by Peggy Lee (popular Jazz song-stylist of the 1970-80 era) as she sang, "Is that all there is?"

I think this is a good time for you the reader, to pause and contemplate where you are. I offer the following questions to help you with this inventory.

QUESTION: Do you often have that "is that all there is" feeling?
QUESTION: Do you feel overwhelmed by "These times are achanging?"
QUESTION: Do you feel you have a having/doing or Being orientation toward life?
QUESTION: Do you find yourself enjoying what you have or obsessing about what you do not have?
QUESTION: Do you feel like you are missing the mark?

If you answered yes to any of these existential questions, keep reading—there is an answer. If you answered no to all of these questions, you are either in denial of your condition or you are solidly ensconced in BEING (SELF). If you are ensconced in BEING, it's quite alright with me if you throw this book in the trash can because you will be better informed by your Inner Reality than this Book. If you don't know whether you are in denial or ensconced in BEING, you are probably in denial and you should keep reading and pray for the willingness to have an open mind. If you don't believe in prayer, do it anyway. The results might surprise you. Pray for the willingness to have an open mind and keep reading!

Chapter 11

SICKNESS OF THE MIND

If you want to get to the plain truth,
Be not concerned with right and wrong.
The conflict between right and wrong
Is the sickness of the mind.
(Zen Poem)

From time to time we hear social commentators use tragic events such as the Oklahoma Federal Building bombing, school shootings, and work place massacres, as an opportunity to tell us that we live in a sick society; and these events are symptoms of that sickness. Most of us would agree that there is truth in this statement. Our society does exhibit sickness. But when these commentators take the next step and say that each of us bears some responsibility for these bizarre events, we are inclined to reverse the tables and call the commentator sick for coming to such an asinine conclusion. For how, indeed, could we who are regular law-abiding, taxpaying folks in any way be responsible for the fact that two wackos decide to bomb a building or a deranged child starts shooting up his school? I must admit this is my reaction. However, if I take a moment and do some self-analysis and see myself as a participant in society (as one who is part of rather than apart from), I catch a glimpse of what the commentator is trying to communicate.

If I then factor in the observation referred to by scientists as "field consciousness," I find the noose of culpability tighten around my neck. Field consciousness indicates that consciousness is not an individual thing, but something we share. My consciousness affects you; and your consciousness affects me. In the middle of the twentieth century, Carl Jung, the renowned psychiatrist, presented us with the notion of the collective unconscious. He developed this notion after analyzing the dreams of thousands of people. In so doing, he noticed certain themes recurring repeatedly. He called these recurring themes, "archetypes." He then asked a question regarding where these archetypes come from. Because they were themes that cut across cultural boundaries, he felt they must come from a common collective unconscious.

Today's field theories seem to go even farther. They indicate that we share the conscious, not just the unconscious. Studies using E.E.G. to test brain waves suggest that events involving large numbers of people also affect people who are not directly involved. For example, when the nation heard the O.J. Simpson jury verdict, people who were not tuned in and not aware that the verdict was going to be announced had brain wave reactions similar to those watching and listening to the announcement. Field theory would suggest that all minds are somehow joined.

Finally, the reaction of a number of astronauts to their experience of looking back to earth from space, claim that it changed their consciousness. If I understand them correctly, they are saying that the experience caused them to change from a we/they orientation to an us orientation. They looked back at the planet and realized we are all in this thing together. They came face to face with "deep ecology," "the web of life."

The point is, the less contact we have with our core essence, the more our minds find ways of seeing ourselves as separate. Our core essence binds and unites us and tears down the false barriers, divisions, and walls that our minds have constructed. When we are separated from our core (who we really are), our minds delight in the game of divide and conquer and are always finding new ways to define ourselves based on our differences. Few have seen this more clearly than the 18th century English poet and artist, William Blake. Blake was very critical of institutions such as the church, state, and education. He felt that these institutions should be the ones who point to the solution, that they should be helping humankind become aware of what makes us one rather than being a part of the divide and conquer mentality. He noted that the institutions of his day were continually erecting new divisions and setting up new boundaries.

Blake is often called a visionary or mystic. The painter, Samuel Palmer, said this about his friend Blake. "In him you saw the Maker, the inventor. He was energy itself and shed around him a kindling influence, an atmosphere of life, full of ideas. He was a man without a mask."

Gregory Bateson (1904-1980), a psychological anthropologist, saw the sickness of man in much the same way as Blake. Bateson said, concerning the sickness of the mind, that society suffers from a pathology of wrong thinking—thinking that doesn't recognize the unity of life. (For more on Bateson See: Appendix I-TRANSITION I.)

For all of the above reasons, I have decided we should go out in space and have an astronaut experience. We should look back at earth and take our individual and collective inventories in hopes that we become aware of our sickness (the illusion of our separateness) and see anew our unity.

****

Fellow citizens of planet Earth, as we continue into the twenty-first century, let us look at the century just passed to assess the state of our planet. To do this, I would like you to join me on an imaginary space platform part way to the moon. This viewpoint should give us an objective perspective. With it we will turn back time and rerun the twentieth century. Just suppose we can do this in the same way we use our VCRs. We can run it slow, fast forward, or play back and rerun. When you do this, what do you see? In our first rapid run-through, the thing we probably would notice most would be technological change.

In just over a century transportation literally moves from the horse-drawn carriage to the supersonic jet. Communication progresses from Pony Express* to e-mail, fax, and wireless telephone. We see the transformation from the hand-processed file folder to computers with blazing speed and almost unlimited storage capacity. We see narrow roads, often unpaved, to modern super arterials, skyscrapers and cars, cars, cars everywhere.

Nostradamus, in the sixteenth century, was said to have prophesied that the twentieth century would be brutal and bloody and it was! We see two major world wars and hundreds of lesser wars (civil and border wars), exterminations, ethnic cleansing, terrorism, atomic bombs dropped on Hiroshima and Nagasaki, the use of poisonous gas and germ warfare, and a long cold war. We note the stockpiling of missiles and warheads so numerous that life on earth could be destroyed several times over.

A review would not be complete without noting the breakthroughs and triumphs of man such as the discovery of penicillin and the near elimination of polio and measles, advances in cancer and heart disease treatment, and the ability to save lives by transplanting organs.

In the first chapter I talked about the idea that we share consciousness. We share much more than consciousness. If a physicist joined us on our space platform he or she would point out that Earth is a ball of energy, whirling molecules held together by the force of gravity. He or she would tell us that these particles are held together in a cosmic ball, and they are constantly being shared. We would be told that molecules, once in the bodies of people like Moses, Plato, Caesar, Jesus, and Confucius are now in our bodies, and the air we breathe into our lungs this minute is composed of molecules shared just hours ago by someone in a country an ocean away. In our lifetime we share the same molecules used by millions of other people, past and present, and from every corner of the globe!

Now, if we look at this cosmic ball as a biologist, we see a biosphere. Take a quick look at the sun and the moon. Is either one a biosphere? No! Both the sun and the moon are without life. Bio

---

* The regular Pony Express service was discontinued in October, 1861, after the Pacific Telegraph Company completed its line to San Francisco.

74

means life. So the earth is a sphere of life. A biologist might also refer to the earth as an ecosystem (ecosphere). In other words earth is a sphere of life in which the various systems are dependent on one another for their survival. With this in mind, let us rerun our century one more time watching the oceans, lakes, rivers and air become polluted, habitats destroyed, and species becoming extinct. Viewing this century of deterioration, we should develop some appreciation for the alarm exhibited by our environmentalist friends. We note in 1997 a group called "Union of Concerned Scientists" published an environmental warning to the world. It was signed by 1700 scientists including many Nobel Laureates. (See Appendix III: WEBSITES, Union of Concerned Scientists)

From the perspective of our space platform, take another look at planet earth in the way that one of the leading lights of the twentieth century, Buckminster Fuller suggested, as a space ship. This space ship is a closed environment that provides us with everything we need, except the energy we receive from the sun. This space ship must not only provide for our current needs but also for the needs of those in the centuries to come.

In his book, *PHYSICS AND IMMORTALITY*, Frank J. Tipler (Professor of mathematical physics at Tulane University) believes that in order for life to survive in the universe, there will come a time when humankind will need to abandon earth. To do this, he says, we will need to send out von Newmann probes (miniature rockets equipped with all that is necessary to start life on far off planets) to colonize the universe. According to Tipler, we will have the technology to send out those probes by the middle of the twenty-first century. However, colonization of the Milky Way will take 600,000 years. When we consider the amount of devastation that has taken place in the last one hundred years, it is apparent that we need to take better care of our space ship.

Before we leave our space platform and return to earth, I encourage you to think about your individual life and how the events of this century have shaped your mind. You may have experienced only a small portion of the twentieth century, but all of the century has had an effect upon your life. Your parents and grandparents were shaped by these events. You, in turn, were molded by society in the person of your parents, grandparents, teachers, T.V., etc. Now, like Scrooge in Charles Dickens' *CHRISTMAS CAROL*, I encourage you to be assisted by the spirit of past, and allow yourself to be guided in a review of your past and its effect on your mind and life. The following vignettes and experiences are intended to help you in your own evaluation of the impact history and culture had on yours. This is not to imply that these influences are always negative. It is meant to suggest that we don't have a choice until we are aware of the problem.

****

Knowing the importance of feedback is one of the advantages we have in the twenty-first century. With feedback we are able to evaluate new information and make course corrections. Even with smart arrows (missiles) one thing is very important—aiming at the right target! We know in the Gulf War some mistakes were made. We targeted our own tanks and our own people were killed. The bomb was smart, the feedback was good, but the target was very wrong. This fact points out the importance of evaluating our programming. Often times we have been programmed to hit the wrong target. Sometimes only a subtle correction is needed, and sometimes a complete change of course is required.

****

The final speaker at a twelve-step meeting said that this was his first time at this meeting, and he didn't know anyone there. He shared that he was apprehensive when he first entered the meeting, but as the meeting progressed his fears started to go away. He realized he was equal with all in attendance—not better than and not worse than, but equal. He said, "That's spirituality." Spirituality is the experience of oneness with our fellow man and the peace that accompanies that experience.

****

Which of the following two people are you most like? The first, in the midst of a discussion about terrorists, the sagging stock market and the Church who protected priests who molested children said, "You know, I look at the world as a sh-t sandwich and each morning I get up and take a big bite out of it!" The second one – When I asked him how things were going said, "Oh you know, the same old thing— one miracle right after another."

I suspect most people do not relate to either of these extremes; but people who have experienced the phenomenon we have referred to as "deep ecology" like Einstein, see life as a wondrous mystery, "one miracle right after another."

Chapter 12

THE PLAIN TRUTH

If you want to get the plain truth
Be not concerned with right and wrong.
The conflict between right and wrong
Is the sickness of the mind.
(Zen poem)

Yes, we started this chapter with the same Zen poem we used in the last chapter. In the previous chapter we highlighted "the sickness of the mind" and in this chapter we highlight the "plain truth." These two phrases reflect two different worlds – two different realms – the relative (the changing aspects of life) and the ABSOLUTE (unchanging realm). These two terms were first used in Chapter 9 when we metaphorically related them to the two aspects of the clay-covered Golden Buddha. We also indirectly referred to these two realms in Chapter 10. In that chapter we were talking about having/doing, another way of referencing life lived in the relative (the changing aspect of life) and Being, clearly a reference to the unchanging or ABSOLUTE aspect of our nature.

Now we turn our attention to perceiving truth in the context of these two different realms. The Poet says that the pursuit of truth is very simple. He says quite clearly that if you want to experience truth, don't look for it in the realm of the relative, "in the realm of right and wrong." He says to look for it, beyond the realm of conflict, in the ABSOLUTE. Let me hasten to add that this is not just a Buddhist teaching or even a teaching found only in eastern religions. It is a teaching found in all major religions. In a discussion with Pontius Pilate just prior to his crucifixion, Jesus told Pilate, "My kingdom is not of this world: - To this end I was born and for this cause I came into the world, that I should bear witness unto the truth." (Excerpts from John 18:36-37) Jesus also said, "Know the truth and the truth shall set you free." (John 8:32) Jesus was talking about being set free from the limitations of the relative realm which is defined by conflict, and by "right and wrong."

Anyone who has been set free by exposure to "the plain truth" will tell you that it is a beautiful and sublime experience. But, the word, "truth" in our day covers a lot of territory and not much of it refers to what the Poet calls "the plain truth." Nor does much of it have the power to set us free.

The following ideas are set forth in order to help us discern the difference between the "plain truth" which has the power to set us free and the relative truth which can titillate our brain but often lays impotent at the doorway of our sick soul.

The concept of truth is so central to the theme of this book that I once thought the title would be either, "A Search for Truth," or "My Search for Truth." Therefore, it seems appropriate that we should pause and discuss the word, "Truth." What do people mean when they use the word "truth" and what is it that sets you free?

The following sets forth some of the major themes regarding the word "Truth." First, let's look at it as something revealed by God. This is a notion that is common to most religions. This idea of truth says there is much more to life than that which is obvious. According to this notion, man is naturally blind and/or ignorant of the real purpose of life. Thus, measures had to be taken by God for humankind to get back on course. This scenario depicts a God who intervenes into the affairs of humankind and often takes unusual measures to reveal himself and his purpose—His Truth!

In Judaism such measures involved the choosing of a people that could be nurtured and guided. This intervention included the exodus from Egypt, the gift of the Ten Commandments through Moses, and the forty years of preparation in the wilderness. It provided them with a land and the prophets necessary to make them "a Holy Nation and a Kingdom of Priests."

In Christianity, according to tradition, God reveals himself by becoming a man. Born of a virgin, he grew up to teach, suffer, and die for the people. Being God, Jesus overcame death and declared newness of life for everyone.

In Islam God (called Allah) revealed himself to Mohammed through an intermediary, the Angel Gabriel. These revelations began in 610 A.D. when Mohammed was forty and continued for several years. These revelations of Gabriel defined the precepts of the religion and outlined acceptable conduct of those who would follow Allah and thus are received into paradise.

Individuals claiming to have communications from God, Jesus, or an Angel have started many sects, orders, and denominations. One example of this is the Mormon Church that was founded by Joseph Smith following revelations from the Angel Moroni.

The second concept of truth grows out of the development of religious institutions. These "truths" include interpretation and doctrines based on the original "revelations." In the following chapter we sketch some events in the long history of the Roman Catholic Church and glimpse how doctrine and tradition were formed. Churches are certainly not the only example of what we are calling institutional or doctrinal truth. We see this in government, schools, and other bureaucracies that have evolved over time. They become their own authority. The Roman Catholic Church established its teachings and doctrines through Councils and Papal decrees. We shall also see in the next chapter how scientists, who felt that they were uncovering God's revelations in nature, came into conflict with the teachings of the Church.

The doctrines and interpretations of the Church were also challenged by others, both within and without the institution of the Church. These individuals claimed to have their own contact with authority, be it God or the Bible. One of these individuals was a

Monk named Martin Luther. His protests gained momentum and resulted in the Protestant Reformation. The Reformation attempted to take the Church back to earlier authority and to cut away some barnacles of tradition. That earlier authority, for most Protestant churches, is the *BIBLE*. One problem with this is that the New Testament was written well after the events of Jesus' life and death and may contain interpretations of those events. It also is clear that the *BIBLE* itself was open to interpretations; and the Reformation resulted in not one but many protests, thus many denominations. Over the past three hundred years, the interpretations have continued and the result has been the further splitting of Christianity into churches and cults.

Thirdly, scientific truth is the truth that comes from the scientific method, facts, and data that result from experiments that can be replicated with the testing that is done according to accepted scientific protocol. This kind of truth, although extremely important for science, is not without its problems and limitations.

No area demonstrates the problems connected with scientific truth more than that of the modern-day health and nutrition scene. My mother, a registered nurse, told me a few years before she died at the age of eighty-one that she had concluded, based on modern science, if something tasted good you should spit it out because it's probably bad for you. This, of course, was a jest directed at the continual reports of food and other items which are said to cause cancer, heart disease, premature aging, etc. We all know, in recent years, these reports are often disputed, changed, and even nullified by subsequent studies. It does not take much analysis to conclude that the confusion in this and other areas is not all due to science. It is sometime the product of politics, special interest groups, and an overzealous press.

Most of us in the United States are the benefactors of a marketplace economy. It has many positive benefits but is not without its shortcomings. One of those shortcomings is the pressure put on truth. Truth, in the hands of advertising agencies, can be blurred. The truth, in the hands of the Press, motivated by the marketplace (ad agencies and media ratings) takes a beating on a daily basis. Truth, in the hands of politicians and their cousins, special interest groups, with one eye on the polls and the other eye on the press soon becomes cross-eyed. Scientists whose research budgets often come from governments can lose their clear vision as well from time to time.

Institutions, like church and government, are not the only ones that become set in their ways. Modern science appears to have problems in this area as well. This is true because much theoretical and experimental science is conducted at universities and because scientists are human and not above protecting their own turf. Honest skepticism should be a part of the process when it comes to evaluating new theories and new areas of inquiry. Closed-mindedness should not be a part of the process. If, however, you look behind the scenes, you will see closed-mindedness is not foreign to scientific circles. The following statement sometimes tossed about by younger scientists makes this point: "There must be a few more funerals before these new theories and ideas will be able to take root and grow." The meaning of this is that those who are entrenched in the system are impeding the growth of new ideas. The older scientists are often the ones with the authority, the clout, and the purse strings.

Two items illustrate this point further. A newspaper article brought to light resistance and infighting at the local university over the hiring of a new professor. The professor is prominent in the field of consciousness. The resistance to his appointment was, in part, because some of his research is in the area of the paranormal. One professor said, "Here we are at the end of the twentieth century and the University of Nevada, Las Vegas is officially sanctioning nineteenth century nonsense." Secondly, there is the phenomenon known as "confirmation bias." Dean Radin, Ph.D. and author of *THE CONSCIOUS UNIVERSE*, defines this as, "using guidelines that worked fairly well on similar problems" and getting locked into those ways of attempting to solve the problem. Radin says that the "confirmation bias" is at least one of the reasons why younger scientists make the most earth-shaking and ground-breaking discoveries..

The fourth concept of truth called "the plain truth" in the Zen poem: "If you want to get to the plain truth, be not concerned with right and wrong." This is the poet's way of saying if you want truth you must get beyond the realm of opposites, beyond the realm of ethics, yes, even beyond the realm of physics. This then would be the realm of metaphysics (beyond the physical world). Accessing this realm is a subjective, human experience. The scientific community puts little stock in the subjective experience. Recently, however, there has been some effort to verify the personal experience by scientific means. This is true in the case of meditation. Meditation is at least one of the techniques historically considered effective for individuals who desire to pierce the veil between physics and metaphysics.

In recent years scientists have sought to verify the meditation experience. While meditating, breath, brain waves, heartbeat and blood pressure can all be monitored. In addition, long-term studies can verify changes in health and behavior. In the last thirty years, many studies have been carried out and much data has been collected. The data seems sufficient to say that meditation can and does produce a fourth state of consciousness—the other three being deep sleep, dreaming, and the waking state.

Changes in brain waves and brain chemistry cannot confirm transcendence (conscious contact with the unmanifest), but they do tell us something is happening; and that something is quite different than that which takes place in either dreaming, deep sleep, or the waking state. Long-term studies relating to health and behavior verify that meditation has a positive effect.

Researchers at the University of San Diego (brain and perception laboratory) recently dubbed a portion of the temporal lobe as the "God module." They claim that their work is addressing the neural basis of religious expression. This kind of consciousness research that is in its infancy may never convince the skeptic that humankind is hardwired for conscious contact with the unified field (God). My response to the skeptic is in the words of Herbert Spencer:

"There is a principle which is a bar against all information which is proof against all arguments and which cannot fail to keep man in everlasting ignorance—that principle is contempt prior to investigation."

It is my belief that the true researchers in human consciousness are those, past and present, who have regularly used some sort of technique, such as meditation, to reach a higher consciousness. With the tools of modern science the validity of this subjective experience can and will become more evident. This subjective experience puts us in contact with the highest form of truth. Whereas science and education, as well as religious doctrines, can and do discover and convey truth that frees, it is only the experience of the realm beyond physics, beyond the realm of opposites that truly frees the human spirit. Thus, the Zen poet calls this higher consciousness, "The plain truth."

A fifth concept of truth is usually called "pragmatic." The question the pragmatist asks is, "Does it work?" For the pragmatist, if it works, it is true. Abraham Maslow, one of the first psychologists to analyze healthy people, noted that a person with an integrated personality is self-actualizing and that such people tend to have what he called "peak experiences." If we combine the concept of the "God Module" and self-actualization with the practice of meditation we have pragmatic truth. It seems evident to me that meditation is a technique for activating the module, producing peak experiences, and in turn, results in self-actualization. If this is true, and we have studies to say it's so, meditation is not just subjective but also pragmatic (true).

Now that we have attempted to identify at least five approaches to truth, it is important that we clarify a couple of areas. First, the concept of the God Module: My personal experience tells me that humankind is hardwired to experience and have a conscious contact with that which is beyond the physical. It also tells me that this hardwiring needs to be activated. I am not sure if a portion of the temporal lobe is the hardwiring as the San Diego scientists suggest. My intuition tells me that if this portion of the brain is involved, it is probably just part of the physical system that could be dubbed the "God Module." I am certain that further investigation will tell us much more about this system.

Secondly, I think there needs to be a distinction made between those who claim to have audible communication with God and those who have the experience of God. For want of a better way to make this distinction, I have divided them into religious, and spiritual. I personally have never had an audible communication from on high and therefore I am probably not qualified to evaluate such experiences. For the most part, I remain a skeptic. I am open to such possibilities, but I feel most people who make such claims are either self-serving or mentally ill. Several sects and their leaders have given us ample and tragic evidence that this is true. The messages of these people have often been destructive, self-serving, and divisive.

On the other hand, the message of the mystical experience is not one of words but an experience that universally communicates love, unity and timelessness—a universal experience that cuts across the history of time, creed, religion, and ethnicity.

Early on in this chapter we talked about the condition of humankind, a condition we described as both blind and ignorant regarding a higher value of life (spiritual). It was because of this condition that religion says that God intervened. My experience tells me God is immanent, also transcendent and that essentially we are ignorant and blind to the unity of life. Because God is immanent and because we have the hardwiring to be in contact, all we need to do is to activate and use that hardwiring (our God Module). Teaching and nurturing the use of techniques that activate should be the primary purpose of religion. Teaching doctrine and tradition should be secondary, fostering the use of those tools that can lead to conscious contact.

I have intimated that the institutions of the church and science have the opportunity to work together in this area. When they do, they will both discover the truth (the unified and the unifying field). At this point, humankind will be much closer to understanding the difference between having/doing and being. Then, we will realize that we do not do the truth or have the truth, but in the deepest sense, when we experience the Imago Dei, we are the truth.

"When I was a child, I spoke like a child, I thought like a child, I reasoned like a child. When I became a man, I gave up childish ways. For now we see in a mirror dimly but then face to face. Now I know in part: then I shall understand fully, even as I have been fully understood. So faith, hope, love abide, these three; but the greatest of these is love." (1st Cor: 13, 11-13)

Krishna's words to Arjuna in the Bhagavad-Gita:

"Still your mind in me, still yourself in me,
And without a doubt you shall be united with me,
Lord of Love, dwelling in your heart.
But if you cannot still your mind in me,
Learn to do so through the practice of meditation.
If you lack the will for such self-discipline,
Engage yourself in selfless service of all around you,
For selfless service can lead you at last to me.
If you are unable to do even this,
Surrender yourself to me in love,
Receiving success and failure with equal calmness
As granted to me.

Better indeed is knowledge than mechanical practice.
Better than knowledge is meditation.
Better still is surrender in love,
Because there follows immediate peace."

The Perennial Philosophy says, "The Kingdom of Truth is within you."

As we continue to search for the truth about the nature of man, I would like you to imagine that we are looking at a diamond, one facet at a time, in order to determine its authenticity, grade, clarity, and color. By the time we finish I hope you will clearly see much of the diamond (man's nature) which will enable you to determine the truth for yourself on the subjective level the level of direct contact.

****

On April 11th, 1998 while browsing in a large bookstore I found a book that has had a great impact on me (more than I could imagine) and consequently on the ideas that I had been working on for the last twenty-five years. Although the author is well known, I had never heard of this particular book. It was written in 1893 and points to the most powerful reality man has ever experienced.

History tells us that a young man, an East Indian attorney living in South Africa, read this book and was overwhelmed by it. Over a period of twelve years, he reread it a number of times. The book was key in the transformation of his life. This man returned to his homeland on January 19th, 1915 and was greeted as the hero of Indian struggles in South Africa. From that time until his assassination on January 29th, 1948, he captured the attention of the world and changed a nation.

Less than ten years after the death of this man, a group of Americans started studying the principles found in this book. When they put the principles into practice, another nation was changed. Some years later the powerful ideas contained in this book came back home to Russia and the Soviet Union. It wasn't long before walls literally came tumbling down—the whole world was changed.

Leo Tolstoy, Russia's greatest novelist, wrote this nonfiction book. His better-known books include *WAR AND PEACE, ANNA KARENINA* and *THE DEATH OF IVAN ILLYCH*. The young attorney whose life was transformed by the ideas in this book was Mahatma Gandhi and the country that he led and changed was India.

The group in America who embraced these ideas was the early black civil rights activists led by Martin Luther King Jr. Later day events in Europe resulted in the tearing down of the Berlin Wall and the dissolution of the Soviet Union.

The powerful reality for good that Leo Tolstoy wrote about in his book was the "concept of truth," the truth that each of us has deep down inside. This truth includes the truth of love, the truth of life, the truth of metaphysics, and the truth that it is available to each of us—the truth that can set us free. The name of the book is *THE KINGDOM OF GOD IS WITHIN YOU.*

You may remember that in the early pages of this book I spoke of Aldus Huxley and his novel, *ISLAND.* It was there that I made a statement about Huxley that could well be considered the "thesis statement" of this book. That statement was "he (Huxley) saw the perennial philosophy as the bedrock of truth and the expansion of consciousness as the path to that truth."

THE KINGDOM OF GOD IS WITHIN YOU, at least to the western mind, is the most concise way to describe the perennial philosophy. In 1944 Aldus Huxley published a book entitled *PERENNIAL PHILOSOPHY.* Huxley fills it with the quotes of mystics of every religion and follows with his own commentary. The book contains a number of themes; but for the most part, they come together in the term, "The Kingdom of God is within you." The phrase itself is based on the words of Jesus as found in the New Testament, but the philosophy as so aptly shown by Huxley cuts across time, culture, race, and religion.

This philosophy not only binds together the great mystics of all religions throughout the ages, but became the bridge that linked the Russian Christian Tolstoy to the Indian Hindu Gandhi. It linked Gandhi to the American Baptist Preacher Martin Luther King Jr. In turn it linked them to those who led the largely peaceful revolution that is epitomized by the tearing down of the Berlin Wall.

This philosophy not only links Englishman Huxley and the Russian Tolstoy, it also links most of the people who we will talk about in this book. Those people include the likes of mythologist and scholar Joseph Campbell, famous psychiatrist Carl Jung, futurist Buckminster Fuller, Jesus and the authors of the *I CHING* and the *BHAGAVAD-GITA.*

Now let us return to Tolstoy. Tolstoy was converted to Christianity late in his life. His conversion was not to an orthodox belief system but to a resonance in the core of his being with the words of Jesus, especially those in the Sermon on the Mount and the parables about the Kingdom of God.

Following his conversion, Tolstoy looked at the people and society in which he lived, a society that claimed to be Christian, and he was dumbfounded. He, in effect, said if these people are indeed Christian, how could they cooperate with evil? How can they cooperate with an evil, abusive, and corrupt government? How can they cooperate with a corrupt church? How can they allow themselves to be abused by these institutions? The government at which he was looking was that of the Tsars, soon to be replaced by Communism. The church that he was looking at was the Russian Orthodox Church that would soon be driven underground by Communism.

Tolstoy concluded that Russia and its people were not in touch with the Kingdom of God within. Therefore, he wrote his book to show the people that they were cooperating with evil and that their lives were miserable because of it. His own conversion told him that God's truth and power were available to them and when tapped would enable them to resist evil without armed force and without violence.

This is the idea that Gandhi found to be so fascinating and the idea that he ultimately demonstrated so effectively. This is the idea that Martin Luther King Jr. and fellow civil rights leaders found and used with such success. This truth was instrumental in bringing down the Berlin Wall and the Soviet Empire. However, this truth, with its transforming power, can only be demonstrated when it is first known from within.

Tolstoy was not content with the transformation of the individual. His reading of the New Testament, especially the Sermon on the Mount, led him to conclude that humankind need not only experience the Kingdom of God within but also needs to establish it on earth. It is this latter thought that turned me in a direction that I had not expected. I had become obsessed with the idea of sharing my own individual transformation and wanted others to experience theirs. Even though I had personally been involved in the Civil Rights Movement of the 1960s, I had never made the direct connection between the discovery of the Kingdom of God within and the social ramifications of that discovery. Yet it is clear to me today that this and this alone is the basis for talk about human rights and the statements contained in the U.S. Declaration of Independence which says "all men are created equal" and have "unalienable Rights."

****

In spite of this look at the impact of Tolstoy's book on the twentieth century, it is not my intention to further explore the ramifications of individual transformation vis-à-vis society at this time. However, I want to underline that there is a definite relationship with the following story. Thirty years ago, shortly before psychiatrist/author Harold Bloomfield published his first book, I attended a month-long seminar at a retreat center at which Dr. Bloomfield was also spending some time. I had the opportunity to speak with him on several occasions. One story he related was a conversation between futurist Buckminster Fuller or Bucky, as he was known to his many friends, and Maharishi Mahesh Yogi. (Fuller is best known as the inventor of the geodesic dome, but he was involved in many other projects, which continue to have a positive impact on our society. One of his major themes was conservation and the idea of "doing more with less." He applied this principle in many areas including automobiles and aircraft as well as building architecture.)

Apparently Bucky resonated with the Maharishi because he, as a young businessman, had a transformational experience that led him to a practice of meditation and what he called transcendental thinking. He gave great credence to these practices and credited them for his visionary thinking.

He had one misgiving, not so much with the practice of meditation but with those who practice these techniques. He expressed this misgiving to Maharishi at a symposium sponsored at Amherst College in 1972. According to Bloomfield, Maharishi and Bucky had a protracted dialogue about this subject. They found themselves in substantial agreement. Bucky's problem was his observation that most people who practiced meditation did so solely for their own benefit. He cited the tendency for such people to become isolated, to join monkish orders, and to separate themselves from society. Maharishi agreed and told him that it was this same concern that caused him to leave India and to begin to travel the world teaching his technique to those who could, in turn, bring the transcendental dimension to society.

Chapter 13

THE BROKEN WEB

In the Introduction we addressed the concepts of "Deep Ecology" and the "Web of Life." In Chapter Eleven, entitled "Sickness of the Mind," we took an imaginary trip into outer space and looked back at our "Home," Planet Earth. We looked deeply into its interconnected ecology. At the same time we also saw the ever-increasing threat to the "Web." We saw the ecosystem being destroyed. The reason for this destruction is clear; the fractured mind of humankind. In this Chapter an attempt is made to look even deeper into the reasons for the fractured mind and its relationship to the broken web.

One reason we are so confused about the "plain truth" is the battle that has raged between science and religion for the past four hundred years. It is a battle that has great significance in forming the modern Western mind or mindset. In this chapter I attempt to give the nonscientific reader (myself included) a brief overview of the march of science from the days of Plato and Aristotle in ancient Greece to the cosmology represented by Einstein and Steven Hawking in the present day.

In so doing, I have put science in juxtaposition with the teachings of religion, specifically, Christianity. Interestingly enough the Christian church (Roman Catholicism) chose for the most part to use the philosophy and science of Aristotle to develop its theology. This came to an ultimate fulfillment in the theology of Thomas Aquinas. A case can be made that if the church had allied itself with Plato and the neo-Platonists (as some wanted) rather than Aristotle, Christianity today would be much more in line with the perennial philosophy and the concept of the "plain truth."

At the end of this article, as you will see, I throw my support behind the neo-Platonists (many were mystical in nature) and show you how my own experience of meditation lends itself to some identification (in a mystical way) with the theories of Steven Hawking. The main reason for this review, however, is to point out how the history and the relationship between science and religion have helped to obscure our knowledge of the perennial philosophy and to minimize, yes in some cases even demonize mysticism.

In the chapter entitled, "Missing the Mark," we introduced the idea that there are two orientations to life, having/doing and Being. Before we go further, I state emphatically that I do not consider either having or doing to be wrong. Both can be good! However, the good can and often does become the enemy of the best. Having/doing, can become the enemy of Being, when the proper value of each does not remain in the forefront. Jesus said it this way, "Again, the kingdom of heaven is like unto a merchant man, seeking goodly pearls: who, when he had found one pearl of great price, went and sold all that he had, and bought it." (Matthew 13:45-46.) I am suggesting that there is a proper or preferred relationship between the two orientations.

Secondly, I intimated various areas within the having/doing mode that have a tendency to consume and confuse us. They tend to get us off-target and to shoot down our own best interests. I believe that both science and religion can and should serve us in our quest for the best. However, history demonstrates that it is not always so. It seems obvious that at least part of our confusion concerning our proper target has been caused by the long battle between science and religion and thus—this chapter.

****

One effect of my healing was to open my mind. Having had my mind opened, I never wanted it to shut again. Keeping an open mind is not as easy as it might seem. It means not having fixed ideas that do not allow change. This I found at times to be uncomfortable. Let me illustrate the difficulty of keeping an open mind with a recent event in my life.

I went back to my hometown for a high school reunion. Before the reunion I contacted an old friend, George, who I had known since the eighth grade. We were both trombone players in the high school band, and we both intended to become engineers. George did become an engineer with a doctor's degree from Stanford University. Today he holds patents on a number of alloys he invented and is a consultant to most of the companies that make jet airplane engines. Knowing that George had been rubbing elbows with mathematicians and scientists in various fields for many years, I wanted to pick his brain a bit. One of the questions I asked him was, "Do you know any mathematicians who regard math as a spiritual pursuit?" George, who is not particularly religious, laughed and said, "Mathematicians are definitely a breed of their own." He went on to say, "I do not know if spiritual is the right word; but after an extended period of calculating, some mathematicians can look at the results and say, 'oooooh, that is sooooo beautiful!'"

After that it became obvious that George was not going to let me pursue this line of brain-picking any further. He cut me off by saying he had a book that he would lend me entitled *THE PHYSICS OF IMMORTALITY* by Professor of Mathematical Physics, Dr. Frank Tipler. This book includes three hundred and thirty-nine pages that can be understood by most people with a high school education. It also includes an extended appendix for scientists, composed of notes, theorems, and formulas. The author says of this appendix, "To comprehend it all without references to a research library would require Ph.D. s in at least three disparate fields: (1) Global General Relativity, (2) Theoretical Particle Physics, and (3) Computer Complexity Theory."

George's answer to my question about mathematicians was more than I wanted or was ready to receive. Dr. Tipler's first sentence in the introduction said, "This book is a description of the Omega Point

Theory, which is a testable physical theory for an omnipresent, omniscient, omnipotent God, who will one day in the far future resurrect every single one of us to live in an abode which is in all essentials, the Judeo-Christian heaven." Dr. Tipler goes on to say that theology should, and he predicts will, become a branch of physics.

My healing led me to conclude that there is integrity in the universe, and man has access to this knowledge. In the twenty-five plus years since arriving at that conclusion, I have moved slowly to include some knowledge about the nature of that integrity. However, I was not ready for Dr. Tipler's scientific theory. In fact I found myself resisting, and I finally had to stop reading. I spent time analyzing my resistance. Was I resisting because some of my own slowly constructed ideas were being challenged? Was my mind once again closed to truth? Was I afraid of the truth? The answer to all three questions was, "To some extent, yes." Once we make an investment in certain ideas or beliefs, we are vulnerable and when we are vulnerable, we tend to cling. If this is true of the individual, then it can be seen how easily institutions can become entrenched in their own ideas of reality as well. Sometimes, these institutions have invested and reinvested, year after year, decade after decade, in their own idea of truth. This is a problem we have already discussed—"truth" becoming institutionalized.

Also in the chapter, "Missing the Mark," we experienced some quick snapshots of the twentieth century. One purpose for those snapshots was to show that the last one hundred years has been a century of transition. These transitions include:

The impact of modern science (quantum mechanics, cosmology) vis-a-vis, Newtonian physics
From low tech to the high tech - transistor age
From local economics to global economics
From the industrial age to the information age
From the generalist to the specialist

It should also be apparent from those snapshots that the transition is far from complete. A century mark, however, is a good time to make an assessment. In a period of rapid change it is also a good time to reestablish our bearing. As we look back over the past century we see in this transition phase times when things seem completely out of control followed by moments when we appear to see the light at the end of the tunnel and only then to be awakened to the reality that the light we see is the train coming toward us.

You need only pause a moment to realize the magnitude of these transitions and how each has benefited humanity. However, go through the list again and ask yourself, "What price are we paying for this progress?"

Let's look at the health-care industry as an example. It has been affected by all five transitions listed above. Out of this has come tremendous progress—the eradication of certain diseases, new and effective treatments, a longer life span, etc. On the other hand, few would disagree that modern health care in general provides care that is less personal, very expensive and at times, dehumanizing. One startling statistic recently revealed underlines this reality: over one hundred thousand people die each year in our United States hospitals from medical mistakes including improperly prescribed drugs.* (At the time of this writing, these figures are being disputed, but no one disagrees with the fact that deaths due to medical error are way too high!)

As I suggested earlier, "To what we are connected is, by what we are directed" and that a "center post" is available that can lead to both individual and global transformation and to greater human civility. We will be looking at science, psychology, mythology, religion, and philosophy for clues to that "center post." It seems appropriate that we start this discussion with a brief review of the historical factors that contributed to the split between science and religion.

Physicist/mathematician Tipler says that the twentieth century was the first century in which theological thought was divorced from the prevailing science. (You will remember that I mentioned that Gabriel Marcel was grappling with this same problem.) My brief assessment would indicate that he is essentially correct, at least regarding

---

* One version of this statistic was published in "Jama" stating that 106,000 patients died in hospitals from properly prescribed and properly utilized pharmaceutical agents.

Christian theology. Almost all of the Christian philosophers and theologians were familiar with Greek thought, especially Plato (429-347 B.C.) and Aristotle (384-322 B.C.). Aristotle's view of the universe was widely accepted until it began to unravel in the 17th century with the science of Nicholas Copernicus (1473-1543) and later with Galileo (1564-1642). With the publication of Sir Isaac Newton's (1642-1727) *PRINCIPIA*, Aristotle's universe was dealt its final death-blow in the scientific community. The most complete and influential theology based on the Aristotelian science was that of St. Thomas Aquinas (1224-1274). His writings and teachings have a significant place in the theology of the Roman Catholic Church to this day.

We should note that both Copernicus' and Galileo's ideas ran into trouble with the church authority. Copernicus, a canon of the Church, was dissatisfied with the Aristotelian view of the universe that had been reworked by Ptolemy in the second century. Copernicus observed that the sun, not the earth, was the center of the solar system. This, in turn, set the stage for Galileo's discoveries concerning falling matter as well as Newton's theories of mechanics and gravitation. It is not surprising that both Protestant and Catholic Church leaders became alarmed about these ideas and tried to suppress them. It was felt that these new scientific theories undermined the idea that man was the center and focus of creation. The focus of this suppression was so serious that science became one of the targets of the inquisition.

The laws that formed the basis for the Roman Catholic Church inquisition were well established by the sixth century, but the Inquisition itself was relatively inactive until the fifteenth century. The laws imposed a broad range of sanctions against heretics similar to those that were imposed against other criminals. The sanctions included fines, confiscation of goods, exclusion from inheritance, exile, deportation, and death. The same tyranny that once was directed toward Christians (by the Romans) was now being directed by Christians toward those who were regarded as unfaithful to the teachings of the Church.

From the sixth century on, even death by crucifixion and beasts in an arena were re-instituted to punish and intimidate the unfaithful.

The difference between Rome's persecution of the Christians and that of the Inquisition was the idea that this kind of coercion was justified and righteous because it had the potential to bring the unfaithful back into the fold.

The targets of the Inquisition, especially in the fifteenth century, were Jews, Protestants, Mystics, and those whose scientific ideas were contrary to the acceptable teachings of the Church. In 1600 a former Dominican, Giordano Bruno, was put to death for heresy that included his views on the science of Copernicus. Galileo in 1610, after the publishing of his research that accepted as correct the Copernican theory, was warned by the Inquisition to "Neither to hold nor to defend the thesis that the sun is the immovable center of the universe and that the earth is movable and not the center."[*] Galileo continued his work and his writing and in 1633 was brought to Rome where he was tried and sentenced. He was forced to recant his writings and spend the rest of his life under house arrest.

The death of Bruno and the trial of Galileo cast fear on the scientific and academic communities. This is best documented by the fact that René Descartes was apparently afraid to publish his scientific treatise, *DU MONDE*. The book was published only after his death.

****

The Newtonian view of the universe is described as an enclosed, perfect, clock-like machine. The theological system based on this mechanical universe was called "deism." Deism, as you may remember, is the belief that there was a creator and after the creation the creator was no longer involved. The creator didn't need to be involved because like a clock, all was set in place. Deism was popular with many of the founding fathers of the United States. However, deism's popularity waned quickly in spite of adherents like Thomas Paine, author of the pamphlet, *COMMON SENSE*. This pamphlet contributed significantly to the revolt of the Colonists against England. Other adherents included Thomas Jefferson, author of the Declaration of Independence and the third President of the

---

[*] *INQUISITION by Edward Peters, p.245*

United States, and George Washington, commanding general of the Revolutionary War and the United States' first President.

It is generally believed that deism was not an enduring theology because its underlying Newtonian science did not leave room for the concept of free will; neither could it compete with Christianity's concept of a personal and merciful God. By the middle of the nineteenth century the relationship between theology and science was in chaos. The Church had backed itself into a corner with its persistent clinging to the Aristotelian science, and the new theology based on the Newtonian science (deism) had failed. That was just the beginning. This period also marked the advent of the evolutionary theories in science. The result was further entrenchment by the Church.

The problem is that the Church was not only locked into a belief system, but in so doing was sidetracked. We have made the point that a belief system should always be secondary to a connection with Being. The following illustrates this fact. I have a number of electrical outlets in my house. If I pay my electrical bill, I can plug appliances into any of these outlets; and they will operate as designed. I have underground wiring, and I have no idea where these wires go. I do not know if my electrical power is hydroelectric, coal powered, diesel powered or sun powered. I just know that if I pay my bill and make the proper connection, I get power! Now, suppose I learn that the power I get is hydroelectric coming from a nearby dam. Let's suppose I go to the dam, take their tour, learn about the history of the dam, learn how many generators it has and how many kilowatts of power it produces, etc. The question now is, will all that knowledge enable me to get more power than I am already getting? If I form a belief system about which kind of generating system is best, will that improve the service I get in my home? On the other hand, if I do not pay my bill, or I do not attempt to plug in, will this belief system alone provide me with any power? Humankind is hard-wired to plug into the ABSOLUTE! A good belief system can, no-doubt, help us plug in, but it is primarily informative, not experiential.

Two publications in the nineteenth century capped the growing division between religion and science. Auguste Comte (1789-1857) published *THE POSITIVE PHILOSOPHY* that lead to the largely antireligious, rational philosophy of logical positivism. The second, *ORIGIN OF SPECIES* by Charles Darwin (1809-1882) really upset the theological apple cart! The reaction of the Church, both Catholic and Protestant, to theories of evolution was hostile and remains hostile in fundamentalist camps to this day.

This brief overview of the relationship between science and religion should give you a fair understanding of the juxtaposition of these two as they entered the twentieth century. In that century both had to come face to face with the new paradigm in physics as presented by Albert Einstein and Niels Bohr and carried on by the likes of Steven Hawking, et al.

****

In the past years I have heard preachers and gurus talk about the "unified field" in a way that makes one think that science has found God or soon will. I recently read several books relating to twentieth century physics. In these books I read about qwiffs, Schredinger's cat, Wigner's friend, quantum leaps, neutron stars, black holes, singularities, and God shooting dice. For the most part these books were for laymen, and still I must admit there was stuff way over my head.

When I finished the last book, I picked up a piece of paper and outlined what I had learned. Here it is: Today we have quantum mechanics, Newtonian physics and cosmology. Quantum mechanics has to do with the small stuff like protons, neutrons, and atoms. A quantum is a unity of energy. So quantum mechanics is about working with the energy of the small stuff. With the dropping of the first atomic bomb on Japan during World War II, we got our first graphic look at the energy (power) of an atom. Newtonian physics applies to our everyday life. His physics is really passé, but it still works fairly well for most of us. It applies because we are slow, and do not move anywhere near the speed of light. A good way to observe Newtonian physics is to play a game of pool or billiards. Notice the balls taking energy from each other. Notice how they react when they hit the cushion. Notice that a ball in motion keeps going until it hits something, and stationary balls stay put until they are hit.

101

That is the stuff of Newtonian physics (force, inertia and all that) and it still works pretty well because the balls are not going at the speed of light either.

Cosmology is the science born out of Einstein's theory of relativity. It has to do with gravitation, and it deals with the big stuff like galaxies and the universe as a whole. The formula, $E=MC^2$, has provided opportunities for many cosmological experiments in the past eighty years. One such project was the concept of black holes. $E=MC^2$ predicted there could be such a thing. A black hole is a mass so large that it turns in on itself and does not let anything escape, not even light. Although the Einstein formula suggested the possibility of black holes, scientists felt that the probability of such a phenomenon was small. Little by little, however, the scientists started getting clues that such a thing might exist. Steven Hawking, the man many call the Einstein of the second half of the twentieth century, seems to have taken this concept to the ultimate. (We will return to this presently.)

Quantum theory and cosmology are the twin pillars of modern physics. Both sciences are filled with surprises that could not be accounted for in Newtonian physics. For instance, in cosmology light bends and in quantum mechanics, particles become waves. The cause and effect mechanical system of Newtonian physics could never allow for such anomalies. Almost from the time that quantum theory was developed, scientists tried to bring the twin pillars of quantum mechanics and cosmology together under some common formula. Einstein worked on his unified field theory for over twenty years without success. Today scientists like Steven Hawking have taken up this quest so adamantly that it is defined by some as the quest for the Holy Grail. At this time, the unified field theory is usually called the theory of everything. Many believe that Steven Hawking has come as close as anyone to uniting the twin pillars. He has done so by applying quantum mechanics to the big bang theory. In his study of black holes, he hit upon the idea that the universe in which we live is itself a black hole in reverse. He and other cosmologists have now established a model that takes us back fifteen billion years to a tiny portion of a second before the big bang. Hawking says at this point there was a super dense piece of matter the size of a proton. At that moment it was expanding to the size of a grapefruit. This first state is aptly described as expansion. According to the model, when the universe reached the size of a grapefruit, expansion was exhausted but continued to move outward in a slow steady manner.

Einstein's theory says that the universe must either be expanding or contracting. Some cosmologists today believe that at some point our universe will stop expanding and the contraction process will begin. This contraction will end in a way that is opposite to the big bang. They call this the "big crunch." At least one huge question remains. Where does that tiny dense proton of matter come from? Many believe that the answer to this question is: "From nothing." If we accept this, the big bang model of the universe says that we start with nothing and in the end there will be nothing again.

Hawking, who does not like to talk of God, curiously ended his popular book, *A BRIEF HISTORY OF TIME*, with a paragraph about God. While on a 20-20 ABC Television broadcast Hawking said, "It is difficult to discuss the beginnings of the universe without mentioning God. My work on the origin of the universe is on the borderline between science and religion, but I try to stay on the scientific side of the border. It is quite possible that God acts in ways that cannot be described by scientific laws. But in that case one would just have to go by personal belief."

In the same vein, Pope John II said at a conference on cosmology in 1981 regarding the big bang theory and the origin of the primeval atom, "Science cannot by itself resolve the question; what is needed is that human knowledge that rises above physics that is called 'metaphysics.'" It should be noted, Steven Hawking also gave an address at this conference.

****

My original intention was to discuss meditation in the later chapters of this book. However, after writing the above, especially the section on black holes, the case for writing about meditation at this point became impelling. Before doing so, let me review. Roger Penrose, mathematician and college friend of Hawking, told Hawking about his calculations indicating the possibility of a collapsing star. With this information Hawking started thinking that reversing the process might give some information about the universe as a whole. Simply put, a black hole is a massive star whose nuclear fuel has become exhausted. Due to its great mass, gravity causes it to collapse in upon itself. It continues to collapse, squishing its molecules, electrons, and protons together until it gets to what the scientists call a "singularity."

Hawking then reversed the dying star process and started with the singularity. (Remember, a point of infinite density and zero size). In his theory, the singularity becomes as we have already noted, the stuff of the big bang. Using Einstein's theory of relativity and quantum mechanics, Hawking was able to trace the expanding universe back to just before the big bang. At that point he says all the laws of physics appear to break down.

Now you may ask, how does this relate to meditation? Good question! For me, it relates in two ways: The intellectual understanding of meditation as taught by Maharishi Mahesh Yogi and my personal experience. Kae and I were among thousands who were taught this technique in the 1960s and 1970s.

Just as Hawking traces the universe from its present state back to its inception, Maharishi taught his students to introduce a thought (a word or mantra) into the mind on the gross level. Then, to follow that thought through finer and finer states until the thought is transcended. He says transcending is going from the finest aspect of thought to the source of thought; from the realm where everything changes to the realm of the ABSOLUTE where nothing changes; from the manifest to the unmanifest; from the world of diversity to the realm of the unified field. The proof, Maharishi said, is the experience of the person meditating. Each time one transcends and returns from that unified field, one returns with the values of that field. Those values accumulate and become noticeable over time.

My own experience of meditation, which I have practiced for more than thirty years, has proven to my satisfaction that what Maharishi said about meditation is correct. I start with a word, without any effort, allowing it to grow finer and finer. As this process proceeds naturally, I am often aware of silence and at times a moment when the laws of physics seem not to apply—a period when time and space seem to be transcended. When I first started meditating, the most noticeable effect was that I felt rested. Over time, I have noticed a gradual change in feeling tone. My life has slowly taken a new sense of meaning and my behavior is no longer self-destructive. Today I am aware of the accumulating effects of tracing a thought back to its singularity and beyond. I once heard Deepak Chopra say that you can expand your consciousness until you touch the womb of the universe. I believe this to be true.

Maybe mathematics and physics will someday (hopefully soon) arrive at a complete understanding of the unified field. Maybe the concept of God will be proven by experiments in a supercollider. "Physics is no longer limited to the finite; technical advances inside physics itself have forced physicists to become concerned with the physics of the infinite." (Tipler, page 5)

Still, coming up with a unified field or a God proven by mathematics or in a supercollider is not transcending. I believe that only humankind and not his/her science or religions have the capacity to transcend, to experience the realm beyond the singularity, beyond the big bang and beyond that tiniest particle of matter. Only man has the capacity to enter the realm behind thought. Only man has the capacity to enter the Kingdom of God. Only man has the capacity to experience "the plain truth" and only a greater manifestation of "the plain truth" can begin to heal the "broken web."

Note

Appendix I The Perrenial Philosophy adds a good deal of detail to this period and illustrates further how the conflict between the emergence of modern science and its conflict with religion have added layers of clay to the modern western mind.

Chapter 14

SPIRITUAL EVOLUTION

We live in an age when millions of people still believe that some five to six thousand years ago God knelt down and breathed into a lump of clay the breath of life, and men and women began to walk the earth. On the other hand we have those (many of them influential scientists) who believe that man is the result of an evolutionary process called "natural selection" and that a superior intelligence has nothing at all to do with the process.

The research for *THE EVOLVING SELF* by Csikszentmihalyi was done largely against a backdrop based on the study of both biological and social evolution. One conclusion implied in the first chapter of this book is that humankind has come to a crossroads, one road leading to greater glory and the other to annihilation. Csikszentmihalyi also shares his conviction that if we are to take the road to continuing and expanding evolution, humankind must become consciously involved in the process.

Not long ago I independently arrived at the same conclusion. However, until I read *THE EVOLVING SELF*, I did not yet have the courage to express my convictions. I thought maybe I was way out on a limb and was not sure this matter should be discussed in this book. But, because I found Csikszentmihalyi's argument to be so persuasive, I have become emboldened in my convictions and assuaged of my timidity.

I do believe humankind has come to a crossroads. The road we take from here will largely be determined by how we view and understand the road we have just traveled. If the majority of humankind remains indifferent to this question while a minority of people take strong polar positions, we may miss our opportunity to move forward toward an understanding of SELF that will be viable for the third millennium. As we have already stated, this could have catastrophic consequences for the survival of our race and environment.

I feel the solution to our dilemma lies neither in the denial that there could be intelligence involved, nor in the denial of an evolutionary process. The road to the solution does not consist of having a popular vote to find out who we will follow—religion or science—ancient wisdom or modern knowledge. The answer does not lie in the choice of one or the other, but in a synthesis of the truth in each. I believe the following information points to the road we should travel and shows this synthesis may have already begun.

EVOLUTIONARY CROSSROADS

Having dealt with our subject largely using analogy and metaphor, we must now ask what is the "life force" and what is its relationship to matter. Listen to these words. "Without any doubt there is <u>something</u> which links material energy and spiritual energy together and makes them a continuity. In the last resort, there must <u>somehow</u> be but one single energy active in the world." These are the words of Pierre Teilhard de Chardin (1888-1955) taken from his *HYMN OF THE UNIVERSE*.

He was a man that combined many elements that we are looking at in this book. He was a scientist (paleontologist), devoutly spiritual (a Roman Catholic Jesuit Priest), a mystic, and an evolutionist. In addition, he was a man experienced in life. He was a stretcher-bearer in the First World War, and in the Second World War he was a virtual prisoner-of-war in China. It seems certain that he was a self-actualized man for what he did, he did out of conviction rather than any self-serving motive. His writings attempted to synthesize both his scientific and religious convictions and ended up pleasing neither the scientific nor the religious communities. Nor did his writings please his superiors who forbid him to have them published, and consequently they were not published until after his death.

According to Ken Wilbur, de Chardin picked up a strain of thought that was only a few hundred years old. Wilbur says, "The idea of evolution as a return-to-spirit is a part of the perennial philosophy, but the idea itself in any adequate form is not old." Wilbur says that we see it's beginning in a more adequate form with philosophers Schelling (1775-1854) and Hegel (1770-1831).

De Chardin learned about evolution by reading the works of his fellow Frenchman, Bergson (1859-1951). Bergson, too, seems to be a man with mystical vision. He lays great stress on the power of intuition and the ability to know a thing from within. He specifically speaks of knowing the SELF, the "one-reality—which we all seize from within."

Bergson found that evolutionary theories expounded by Darwin, DeVries, and Spencer to be lacking and set out to put in place a satisfactory explanation of how and why evolution takes place. At the beginning of this piece, we quoted de Chardin saying, "There is something which links material and spiritual energies together." De Chardin, no doubt, first got this notion of this something from Bergson, or at the very least shared it with him. This link Bergson calls "élan vital" (vital impulse) and says we first discover this through our own SELF. Finally, Bergson talks of the élan vital as that which resembles consciousness and says it is certainly "of God, if it is not God himself."

In THE PHENOMENON OF MAN and with the concepts of his own faith (Christianity), de Chardin traces the élan vital from the beginning of matter to the dawn of life and into the blooming of consciousness. He doesn't stop when he gets to the present day. He continues, projecting into the future a vision that he calls the "omega point." He says the omega point is the fulfillment of John 17:21. "That they may all be one even as thou, Father, art in me, and I in thee, that they also may be in us..." In this work he does that for which Joseph Campbell pleads. He takes myth and revitalizes it into a vision of hope. He blends scientific knowledge and theological truth into a mystical vision. This vision can, no doubt, be fully appreciated only by those who have themselves tasted the mystical and have become somewhat conscious of the élan vital.

Another man from whom we can catch a glimpse of the evolutionary future, beyond the present crossroad, is Aurobindo (1872-1950). Aurobindo was a Hindu Mystic, educated at Cambridge where he was a brilliant scholar. Like de Chardin, he blended his faith with the Western understanding of evolution. Also, like de Chardin, he knew something of life's hardships having been jailed for his political views after returning to India. I feel there is no better way to highlight this short section on evolution than to share with you the visionary words of both de Chardin and Aurobindo. As you read these quotes note, even though one is Christian and the other Hindu, for both men spiritual evolution means recognition of the divine interior in Humankind, progress toward unity, and the growth of consciousness in the direction of the COSMIC SELF.

FIRST: Pierre Teilhard de Chardin – a Christian

"Because of the fundamental unity of the world, every phenomenon, if it is adequately studied even though under one single aspect, reveals itself as being ubiquitous alike in its import and in its roots. Where does this proposition lead us if we apply it to human 'self awareness?'"

"We might have to say, 'Consciousness manifests itself indubitably only in man; therefore it is an isolated event of no interest to science.'"

"But no, we must correct this, and say rather, 'Consciousness manifests itself indubitably in man and therefore, glimpsed in this one flash of light, it reveals itself as having a cosmic extension and consequently as being aureoled by limitless prolongations in space and time.'"

"This conclusion is big with consequences, but I cannot see how it can be denied if sound analogy with all the rest of science is to be preserved."

"It is a fact beyond question that deep within ourselves we can discern, as through a rent, an 'interior' at the heart of things; and this glimpse is sufficient to force upon us the conviction that in one degree or another this 'interior' exists and always has existed everywhere in nature. Since at one particular point in itself, the stuff of the universe has an inner face, we are forced to conclude that its inner structure—that is, in every region of space and time; it has the double aspect, just as, for instance, in its very structure it is granular. In all things there is a Within, co-extensive with their Without."

HYMN OF THE UNIVERSE - Pierre Teilhard de Chardin.

"Since Jesus was born, and grew to his full stature, and died, everything has continued to move forward; Christ is not yet fully formed; he has not yet gathered the last folds of his robe of flesh and of love which is made up of his faithful followers. The mystical Christ has not yet attained his full growth, therefore the same is true of the cosmic Christ. Both of these are simultaneously in the state of being and of becoming; and it is from the prolongation of this process of becoming that all created activity ultimately springs. Christ is the endpoint of evolution, even the natural evolution, of all beings; and therefore evolution is holy."

HYMN OF THE UNIVERSE - Pierre Teilhard de Chardin

Now we turn to Sri Aurobindo – a Hindu

THE NEW RACE

"The gnostic individual would be the consummation of the spiritual man; his whole way of being, thinking, living, acting would be governed by the power of a vast universal spirituality. All the trinities of the Spirit would be real to his self-awareness and realized in his inner life. All his existence would be used in oneness with the Transcendent and universal Self and Spirit; all his action would originate from and obey the supreme Self and Spirit's divine governance of Nature. All life would have to him the sense of the Conscious Being, within, finding its self-expression in Nature; his life and all its thoughts, feelings, acts would be filled for him with that significance and built upon that foundation of its reality. He would feel the presence of the Divine in every center of his consciousness, in every vibration of his life-force, in every cell of his body. In all the workings of his force of Nature he would be aware of the workings of the supreme World-Mother, the Supernature; he would see his natural being as the becoming and manifestation of the power of the World-Mother. In this consciousness he would live and act in an entire transcendent freedom, a complete joy of the spirit, an entire identity with the cosmic Self, and a spontaneous sympathy with all in the universe."

Sri Aurobindo

Aurobindo, de Chardin, and Bergman had several things in common. They were all highly intelligent, had academic backgrounds, studied science, had religious orientations, were steeped in life's vicissitudes, and experienced the mystical. I feel the key to their effective assimilation of all these elements was their mystical experiences. Now the word mystical is not well understood in our society. In fact, when I told a clergyman friend of mine that I was going to write a book that included an emphasis on the mystical experience, he cautioned me saying, "You know talking about the mystical is not very popular."

I define mystical experience as a conscious experience of being in contact with pure consciousness. This harkens back to what Bergman said about the élan vital - that it resembles consciousness and that it is "of God, if it is not God himself." I repeat that I define mystical experience as a conscious experience of BEING. One further thought: contact with BEING does not have to be pure to be contact with pure consciousness. In other words, our contact may well include some static, some thoughts, but it is a contact nonetheless.

Chapter 15

HIGHER CONSCIOUSNESS

In an earlier chapter entitled, "The Broken Web," we looked briefly at cosmology or outer space. In this chapter we are looking at inner space, the space associated with the realm of the mind; not the thinking mind but the mind that can move beyond thought, the mind that has the potential to experience pure consciousness. It should be noted that both the cosmos and the mind are relatively unknown quantities. However, we probably know more about the mysteries of the cosmos than the mysteries of the mind. Indeed, in comparing the two, the study of consciousness is a mere infant. The first telescope was invented in 1608 and first used to study the heavens by Galileo. The technology that enabled us to start studying consciousness is the electroencephalograph (EEG). It was introduced in the early 1920s.

EEGs were first used to detect abnormalities in the brain such as tumors. However, before long they were being used in experiments with individuals who were dreaming, sleeping, and awake. These three states were recognized as three different states of consciousness. With the use of the EEG each state was proven to have its own unique brain wave pattern. With this new device at their disposal, it was not long before scientists were using it to verify the so-called fourth state of consciousness. Scientists as early as the 1930s took EEGs to India in search of meditators who could be monitored. Early results of these experiments suggested meditation produced a state of deep rest, but the overall results were inconclusive regarding a fourth state.

In the 1960s Maharishi Mahesh Yogi came to the West and introduced his Transcendental Meditation Technique to a large number of people. With this increased interest in meditation there also came an interest, by scientists, to study its significance. Even though this study was being done in places like Harvard University, the conclusions carried a cloud of suspicion with them because many researchers themselves were involved in the T.M. movement.

However, over time, much of the suspicion has been alleviated, as corroborating research by non-T.M. scientists has been published. There is growing evidence, based on brain wave studies, that meditative techniques produce a fourth state of consciousness and this fourth state can, in time, with persistent use of a meditative technique, be stabilized. This may not be widely accepted but the science of consciousness itself is not widely accepted. Like any new science, it must go through a period of trial, of doubt, and skepticism. Dr. Dean Radin, a researcher in this field, in his book, *THE CONSCIOUS UNIVERSE* says, "There is every reason to expect that the same methods that have given us a better understanding of galaxies and genes will also shed light on experiences described by mystics throughout history." He also says, somewhat cynically concerning the skeptics, "History amply demonstrates that science progresses mainly by funerals, not by reason and logic alone."

Just as the use of the telescope cannot tell us everything we want to know about the Universe, neither can an EEG tell us all that we would like to know about consciousness. In fact, Stanislav Grof (a man whom many think is our greatest living psychologist) says that although the brain mediates consciousness and human experience, it does not originate there. He says, "Consciousness clearly can do things that the brain and sensory organs cannot." He goes on to quote the famed neurologist Wilder Penfield in support of his contention that consciousness does not have its source in the brain. (*THE HOLOTROPIC MIND*)

Prior to the EEG and consciousness research being conducted in a laboratory a number of individuals investigated this area. In the last one hundred years three of these individuals gained some prominence with their observations.

Before we look briefly at these studies, let's consider another metaphor—that of metamorphosis. We are all familiar with metamorphosis. It is the process of physically changing from one form to another. The process is what the caterpillar goes through to become a butterfly and the tadpole goes through to become a frog. These two are probably the most familiar, but did you know that thousands of nature's lesser-known creatures also go through this process?

The more I have studied this business of human consciousness, the more I am convinced that humankind in its present state of development can achieve metamorphosis. Our metamorphosis is not intended to be a physical change but a psychic one. Although it is not on the physical level, it is every bit as important. If indeed Csikszentmihalyi's evaluation of our present condition is correct, our very survival depends on this metamorphosis.

I am also convinced that almost every religion has something to say about this. Unfortunately, the message is often hidden, misinterpreted, covered up, or otherwise lost. I have little doubt that Jesus of Nazareth was a man who experienced in his lifetime this metamorphosis, a throwing aside those aspects of culture and genetics that limited his perception of reality and took on a new identity that he called the Kingdom of God. Jesus kept telling his followers about this new identity hoping they would get a glimpse of the metamorphism for themselves. Repeatedly he said the Kingdom of God is like this or like that. He used many parables (metaphors), for how else could he talk about a psychic change including a whole new identity? In another setting, he shared with an inquirer what it was like being born again. Now, present day Christian Churches talk about being born again, but I cannot honestly say they are (in most cases) talking about the same thing Jesus was talking about.

Now, let's look at three individuals who studied the idea of a fourth state of consciousness. The first is Richard Maurice Bucke. He was a Canadian Medical Doctor and a Superintendent of an asylum for the insane. (Note: The relationship between Walt Whitman and Richard Maurice Bucke was documented in a 1992 film called "Beautiful Dreamers." Walt Whitman is played by Rip Torn. Home Hempdale Home Video, Inc distributes the film. The film is a deeply moving triumphantly optimistic story based on actual events.) Bucke fell under the influence of the writings and person of Walt Whitman. He found Whitman to be a most unusual and unique personality. Under Whitman's influence, he realized a psychic metamorphosis. He also became aware of others who had experienced a radical transformation by being around Walt Whitman and/or his writings. Bucke was so intrigued by this phenomenon that he set out to explore it further. He started by contacting other people who were greatly influenced by Whitman. With the information he garnered, coupled with his knowledge of Whitman and the awareness of his own illumination, he started to look back in history for others who might fit into this picture. In 1898 Bucke published his findings in a book entitled *COSMIC CONSCIOUSNESS*. The limited edition of five hundred copies described what he considered a new, fourth state of consciousness. He apparently appropriated the term, "cosmic consciousness," from Edward Carpenter, one of those he studied and who used the term in a book entitled, *FROM ADAM'S PEAK TO ELAPHANTA*.

Bucke sets up criteria that denotes this new consciousness. He said this higher consciousness enables individuals to realize their oneness with the Universe, to sense the presence of the Creator, to be free of fear and to comprehend the law of love. Bucke believed this consciousness was a result of evolution and consequently would appear in more and more people. He felt in time, it would become the norm. The list of those whom Bucke studied and saw as having achieved a high degree of this fourth state of consciousness included: Buddha, Jesus, Paul, Plotinus, Mohammed, Dante, Francis Bacon, Pascal, William Blake, and Lao Tzu.

William James, the author of *THE VARIETIES OF RELIGIOUS EXPERIENCE*, quoted Bucke and gave further credibility to the concept of cosmic consciousness. James also, in his studies, found the mystical experience seemed for the most part a positive, integrating experience. He reports that the testimony of mystics from a broad spectrum of religions and theological backgrounds constitutes a surprisingly consistent message. Theological and religious backgrounds seemed to take a back seat to the experience itself.

The third figure I want to mention is P.D. Ouspensky. He was born in Moscow, Russia in 1878. Unlike James and Bucke who came to the idea of a fourth state of consciousness through psychology and subjective (mystical) experience, Ouspensky came to the idea of a fourth dimension via mathematics. In 1909 he published his first book, *THE FOURTH DIMENSION.* The subject matter was abstract, mathematical theory dealing with the illusory fourth dimension of time. Three years later he published *Tertium Organum* in which he took his mathematical theories into the realm of philosophy, especially the concept of consciousness. (Incidentally, *TERTIUM ORGANUM* was one of the books found in Dr. Bob's library after his death. Dr. Bob is a co-founder of Alcoholics Anonymous.)

Ouspensky spends an entire chapter in *TERTIUM ORGANUM* quoting extensively from and commenting on Bucke's Cosmic Consciousness. While he generally agrees with Bucke concerning the evolutionary appearance of higher consciousness, he takes him to task for not recognizing that humankind must become consciously involved in this evolutionary process. Thus Ouspensky, in the first decade of the twentieth century, made the same case as University of Chicago's Csikszentmihalyi made in the last decade of the century. The case referred to is: that in order to survive, humankind must become consciously aware of its condition and become involved in the process of moving from this condition to one that enjoys greater freedom from the bonds of genetics, society, and ego.

"Allured by the evolutionary point of view, and looking at the future Dr. Bucke, like many others, does not pay sufficient attention to the present. That new consciousness which men may discover or unfold in themselves is indeed far more important than that which may or may not appear in other men millenniums hence." (*TERTIUM ORGANUM*, 296-297)

"The higher form of consciousness is not necessary for life; it is possible to live without it. But without it, the organization and orderliness of life is impossible. Long under the domination of materialism and positive thinking, forgetting, and perverting religious ideas, men thought it was possible to live by the merely logical mind alone. But now, little by little, it is becoming quite evident to those who have eyes, that merely by the exercise of logical reason men will not be able to organize their life on earth, and if they do not finally exterminate themselves, as some tribes and people are doing, in any case they will create (and have already created) impossible conditions of life in which everything gained will be lost—everything that was given them in the past by men of self-consciousness and cosmic consciousness." (*TERTIUM ORGANUM*) (Once again we are reminded of the validity of the acronym for God – Good Orderly Direction)

I think it is interesting to remind ourselves that these comments of concern about our survival were written in a pre-atomic and pre-missile age. Ouspensky says that the mass of humanity experiences only two states of consciousness, sleep and waking sleep. He uses the term "self-consciousness" to describe a state of higher consciousness not experienced by the mass of humanity. Regarding evolution, Ouspensky developed a classification that ends with an interesting observation concerning the inability of science to study higher states of consciousness.

In 1915 Ouspensky met the great Russian Master and Mystic, G.I. Gurdjieff. This meeting greatly influenced Ouspensky. He subsequently devoted the rest of his life to the pursuit of knowledge and techniques that could help people to realize higher states of consciousness. His lectures in London and the United States from the early 1920s until his death in 1947 are published in a small book called *THE PSYCHOLOGY OF MAN'S POSSIBLE EVOLUTION*. The technique he espoused is chiefly that of self-observation and self-discipline. One of those who attended his lectures was author and philosopher, Aldus Huxley, whom we have previously mentioned in connection with the perennial philosophy.

Finally, it should be said that the term cosmic consciousness was used and popularized by Maharishi Mahesh Yogi at the time he brought Transcendental Meditation to the West. Maharishi used the term to indicate one of three states of higher awareness within humankind's capability. Cosmic consciousness is the first of these three states. The other two are: refined cosmic consciousness and unity consciousness. He related his teachings to the *BHAGAVAD-GITA* in which each of these three states is described.

Maharishi's commentary on the *BHAGAVAD-GITA* points out, when one practices the technique of Transcendental Meditation over a reasonable period of time, transcendental consciousness can be stabilized in the nervous system. This stabilized condition, called cosmic consciousness, allows the practitioner to be aware of the transcendental value in his consciousness. Continuous use of the technique develops refined cosmic consciousness, enabling one to recognize this value in others. Finally, through what Maharishi calls devotion, one reaches the state of unity consciousness. This is a state of awareness in which the individual clearly sees that all of life is a manifestation of this transcendental value. These three states are summarized in the words found in the *BHAGAVAD-GITA*: "I am that, thou art that, all that is, is that."

All those who have used the term cosmic consciousness in the past century have not done so in any consistent way. A study, more detailed than the one we have here, would make that clear. However what is clear, is all those who have used the term have used it to suggest an experience and a state of consciousness that is a moving beyond ego conscious. It is also clear, this moving beyond ego consciousness serves to make life more interesting, more spontaneous, and more satisfying. It should be noted both Ouspensky and Maharishi believe that ordinary humans through discipline and practice can obtain these higher states of consciousness. We will revisit this subject when we review Aldus Huxley who also supports the idea that higher states of consciousness are available to ordinary human beings. To conclude this chapter we return to our discussion of metaphor.

WHAT'S A META FOR?

We have already mentioned the butterfly, the frog, and the phenomena of nature known as metamorphosis. We have indicated that humankind may very well have been created to or has evolved to the point where he/she is able to experience metamorphosis, not on the physical but on the psychic level. In this discussion above, we have given evidence that this very thing has been happening. I would like to break it down even further and for a few moments make it very simple.

In Seattle there are buses with two completely different operating systems. When out on the streets and highways, the buses operate on diesel fuel. When they come into the downtown area they go underground and travel on streets built under the city. Just before these buses go underground, they stop at a transition area, turn off their diesel engines, and attach overhead connectors to electrical cables. This, then, allows the operator to start the buses' electric motors. This transition takes a very short time and the buses are ready for a trip under the city operating on an entirely different propulsion system. This new system is quieter, smoother, and less harmful to the environment.

Modern devices with two separate systems are nothing new. We turn on our radios and make a choice between a.m. and f.m. Thousands of people, who own recreational vehicles, are familiar with refrigerators that run on both gas and electricity and other appliances that can operate on both DC (direct current from the battery) and AC (alternating current from electrical power lines).

Now to drive the two-system buses properly, in Seattle, the driver must give attention to the system he is using. There are, of course, some differences, and only by being aware and attending to those differences will the driver be able to provide a safe ride for his/her passengers. By the same token, it is by <u>attention</u> that individuals become aware they have two operating systems, and only by <u>attention</u> can the individual enjoy what Henry Thoreau called, "the road less traveled." Just as the Seattle buses take their passengers down a special road, so does the other system take us down a special path.

Like the Seattle buses, if we are going to go down this other road, we must shut one system down before we can effectively operate on the other. I would like to refer one more time to the tadpole and the caterpillar. Isn't the cocoon stage the transition period? Isn't metamorphosis the shutting down of one system and the starting of an altogether new one? The transition period for the Seattle buses is a minute or two. The transition from caterpillar to butterfly can happen in a matter of days or take as long as a year. The transition for me has been over twenty-five years and it continues. I may not yet be a butterfly but I am no longer a caterpillar.

Unlike the Seattle buses and the caterpillar that shut down during the transition, man does not have a transition center or a cocoon to enter. Humankind must make the metamorphosis, the transition, while on the run. We see this transition on the run in stories like Hermann Hesse's *SIDDHARTHA* and Ibsen's *PEER GYNT*. In both stories you see the transition, and in the end there is a metamorphosis. In both stories the searchers find that for which they are searching. If you were like me, you are asking; what were they searching for? Both were fictional characters, and in both cases I believe the author's intention was not to indicate what they found, but rather to show that there is something to be found, that warrants the search. That something, is at once both the new operating system and the road it permits us to travel.

SYSTEM CHOICE?

Speaking of life support systems,
you systematically derive one is
grounded and keeps you alive.
The other, bobbles and wobbles
and jumps on a stick, pogo of
course, and pogo quite quick!

One moment you're up and the
Next, of course, down. Ego feeds
frantically on what's whirling around.
Why does this system tend to rule
our life, when contact with grounding
would settle the STRIFE?
by Kae

This metamorphosis of two systems is no-doubt an oversimplification. However, it is an oversimplification that is needed, because millions of people in our day go on with their lives without any awareness that a beautiful psychic metamorphosis is available to them and with it, a far more meaningful life. They live like caterpillars living in a very small world with no realization that they can be free like a butterfly. They live like Seattle buses motoring on diesel with no knowledge that a smoother, quieter, less polluting system is available to them.

Chapter 16

A CHILLING THOUGHT

In the last chapter I mentioned I went through a period where I believed humankind had reached a point in its evolution that required a conscious participation in its own continuing evolution. I also said I felt I was out on a limb and was reticent about discussing my feelings on this matter. In truth, my reticence was based on a fear—a fear, that at the time, I was not willing to confront.

There was a point in my study when I began to wonder just where we were in the evolutionary process. I started to wonder regarding higher states of consciousness; if we were using this capacity less, rather than more. There seems to be evidence for this. This evidence shows we are clearly developing the brain and nervous system in the area of scientific pursuits, reason, and logic. The evidence, at the same time, indicates we may be neglecting the path that develops our nervous system in those areas, which enable us to consciously connect with what Bergson calls, the élan vital. I thought it possible that rather than growing toward cosmic consciousness, as Bucke contends, and because of our lack of interest in those things that are mythical and mystical we may be choosing a path where cosmic consciousness is becoming less common.

I hasten to add that I don't know for a fact which path we are taking. I do know, however, that we are hardwired to experience pure consciousness and many of us are not consciously using and developing this hardwiring. Could the message be—use it or lose it? Could we literally be creating our own hell by not using this hardwiring?

When I was a very young boy, I experienced hell. The memory is still vivid in my mind. I lived in an oil camp that belonged to my great uncle. The camp included an office, a machine shop, a foundry, and twelve to fifteen houses (mostly tarpaper shacks). One day my mother, sister and I walked to the shack where my dad's cousin lived (an adult male). When we arrived the cousin greeted us and asked if we would like to have a coke. My mother and sister said, "Yes." I was shy and said nothing. He then asked me specifically if I would like to have a coke and I said, "I don't know." He turned around to get the cokes and said, "If you don't know, I don't either." He came back with three cokes, one for my mother, one for my sister and one for himself, but none for me. I sat by and watched them drink, and it was hell. I now knew I wanted a coke, but the possibility had passed me by.

Could we be creating our own hell? Could humankind be in an "I don't know" stage regarding higher states of consciousness? Could we be sitting by while our opportunity to evolve in a manner envisioned by de Chardin and Aurobindo is being dissipated? Could we be shutting down the very machinery that enables us to become aware of pure consciousness, the élan vital—the Cosmic Christ?

Let me share with you two pieces of information that were in part responsible for this chilling thought. During one twenty-four hour period I reviewed materials on what some call *THE VOICES OF THE FIRST WORLD*, and a book about the brain by an eminent neurologist. The first includes materials from American Indians such as Black Elk (a nineteenth century Chief of the Ogallalla Sioux), Chief Sealth (for whom Seattle was named), Eskimos, Aborigines of Australia, and the words from the African writing, IFA ORACLE. The words of these people who lived so close to nature, who had such appreciation for the earth, sky, water, vegetation, and the animal kingdom seemed to me to be the voice of pure consciousness. The following is an example:

I AM THE WIND

I am the wind that breathes upon the sea,
I am the wave on the ocean,
I am the murmur of leaves rustling,
I am the rays of the sun,
I am the beam of moon and stars,
I am the power of trees growing,
I am the bud breaking into blossom,
I am the movement of salmon swimming,
I am the courage of the wild boar fighting,
I am the speed of the stag running,
I am the strength of the ox pulling the plough,
I am the size of the mighty oak tree,
And I am the thoughts of all people
Who praise my beauty and grace.
(From the ancient Welsh *BLACK BOOK OF CAMARTHAN*)

Another example comes from one of the early Zen Masters, Dogen Zenji: "Delusion happens when we see all that is from the viewpoint of the self. Enlightenment happens when we see ourselves from the viewpoint of the things in nature."

In contrast to the voices of the First World are the modern scientific words of Dr. Antonio R. Damasio, one of the world's foremost neurologists and head of the Department of Neurology at the University of Iowa College of Medicine. Dr. Damasio is the author of *DESCARTES' ERROR*. This book appears to make a positive contribution to our understanding of the relationship between thought and feeling, i.e. mind and body. As the title of his book suggests, he addresses himself to the division of these two entities in our modern world. He, like many others, feels that René Descartes' philosophy is largely responsible for the origin of this dichotomy. I do not find fault with the general thesis of this book, but I am saddened to realize that a modern day authority on the brain has no apparent direct experience with pure consciousness. Let me quickly add, it is my belief in this regard, Dr. Damasio is an example of the rule, not the exception. This, of course, makes the situation much more serious, if not tragic. Allow me to illustrate. The following are quotes from *DESCARTES' ERROR*:

"We almost never think of the present, and when we do, it is only to see what light it throws on our plans for the future. These are Pascal's words, and it is easy to see how perceptive he was about the virtual nonexistence of the present consumed as we are about using the past to play what-comes-next, a moment away or in the distant future." (Page 165)

"Pascal's statement on past, present and future – captures this essence in lapidary fashion. Present continually becomes past and by the time we take stock of it we are in another present, consumed with planning with the future, which we do on the stepping-stones of the past. The present is never here." (Page 240)

When Damasio used Pascal to bolster his argument that we cannot experience the present, he reveals he hasn't the foggiest notion what pure consciousness might be and may, in addition, misunderstand Pascal's intent. Richard Bucke studied the life of Pascal. Using the criteria that Bucke formulated, he declared Pascal to be one of those who experienced cosmic consciousness. If this is true, then Pascal, by definition, knew something of pure consciousness and therefore was conscious of the reality that stands between and behind our thoughts. That reality is the present moment, for one of the experiences of higher consciousness is the conscious experience of that moment. That moment, however, contrary to what Dr. Damasio believes, is not a moving, unobtainable target but a constant reality.

Upon concluding this piece, contrasting the modern mind with that of the First World, I recalled the words of ancient Eastern thought that says, "The mind is the great slayer of the Real." Dr. Damasio's limited observations concerning the present moment serve to prove this truth and underline the basis of my chilling thought. The ancient truth went on to say: "Let the Disciple slay the slayer." In other words, let the Disciple learn to recognize that screen upon which the drama of our lives is played out. In Section Three of this book I will tell you my story. I will tell you how I learned to slay the slayer (the monkey mind that chatters away constantly blocking out the present moment).

In Section Four of the book I will share with you techniques that can help you with your metamorphosis and enable you to become consciously aware of the present moment. One technique I will share is something I do daily. I call it my gratitude walk. In this walk, I attempt to become more like those of the First World. As I walk in nature, I attempt to drink up, not think of the sight and sound about me. This drinking, not thinking, helps me to become one with my surroundings, to transcend time, to become aware of that which lies hidden behind our thoughts much like you might become aware of the screen upon which a movie is being projected. For the present moment is not a moving target, it is a constant. As it correctly says in the book, *A COURSE IN MIRACLES*, "The closest thing in time to eternity is the present."

Talking about drinking, not thinking, gives me the opportunity to clearly state that this entire journey should not be made too complicated. It is not as esoteric as some would have us believe. The reality of which I speak, that which is hidden from many in our modern world is more natural, more abundant, and more common than water. In fact, I believe the voice of pure consciousness speaks of itself when both Jesus and Jeremiah spoke of water—living water.

"I still contend with you, says the Lord, for my people have committed two evils: They have forsaken me, the fountain of living waters, and hewed out cisterns for themselves, broken cisterns that can hold no water. (Jeremiah 2)

In the New Testament there is a story about Jesus stopping in Samaria at Jacob's well after a long travel. There he entered into conversation with a woman from Samaria and it caused some stir because Jews did not have dealings with Samaritans. The woman, in fact, was so surprised that Jesus would ask her for a drink that she said, "How is it that you, a Jew ask a drink of me, a woman of Samaria?" Jesus then spoke to her of living water that he further defines in the following:

"Everyone who drinks of this water will thirst again. But whoever drinks of the water that I shall give him will never thirst, the water that I shall give him will become in him a spring of water welling up to eternal life." (John 4)

Living water is the now – it is the screen – it is the present moment – it is your true SELF – the closest thing in time to eternity. The ego or monkey-mind is a broken cistern that holds no water, that blocks out the present moment, which is your true SELF. This true SELF, this present moment, this screen is the center post of stability for which we all search. Kae expresses it this way:

> The light of dawn portals the day
> And enters the now, the only way
> The joys of life to be set free—
> Coupled in hand with simply to be.
>
> Time is the beggar that stalks the night
> Robbing the SELF when projected beyond,
> Beyond the now or drowning in past.
> The light of now is the infinite last.
> By Kae

NOTE: In the original manuscript the next chapter that was called "The Perennial Philosophy" has been moved to the Appendix. This was done because some readers felt they were being bombarded with an excess of detail. This piece is an overview of a study that took me more than three years to complete. The following are some of the subjects covered: The Unified Field; the Search for Truth in Mythology, Greek Philosophy, and the Church; the Source of High Ideals, Great

Principles and Universal Truth; the Relationship between Philosophy, Health, Mathematics and Music in early Greece. This article deals in some depth with what we have previously referred to as "the broken web." This is illustrated with references by the Poet Blake, Plato and the 20th Century scholar, Gregory Bateson. The article ends with a story about one modern day American Indian who is sharing this philosophy by singing about the ways of his ancestors. For those who hunger for details, I encourage you to at least sample TRANSITION I in APPENDIX I before going on.

THE VISION QUEST HERO

SECTION III

INTRODUCTION

TO THE VISION QUEST

As grandiose as it may sound, we stated in the first chapter that we were going to offer a solution to the problems of humankind. In the subsequent chapters we spelled out this solution. As we see it, the answer to our personal problems, to the problems of organized religion and to our civilization (on the brink of self-destruction) is the individual and collective discovery of SELF - of our INNER BEING! To be sure this answer is not new! It is one that has been suggested over and over again throughout humankind's written history!

Once again I remind you that we do not intend to define the concept of SELF for you. Our intention is to point to it, to show you where it can be found and give you some suggestions as to how it can be accessed. In this regard the answer has always been a matter of self-discovery - of self, discovering SELF. The idea that self discovers SELF is reminiscent of St. Francis of Assisi's statement: "What you are looking for, is what is looking."

The goal of this next section is to describe the journey from self to SELF. Although the journey is always an individual one, the record of such journeys cutting across race, culture and religion are surprisingly similar. One of the classic descriptions of this journey in the Christian tradition is *PILGRIM'S PROGRESS*. (Author - John

Bunyan 1628-1688) This allegory, written while in prison, describes Bunyan's inner struggle. Another, in the Hindu tradition, is about the trials and tribulations of Arjuna and his mentor, Lord Krishna. This story is the basis for the *BHAGAVAD-GITA*, a book that is one of the staples of the Hindu Faith.

Both of these references are included in the broad approach we are going to take. However I have not used them per se. But, they certainly do fall into the category of the vision quest. Instead, I have chosen to use as a guide the wonderful Twentieth Century Mythologist, Joseph Campbell and his book, *THE HERO WITH A THOUSAND FACES* (1949). In this book Campbell looks at the journey from the view point of myth. A myth that is so common and ubiquitous, he calls it a "monomyth - the myth of the hero.

"I do not regard him as a hero who is able to battle successfully against a mighty army; only him I consider a hero who is able to cross the ocean known as the mind and the senses." (THE CONCISE YOGA VASISTHA, Swami Venkatesananda, page 18)

Chapter 17

THE VISION QUEST HERO

During the years 1985 and 1986 Bill Moyers, the one-time Baptist preacher and White House Press Secretary sat down with Mythologist Joseph Campbell to record material for a PBS (Public Broadcasting System) Special. Over twenty-four hours of material was recorded - six hours of the material was used for this Special.

In Moyers' interview with Campbell the subject of the *STAR WARS* movie came up several times as an attempt to convey how ancient mythological themes rightly find themselves in modern times and with modern media. At one point in the interview Moyers tells Campbell that his youngest son had seen *STAR WARS* thirteen times. He went on to say that when he inquired of his son the reason for his going back to see the movie again and again, his son told him it was for the same reason that he (Moyers) went back to the Old Testament again and again.

In another movie, *THE GAME,* (which did not receive good reviews nor did it do too well at the box office) actors Michael Douglas and Sean Penn portray two brothers. Michael is an uptight businessman and Sean, his younger brother, has a devil-may-care attitude. In an attempt to loosen up his brother, Sean buys Michael a birthday present, which as it turns out becomes an elaborate action and suspense filled drama in which Michael finds himself tested to his limits both emotionally and physically. At the end of the movie Michael experienced the transformation that his younger brother had envisioned.

Most people I talked to who saw the movie thought it was a pretty good action film. I saw it, *THE GAME,* as a parable of life. The purpose of life's trials and pain is to get us in touch with "the light within that enlightens us all." Another similar interpretation would be to see it in the light of ancient initiations such as in nature religions, the purpose of which is to shock the initiate into seeing life differently.

The purpose of both of these movies obviously was to entertain but, on another level, they were meant to convey something. The purpose of myth is to inform and to transform. The purpose of myth at its very deepest level is to put us in touch with our essential SELF, "the light that enlightens all men."

Mythology traditionally includes a combination of stories, rituals (including initiations) and consciousness-raising techniques. These techniques vary but many of them are some form of meditation. The religions of the World have generally been the guardians of myth; however, because myths are seen in our modern day as unscientific, they are regarded as just folklore of the past, with little value in the present other than entertainment.

It is at this point that we must distinguish between the information and the vehicle or media that is being used to transmit the knowledge. It wasn't too many years ago that the Indians used smoke to communicate and the white man used Morse Code. Both are no longer used in this day of cell phones and satellite communication. However, the same information is often communicated today by these modern devices as was communicated by the older devices of smoke and telegraph or wireless code - messages like danger and SOS (Help!).

In the case of mythology we have been guilty of throwing the baby out with the bath water. We have relegated myth to the uninformed and unscientific past and have lost the information (the knowledge) while retaining the media (the stories) much the same way as we would retain an old hand-crank telephone or telegrapher's key in a museum. We use mythology to entertain ourselves and at best, to inform ourselves about the past. The problem with this is that mythology is always about the present, not the past! Mythology is about life and death; it's about our connection to nature (Mother Earth). It's about our connection to Spirit (Father, Creator). It's about our connection to each other (Brother, Sister).

The archetypes, which were discovered by Carl Jung in man's subconscious, are receiving receptors and contact points and the means of communication with them is, has been and always will be, myth. To be sure, this means we need to have a new understanding of myth and its purpose. It may mean we need to find new media through which to communicate the knowledge of myth. It also may mean we need to rediscover the purpose, significance and meaning of the old and ancient traditions.

It may well be that science itself will be the new conveyer of this ancient knowledge. Certainly when one gets an insight into the lives, work and character of the individuals included in this Book, such a thought does not at all seem far-fetched. This may come together as progress is made in what is becoming a new field of study - human consciousness. In the ebb and flow of things it appears to me that the pendulum has swung about as far as it's going to go in the direction of dividing and separating. It is my firm conviction as we learn more about human consciousness we will learn more about what Bateson called "sacred unity." and Arne Naess calls "Deep Ecology." As we do we will retain our knowledge and appreciation for diversity but we will yearn to know our underlying unity, not just within humanity but within all of nature. This yearning, together with our new science and new means of communication should enable us to reconstruct and appreciate the function of mythology.

Bill Moyers' son saw *STAR WARS* thirteen times because it said something to him about himself and about the world in which he is connected or perhaps, disconnected. It may well be that it's the yearning to be connected that drives him back again and again. As I said above, this is the function of myth. It is when we are connected we sense the mystery that Einstein talked about. It is when we are one with the mystery that we no longer see ourselves and the world around us as profane but, as sacred.

To carry this one step further, I believe it is only after we have arrived at a consciousness that is aware of the sacred unity that life becomes sacramental. This is the lesson of the Perennial Philosophy and the lesson of the seventeenth-eighteenth century Hasidic Jewish Communities that was brought to the world's attention by Jewish scholar and mystic, Martin Buber. (See Appendix II) The content of myth is the nature of man and his/her relationships. This, then, is of supreme importance whether the study is Physics, Mathematics, Philosophy, Anthropology, Psychology or Religion. For the deeper question is not what is being studied but <u>who</u> is doing the studying! In other words, the important question in each case is, what is the nature of the student?

Myth communicates on the level of mystery, and, as we have noted, there is a mystery about it all. Mystery is not just that which is unknown but, even more importantly, that which can not be known by the rational finite mind. Myth, like poetry, communicates on deeper levels. Myth communicates on the level of mystery and speaks the language "of the Gods."

There is much we could say about Joseph Campbell but we have easy access to both what he has said and what others have said about him in books, tapes and the worldwide web. (See Appendix III – WEBSITES) My goal in this section is to share with you what I have learned by studying Campbell and to do what he did - "open others to a new way of seeing." (*THE POWER OF MYTH,* by Joseph Campbell with Bill Moyers,)

THE CALL TO AWAKEN

The myth of the vision quest hero is the story of how an individual becomes acquainted with the realm that lies beyond the physical realm. It is the realm of the metaphysical, the realm of pure consciousness, the realm of the Elan Vital, the realm of the spirit, the realm of the "plain truth." It is the story of how an individual is made whole, made complete. You may be surprised to know that the Greek word in the New Testament, which is translated "saved", or "salvation" means wholeness or to be made whole. According to

Campbell this is the process by which one becomes whole. This process of becoming acquainted with the realm beyond is how one awakens from "Newton's Sleep." (This is a reference to a poem by William Blake cited in TRANSITION I, see Appendix. I)

Joseph Campbell's book, *THE HERO WITH A THOUSAND FACES*, was first published in 1949 when he was forty-five years old. It is considered by many to be his best book and it makes clear that the story of a "union" with the realm beyond the physical, has surprising similarity throughout time and culture. He makes clear that this story lies at the heart of Buddhism, Hinduism, Judaism, fairy tales, the Moslem faith, folk lore, tribal cultures, Christianity and classic mythology. He also relates these stories to the findings of modern psychotherapy and metaphysics. Finally if we take seriously scientists Fritjof Capra and Arne Naess which we mentioned in the Introduction, it also related to modern physics, biology and ecology.

Campbell dedicated his life to discovering, understanding and teaching mythology. I have no such background. My background in this area has been very limited. My formal training focused on English literature, the Bible and counseling psychology. So it is from these sources that most of my illustrations will come as I attempt to communicate my understanding of the "Vision Quest Hero." In so doing I will, as did Campbell, apply my understanding of modern psychology and metaphysics to the interpretation.

I had a recent discussion with some friends about the problems of Western society, especially in the United States. We recalled many events which had made headlines in recent years such as the Oklahoma bombing and the Columbine School massacre. I asked, "Do we live in a sick society and if so, just how sick do you think it is?" There was a silence, and then one of the group thoughtfully began to speak. "I think our society is very sick and the kind of things we have just mentioned are but the glaring symptoms. The real problem is we are obsessively materialistic and hedonistic. We think money, the things money can buy, and pleasure beyond reason will make us happy." He continued, "We pursue these things with a kind of madness trying to fill an emptiness that used to be filled by the churches. The churches have somehow lost their ability to help people bridge this gap and fill this need." He ended by saying with a note of despair in his voice, "I don't know what is going to replace it."

I don't think my friend had ever read anything by Joseph Campbell but, in a nutshell, he had echoed the conclusion of Campbell's lifework. It should be noted that when Campbell studied these various traditions and cultures, he was not so much taken by their differences but by their similarities. There he discovered what he called the "monomyth." Campbell implies what often divides religions and cultures is surface differences and that which could unite us is the common realm to which each of these varied stories, whether mythological or historical in origin, point and direct us.

Now, to be sure, human conflict based upon religious differences seems to go back to the beginning of recorded history. The Old Testament is filled with the record of such conflicts, but in modern times this fact seems to be especially troubling and anachronistic. Here in the Information Age when we are increasingly linked to one another around the globe by phone, fax and worldwide web, we still argue over and fight about whose God or faith is more viable. The very fact that this is anachronistic (out of place) may well be why religion is out of place in regard to time or chronology. The Churches' positive influence in society continues to wane. Campbell and others offer us an antidote to this anachronistic poison and it is in these next pages I hope to set forth that antidote.

In the early 1980s I spent several years with the Seattle School District teaching kids who were locked up in the County Juvenile Detention facility. Their ages ranged from ten to eighteen years. At one point it was my responsibility to conduct a reading class that included silent reading and journal writing. The young people could select any book we had in our library and read from it silently for thirty minutes. The remainder of the class period was then spent writing in their journals. It was expected that the reading would form some basis for their journal writing although it need only be loosely connected. The journal writing often provided some valuable insights into the psyches of these young people.

In hopes of setting an example, I would read and write while the students were doing their reading and writing. One of the books I read and journalized during this time was *THE AGONY AND THE*

ECSTASY, (by Irving Stone) a historical novel about Michelangelo, arguably the greatest artist of Western Civilization. While writing in my journal I wrote, "Sometime in the future I want to go to Florence and Rome and see some of Michalangelo's work. I especially want to see The David."

Michelangelo was an architect, sculptor and painter. His most noted architectural project was St. Peter's Cathedral in the Vatican. His most famous painting is the ceiling of the Sistine Chapel and his most popular sculpture is that of The David.

Ten years later the dream that started in the midst of a room full of juvenile delinquents was fulfilled. As I stood looking at that beautiful David my thoughts flashed back to those students. Several were now doing time in prison, one for killing a cab driver. Several were dead. A Federal Marshall killed one when he tried to hijack an airliner. Another (a beautiful and bright young lady) was killed by one of her clients after running off to Los Angeles to become a prostitute. How different they were from Michelangelo; how different they were from David. I found myself wondering how our society might make a more positive impact on youngsters like these.

My mind and thoughts were brought back to the present as the guide began to speak. She was an Italian woman about thirty-five years old who had spent a few years living in the United States. Her command of the English language was beautiful and her presentation of Florence was captivating and imaginative. But when she started to speak of The David it was as though she was transformed. She talked about "that moment" in the life of David that was captured by Michelangelo's sculpture. She pointed out that David, although about to do battle with the Philistine giant Goliath, was in a very relaxed physical state. She noted the relaxed nature of the right arm and how the veins in the arm denoted such a state of relaxation. She spoke of the Children of Israel as God's chosen people and of the covenant that God had made with them. She said this moment for David was <u>not</u> one of bombast or even of courage in the usual sense; rather one of quietude, of relaxed readiness, of surrender, of recalling the covenant, of becoming one with SELF, with the divinity within. As she spoke, I couldn't help but think that she too had known such a moment. She knew the David because she knew her SELF, she knew Michelangelo because she knew her SELF.

As I stood there gazing at this wonderful piece of art, listening to this woman talk, I knew at that moment, how heroes were born and I experienced a wonderful communion with all those who had shared that moment when self and SELF become one. A Hero is born when God or the non-ego becomes one's strength. That is the message of the Old Testament. The covenant of the Old Testament is simply "if you will be my people, I will be your strength." David, in that moment before the battle, remembered the covenant.

In subsequent years I was introduced to the mind of Joseph Campbell. In his lifelong study of mythology he became intimately involved with the concept of Hero. He called it, "the mask with a thousand faces." Campbell studied heroes of many cultures. I immediately took to Campbell because I realized that his understanding of hero was like that of the young lady who described The David. Campbell however, adds a large measure of scholarship and detail.

Joseph Campbell identifies nine stages through which mythological heroes move. I am using some of these stages as chapter titles and themes in this section. I will be relating my own story to these stages as well as stories about people I consider to be modern vision quest heroes. I hope that this construct will help you to identify where you are in this process because awareness is often the key to progress.

Long before I knew anything about Joseph Campbell's work and long before I felt the study of mythology could add anything to my understanding of man I remember writing a piece called, "I Am My Own Hero." (It is one of those writings that have slipped through the cracks of my rather slipshod filing system.) I remember that it was written as the result of a certain awareness and sense that I had lived a victorious life. It also acknowledged the victories were not as a result of my own (ego) efforts but as a result of the ego surrendering to the non-ego SELF. When I looked at this I also had to acknowledge that I couldn't even take credit for having surrendered; for even surrender was the result of defeats, not victories or success. I (ego) had invariably surrendered only after the pain of pursuing my own (ego) course had become intolerable.

Now you may rightly ask, "How do you see yourself as a hero?" The answer is quite simple; it is a matter of identification. I no longer identify with the defeated, but with the victor. I no longer see myself (most of the time anyway) as the ego self but as the non-ego SELF. It is no longer I (ego) who lives but the Hero who lives in and through me - the Hero who has overcome virtually every obstacle which I (ego) have set before it.

MY STORY
The Call to Change (1997)

"This first stage of the mythological journey—which we have designated the 'call to adventure'—signifies that destiny has summoned the hero and transferred his spiritual center of gravity from within the pale of his society to a zone unknown." *THE HERO WITH A THOUSAND FACES* (Joseph Campbell, page 58)

When I was nineteen years old and a college sophomore, I made a decision to change my major from engineering to pre-seminary. When I told my advisor about my decision, he had one word of caution for me. He said, "Don't go into the ministry for your own salvation." As I look back on these words, I feel he must have known me a lot better than I thought, and probably better than I knew myself.

Looking back, I believe my motivation for going into the ministry was twofold. I was attracted to a devout Lutheran woman who had just graduated from the Junior college I was attending. She was now studying at a church college some three hundred miles away. Secondly, I believe my attraction for this young woman and the ministry, as my professor seemed to realize, was subconsciously involved with my own survival. I was already (at least in a small way) aware of what I called "a wild hair," something within me that I feared could destroy me. After graduating from Jr. College I transferred to the college that the young lady was attending. My plan was to go on to the seminary. I soon found out the young lady, although nice to me, was not interested in me romantically.

The summer after graduation from college and before going on to the Seminary at St. Paul, Minnesota, I married a woman equally as devout as the first, but not as street wise. I say this because if she had been more street wise, she probably would have seen the trouble ahead.

Four years later and with two children, I graduated from the Seminary and I started my first ministry in rural South Dakota. I served two small churches, one in town and one approximately seven miles out of town. My marriage seemed satisfying and so did my work. I worked long hours and with the support of my wife we seemed to have a good ministry. While there, our family grew with the addition of two more children.

In the third year of my tenure as Pastor of these churches, the country congregation started to turn against me. I continued to have full support of the town congregation and this dichotomy was very confusing to me. As the problem escalated, I was called a "communist." (Back in the 60's, if someone didn't like you or disagreed with you, it was not uncommon for them to call you a "communist.") The idea that I was teaching communism started to grow. At the height of this controversy, I was called home to be with my dying Father. After sitting by his bedside for several days and nights, I went to a bar in my old hometown to see if any of my friends were around. I ended up having a few drinks and a one-night stand with the barmaid.

When I returned to South Dakota the controversy continued to escalate and within a few months I left the parish to accept a one-year clinical residency at Lutheran Hospital in Chicago. This was followed by seven years of ministry at two different parishes in the state of Washington. I can't say that going into the ministry or marrying the woman that I did was a mistake, for both my wife and the ministry served to protect me from the "wild hair." But, the behavior that started that night after leaving my Father's bedside slowly escalated.

I did seek help! I did try to change. I went to group therapy and three different Psychiatrists over the next nine years, but I didn't change. I tried to get out of the ministry gracefully but I couldn't find a ready answer to the financial squeeze it would cause.

When I reviewed this period of my life I tried to relate it to what Campbell called the "Call to Awaken". I felt that making the decision to enter the ministry must have had something to do with a "Call" but when I looked at the whole story it was difficult to see how. Contrary to what I wanted to think in many ways it looked like a big mistake. I had thought that I had a religious conversion; but if I did, it sure wasn't working. I went back and reviewed Campbell to see if I could make any connection at all between this period of my life and the journey of the "Vision Quest Hero." Eureka, I found it! I found it in his discussion of the Herald.

LOREN EISLEY

In myth there is usually a herald that calls the hero to adventure. In myth there may be but one herald; however, I suspect in the life of an individual that the herald calls on numerous occasions and in many forms. There were two heralds that spoke to me during the period referred to in the above story. One of the heralds of my life was Author, Loren Eiseley. He spoke to something inside of me that was either forgotten or hidden. It was a time in my life when I was in trouble but also in huge denial about the extent of that trouble. Shortly I will tell you something about Eiseley and his influence on me.

But before I do that, I must go back and talk about an earlier herald. When describing the herald in myth, the following is one of the descriptions Campbell gives: "The herald is a beast (as in the fairy tale) representative of repressed instinctual fecundity within ourselves." I mentioned above that in my sophomore year of college I started to become aware of something I called it a "wild hair (wild hare)," something within me that was frightening to me, something that I felt could destroy me. I had no idea what it might be. I don't recall thinking that I might be mentally ill or anything like that. But, I do remember an awareness of this wild streak.

147

Some four or five years later, after graduating from college and while attending seminary, I recall revealing this to several fellow seminarians. To a man, they said that they couldn't relate to what I was talking about. I remember thinking that I must be a bit off if none of them could relate to what I was saying. I now see this wild hair, as a herald of the call to become a vision quest hero - as Campbell says, the divinity itself becomes our terror for it is that which can destroy our egocentric system. In such a case Campbell makes it clear it is the ego that has become the monster. This way of looking at the wild hair amounts to two sides of the same coin. It was at the same time, that which could destroy me and that which could free me from my self (ego). In the next chapter it will become abundantly clear just what the "wild hair" was. But, at that point in my life I honestly had no idea.

Back to Loren Eiseley - I wish, as I sit here attempting to write this piece, I could simply say the herald who called me to adventure was Loren Eisley. The reason that I wish it was so simple is because the kind of connection that occurred between Loren Eiseley's writings and myself is virtually impossible to communicate. In order to understand you would have to be captivated by Eiseley as I was. I never met the man face to face, only through his books did we make this connection and what a connection it has been!

When I first read *THE UNEXPECTED UNIVERSE*, I immediately knew that a connection had been made. I started telling all of my friends about the book and encouraging them to read it. Now here it is, over thirty years later, with subsequent readings in the meantime and I am realizing that this book had a far greater impact on me than I first thought. It is not just a literary gimmick when I say Loren Eiseley was the herald who called me to adventure. This is all the more amazing to me when I realize that the adventure to which his words called me was an adventure that in the final analysis appears to have substantially alluded him.

Part of what attracted me to Eiseley was his beautiful prose; another part was his amazing love for nature and his ability to communicate this. Many have referred to him as the Thoreau of the twentieth century. Some even refer to him as a mystic. Belatedly he was recognized as one of the finest writers of the twentieth century. Among his admirers was his friend, the poet W.H. Auden.

When I first read Eiseley I did not try to analyze our connection. I did not ask what is it about this man who looks at old bones, crawls into caves, wrestles with wolf cubs and pokes pencils into spider webs that attracts me. I just knew that I loved the way he looked at things, the way he mused, the way he wrote. I knew there was something deeper about it all and I liked that too.

Today I know what that something deeper is. It is the questions. It is the questions that were only occasionally asked up front but are always hauntingly there beneath the surface. As an anthropologist the question was, Who were these beings that went before us? As a naturalist it was, how can we be so blind, so careless, and so greedy? How can we not see that what nature gives us is so much better than what we seek to be. Eiseley described what we seek to be with the phrase "the asphalt man?" As a man, the question is, What does it all mean? And hesitantly he seems to ask, Who or what is behind it all?

It appears to me in reading his final book published in 1967 (shortly before his death at the age of sixty-nine), that for him the questions were never really answered. The book, *ALL THE STRANGE HOURS,* an autobiography, has three sections: "The Days of a Drifter" - for a decade, as a young man, during the depression he rode the rails and wandered about the country. "The Days of a Thinker" - At the age of twenty-seven, he started college earned a doctorate degree and ultimately headed the Department of Anthropology at the University of Pennsylvania. "The Days of a Doubter" - In this section there is a lot of brooding, a lot of talk about death, his own and of those he has known. There is an attempt to free himself from the past, his Mother, his Father, and his Aunt. There is regret and there is doubting. There is loneliness. Read for yourself!

"I am every man and no man, and will be so to the end. This is why I must tell the story as I may. Not for the nameless name upon the page, not for the trails behind me that faded or led nowhere, not for the rooms at nightfall where I slept from exhaustion or did not sleep at all, not for the confusion of where I was to go, or if I had a destiny recognizable by any star. No, in retrospect it was the loneliness of not knowing, not knowing at all." *ALL THE STRANGE HOURS,* Loren Eiseley

At the time I first read *THE UNEXPECTED UNIVERSE* I was in the throes of a spiritual crisis. The extent of this crisis was not apparent to me at the time. I was in a lot of denial! I believe the crisis and the subsequent denial was the reason that the haunting questions that lie beneath his beautiful prose connected with the archetypes of my psyche. Eiseley's musings clearly reflect the language of myth both ancient and modern. In preparation for this piece, I looked in the bibliography of *THE UNEXPECTED UNIVERSE* (I believe for the first time) and there, much to my surprise, was Campbell's *THE HERO WITH A THOUSAND FACES.* Another connection had been made!

It is obvious to me now (but not at that time) that Eiseley had something that I wanted, It was that quality that underlies his being recognized by some as a mystic - that connection with nature, with the past, with the universe. It was something I did not have, for I was far too blocked off from my SELF to make such a connection.

Regarding Eiseley's haunting questions, Vernon Howard (a twentieth century teacher, mystic, and writer) says that in order to find what we are looking for we must follow the question mark all the way to the end. It appears that Eiseley, much like Moses who looked at the PROMISE LAND from the mountain top, but never got there himself, was a man who was able to call others to the adventure but was not able to follow the question mark all the way to the end. He was a herald who called his readers to awaken from the sleep that allows us to devastate our Planet. For me, he was the herald whose words called down into the far reaches of my own psyche saying, "Come alive! Awaken to the Oneness that is ours."

LESSON: Over Carl Jung's door and later on his tombstone the following words were carved "BIDDEN OR NOT BIDDEN GOD IS PRESENT." In effect he says, believe it or not the spiritual dimension is always with us. It is the one constant in our lives. Religious literature has given expression to this in many ways. One such expression is: "In Him we live and move and have our being."

(Acts 17:28) However, our awareness of this spiritual dimension is another thing; although it is the very essence of who we are, for many of us it is but a fleeting experience. For some of us, tragically, we know it not at all!

The spiritual life can be compared to a beautifully cut diamond. At times we are totally oblivious to the fact that this diamond is at the very center of our lives. At other times a single facet of the diamond can flash through to our "selfness." Huxley says that selfness is a combination of our body and mind and it is, in general, how we identify or see ourselves. But we are more; we are an unseen diamond!

If we are open to these flashing facets, we become more and more aware that we are something else! We become aware that we are not just selfness. If we will but nurture this process, we start to see more of the diamond. As this process occurs, we begin to identify more with the diamond (spirit) than we do with selfness. The monomyth, the "vision quest hero" is a universal picture (code) embedded deep in the mind of humankind that, when nurtured, opens up the process of seeing more and more facets of our hidden nature.

The Call is but a facet or two of the diamond (the objective of the vision quest). In all probability most of us will never experience the totality of the diamond in this life. Nevertheless, even if only in part this diamond can shine through, it will bring a sense of fullness to our earthly lives. It is the Holy Grail, the Pearl of great price, the Golden Fleece! IT IS WHAT WE ARE LOOKING FOR!

151

Chapter 18

THE REFUSAL—OR—ACCEPTANCE
REFUSAL OF THE CALL

"Often in actual life, and not infrequently in the myths and popular tales, we encounter the dull case of the call unanswered; for it is always possible to turn the ear to other interests. Refusal of the summons converts the adventure into its negative. Walled in boredom, hard work, or "culture" the subject loses the power of significant affirmative action and becomes a victim to be saved. His flowering world becomes a wasteland of dry stones and his life feels meaningless—even though, like King Minos, he may through titanic effort succeed in building an empire of renown. Whatever house he builds, it will be a house of death: a labyrinth of cyclopean walls to hide from him his Minotaur. All he can do is create new problems for himself and await the gradual approach of his disintegration. (*THE HERO WITH A THOUSAND FACES*, Joseph Campbell, page 59)

The use of the word "wasteland" above, if not a direct reference to the poem by T.S. Elliot (1885-1965) "The Wasteland" is certainly an oblique one as Campbell relates to Elliot's "The Wasteland" in other contexts. "The Wasteland", written in 1922, is one of the great poems of the 20th century. In it Elliot conveys one of the reoccurring themes of this book. The wasteland is a place where individuals and whole societies are cut off from any depth of meaning and purpose. It is a place where the vitality of life is gone and people take jobs that they don't like because they feel they have no choice. It is a place where one exists rather than lives.

Elliot recognizes some of the shortcomings of modern society, especially the propensity of our societies to cut us off from our spontaneity and imagination. I am not altogether sure that Elliot understood the depth to which we can be cut off from our essential SELF, nor am I sure that he himself was attuned to that SELF. Be as it may, he wrote a poem that many have identified with as the 20th Century problem. It is described as a problem that at its core manifests itself as a refusal to the call to awaken to SELF. In this regard, I am reminded of the scrubwoman in Minneapolis who left a suicide note that read, "Life for me has just become too daily." Certainly she and millions like her in high and low places, with and without money, with and without family and friends have heard the call to awaken but dared not. The point I am trying to make is that the refusal of the call is not only a sickness of the individual soul but also a sickness that entwines the very fabric of our Society. This has been true to a great measure in all times and in all places.

It is said that "he who hesitates is lost" but this by no means is always true. There are many examples of delay and hesitation between the call and its acceptance. Each time we consciously or unconsciously get a glimpse of PURE CONSCIOUSNESS and/or divine love, we are experiencing a call to change, to transformation, to discover more fully our true nature. Nowhere in my experience is the delay between the call, the refusal, and the acceptance of the call better documented than it is with the cofounder of Alcoholics Anonymous, Bill Wilson. The following story is related in *THE BIG BOOK (ALCOHOLICS ANONYMOUS)*. Bill begins his story with an incident that took place soon after he was shipped to England during the First World War. He visited Winchester Cathedral. He says, "Much moved, I wandered outside. My attention was caught by a doggerel on an old tombstone. It read in part, 'Here lies a Hampshire Grenadier who caught his death drinking cold small beer.'"

After the war Bill turned to business and some serious drinking. Before long the drinking took over. Bill was in and out of the hospital. On one of those occasions an old school friend, whom he had not seen for years, came to visit him. He, like Bill, was an alcoholic, but had found sobriety through attendance at an Oxford Group meeting. When Bill learned this he said to himself, "So that's it. Last summer an alcoholic crackpot; now I suspect, a little cracked about religion." With this thought in mind, Bill expected his friend to rant, but he didn't. He just shared with Bill "a simple religious idea and a practical program of action." Bill was a man of science. He had to swallow hard when he heard the word God. His friend sensed this and suggested that Bill shouldn't get hung up on a particular concept of God. He should choose one for himself that he was comfortable with at that time.

As they talked Bill said the "scales of pride and prejudice fell from my eyes. A new world came into view. The real significance of my experience in the Cathedral burst upon me. I had needed and wanted God - there had been a humble willingness to have Him with me - and he came." Bill further explains that this sense of a divine presence was soon blotted out by "worldly clamors, mostly within myself."

Bill's recollection of this moment led to a rather dramatic spiritual experience and a reordering of his life. He never had a drink again. He started sharing those simple ideas with other alcoholics. One of them was Dr. Bob, who like Bill, accepted the message and the two of them went on to found Alcoholics Anonymous (A.A.). The simple message is passed on today much the same way it was then. Through A.A. millions have found relief from the disease of Alcoholism and the hand of A.A. reaches into virtually every country of the world.

Several of the people that I refer to as 20th Century lights or heroes had some connection with each other. I already pointed out at least a casual relationship between Campbell and Eiseley. Joseph Campbell and Carl Jung on the other hand had great admiration for each other's work and found through reading and correspondence that they had much in common. Another very interesting connection is that between Bill Wilson and Carl Jung. A man who is referred to as Roland H. (in AA literature) was one of the first one hundred people to recover in Alcoholics Anonymous. He had been a patient of Dr. Jung. Bill Wilson was curious about some of the things Dr. Jung told Roland, so he wrote Dr. Jung a letter and told him what was happening in the fellowship that he and Bob had founded and queried him further about what he (Dr. Jung) had told Roland. (The story of Roland H. and Dr. Jung is found on pages 26-27 of *ALCOHOLICS ANONYMOUS*. (The Big Book) The letter Dr. Jung sent back to Bill included these words:

"His craving for alcohol was the equivalent, on a low level, of the spiritual thirst of our being for wholeness, expressed in medieval language: the union with God. How could one formulate such an insight in a language that is not misunderstood in our days? The only right and legitimate way to such an experience is that it happens to you in reality and it can only happen to you when you walk on a path, which leads you to higher understanding. You might be led to that goal by an act of grace or through a personal and honest contact with friends, or through a higher education of the mind beyond the confines of mere rationalism. I see from your letter that Roland H. has chosen the second way, which was, under the circumstances, obviously the best one.

"You see, 'alcohol' in Latin is 'spiritus' and you use the same word for the highest religious experience as well as for the most depraving poison. The helpful formula therefore is: spiritus contra spiritum."[*]

I found a number of things worth noting in this letter not the least of which is the reference to the kind of tension that exists between religion and science that we have previously discussed. It is also worth noting that Dr. Jung is disdained to this day in many psychiatric circles for the interest he took in spiritual things. He is also less than highly regarded in many religious bodies because of his interest in eastern religions and his research into Alchemy.

---

[*] spiritus and spiritum are different forms of the same Latin word which means breath, life and spirit. Jung apparently used this phrase to emphasize that drinking alcohol in excess was contrary to the true pursuit of these qualities.

At the time Roland H. met with Dr. Jung there was virtually no successful treatment for Alcoholism; because of that, I believe his understanding of the disease as well as the treatment was uncanny. It is little wonder that Bill Wilson wanted to make contact with Dr. Jung; what Dr. Jung told Roland was essentially the treatment for Alcoholism that was emerging in the fledgling A.A. movement.

In this letter Dr. Jung also wrote about the danger to society of what he called "the unrecognized spiritual need." After reading Jung's *THE UNDISCOVERED SELF*, I am convinced that he is saying the unrecognized spiritual need in most people is the need to discover their ESSENCE, their true nature. I am also convinced that he is saying that this lack of awareness is counter-productive and may lead to ruin both on the individual and societal level. In these words of Jung we hear something reminiscent of Elliot's Wasteland and Eiseley's nostalgia.

Dr. Jung, himself, experienced a call to change. This change led him to champion an understanding of man which I believe more and more stands up well to both science and metaphysics. For a number of years he worked with Sigmund Freud. However, his conscience forced him to break with Freud over this very issue. As Jung grew in his understanding of man, especially that deep within man is the idea or spirit of God, he found he could no longer collaborate with Freud. Consequently, he broke with Freud and started to study, teach, treat and write about his own system based on his own understanding of the nature of man. Jung was no stranger to mythology and the concept of hero, for it was one of the archetypes he discovered in the subconscious. Jung can rightly be characterized as having accepted The Call and consequently, he was adequately prepared to affirm the phenomena taking place in the context of *ALCOHOLICS ANONYMOUS*.

MY STORY- THE BLUNDER

"Blunders are not the merest chance. They are the result of suppressed desires and conflicts. They are ripples on the surface of life, produced by unsuspected springs and these may be very

**deep - as deep as the soul itself. The blunder may amount to the
opening of the destiny."** *THE HERO WITH A THOUSAND FACES*
by Joseph Campbell, page 51.

I returned to review Campbell after recalling the impact that
Loren Eiseley's book had on me. When I read the quote above about
blunders and their significance, I started to rethink the meaning of my
decision to study Theology and ultimately to enter the Lutheran
Ministry. The following may be a more accurate interpretation of
those years than the one that was set forth in the previous chapter.

This segment of my life covers a period of approximately eighteen
years. For a long time I saw it as the period between the refusal of the
call and the ultimate acceptance. I now believe that my response to
the call was not refusal. I now see this period as one of preparation.
It was not a period of running away from the awakening of SELF but
was a period of slowly being lead and guided towards my awakening
and my ultimate destiny. It's quite interesting to me that when I
finally perceived that this period was not so much a wasteland period
but a preparation period, <u>I had a definite psychological reaction of
relief, followed by a sense of exhilaration and joy.</u> This was an
uneasy period in my life and I believe you will recognize why I have
wondered if this period should be categorized as refusal of the call; or
as Campbell says, a blunder which may be an opening of destiny.

This period covers my life from the time I was twenty years old
until I reached thirty-eight. This was a time in which I made my
career choice, chose my mate, fathered four children and, in some
ways, had climbed the ladder of my profession.

Campbell says, "the adventure may begin with a blunder." Mine
surely did! In high school like so many, I started drinking alcohol and
at one point, in my senior year, I was expelled for being drunk. I was
a member of the pep band and before an away football game I got on
the school bus intoxicated. My drinking continued on a fairly regular
basis through my two years of Junior College. During this time, I
turned to the Church. Turning to the Church was no doubt
unconsciously related to my drinking. However, I do not remember
consciously making that connection at the time.

You see, there was also a young woman involved. I was very attracted to her. She was an active Lutheran. She was several years my senior and she was always nice to me. She would go out on dates with me but explained to me that ours was a platonic relationship. For the most part, that is all it ever was even though that was not what I wanted. Consequently, I became a Lutheran, followed her to a Lutheran University and decided to study for the ministry.

My drinking pattern changed. As I look back on those years, I can see I was in the early stages of alcoholism. My affiliation with the Church didn't alleviate my drinking problem but it did change my drinking pattern. I became a closet drinker and what is often referred to as a "periodic alcoholic." A periodic is one that doesn't drink on a regular basis but when he or she does drink, they often get drunk. Closet drinkers are those who hide their drinking from family and friends. I waited for situations to drink when I was alone and where no one knew me. This pattern continued for almost fifteen years; although, towards the end, my drinking pattern was changing again. My drinking was becoming more frequent and I was less concerned about who saw me when I drank.

As you already know the young woman who first drew me into the Lutheran Church was out of my life, and yet I remained close to the church. I went on to seminary and became an ordained minister of the Lutheran Church. After some years of periodic benders, even though married with children, I started looking for female companionship when I was drinking. This, in time, led to one night stands and some longer affairs. This kind of behavior is symptomatic of the disease of alcoholism.

I think you can see (as interpreted in the last chapter) why I felt that, if the awareness of the wild hair was a "call to adventure," then, by becoming a minister and marrying a conservative Lutheran woman, I had rejected the call and sought only personal protection.

Today I recognize that following the young Lutheran woman to the University, joining the church and becoming a minister were all blunders. In other words, a good case can be made that being in the ministry was a mistake. Today, however, I see it as a <u>divine-led</u> blunder of mystical proportions that saved my life and prepared me for my destiny.

LESSON: <u>We</u> <u>do</u> <u>have</u> <u>a</u> <u>choice.</u> Those flashes from the beautiful diamond within are telling us that we have a choice. Those moments when we sense that we are more than we realize - those times when we remember that we are made of higher stuff are all saying to us that we have a choice. The poet Robert Frost said it this way. "Two roads diverged in a wood, and I—I took the one less traveled by, And that has made all the difference." (The Road not Taken {1916}) A psychologist with a spiritual understanding borrowed these words and wrote a book that you may want to read if you haven't already done so. *THE ROAD LESS TRAVELED* by Scott Peck. In part, it is about making choices.

Chapter 19

THE GATE

CROSSING THE FIRST THRESHOLD

In mythology the hero is depicted as one who enters into the region of the unknown, usually a desert, a jungle or an unexplored sea. We need only remind ourselves of King Arthur's journeys to find the Holy Grail, the sea voyage of Odysseus or Hansel and Gretel's journey into the forest. Campbell, Freud, Jung and many others see this unknown region as symbolic of the unconscious, or the spirit realm beyond the conscious.

Campbell says that in virtually all such stories there is a gatekeeper and ogre that warns against such passage. I must say I almost missed the significance of this idea. Indeed, if it were not for a reference to Nicholas of Cusa and his "wall of Paradise" I believe I might have missed the significance of this idea entirely. Nicholas (1401-1464), a German philosopher, was born in Cusa and studied in Heidelberg and Cologne. Among his writings is one called the "Vision of God" and another, "On the Hidden God." In these writings he says God is both transcendent (beyond experience) and immanent (available to experience). He says God is immanent even in the smallest of things. He also believed that every part of the universe was present in every other part; that man is a microcosm of God and as such reflects the total macrocosm. It is interesting that Nicholas, long before the modern understanding of atomic physics and quantum theory, eerily talked about the universe being present in every part. By the same token, it is interesting that in this day when cloning has become a fact, several hundred years before the microscope and the discovery of cells, Nicholas talked about the part being representative of the whole. Now we know for a fact, that a cell of a living thing can be fully representative of its whole.

The "wall of paradise," says Nicholas, is the "coincidence of opposites:" good and bad, beautiful and ugly, life and death, hot and cold. These things are available to our five senses and become fodder for our mind and our reason. They are a description of the world in which we live and as such they become the barriers to the realm beyond. In a real sense <u>we become seduced</u> <u>by this realm of the five</u> <u>senses</u> and we get walled off from the realm of paradise. In order to experience God one must get beyond the gatekeeper (the highest spirit of reason), get beyond the pairs of opposites, get beyond thought - beyond <u>concepts</u>. In order to experience the immanent nature of God we must pass beyond the pairs of opposites and through the "wall of paradise."

Now, the question is, how do we (potential vision-quest heroes and heroines) overcome, get past the gatekeeper and enter into the realm of the unknown, of mystery. Campbell says, in mythology the vision quest hero does it with the help of a supernatural force. He says the hero is joined in his quest by one, which is more powerful than the gatekeeper.

GATHERING ALLIES

One of the stories most often told by a newcomer in the twelve-step programs is while in a state of pure desperation they shouted out something like "if there is a God, please help me." Within hours, if not minutes later, they found themselves talking to someone in recovery, reading twelve-step literature, going to a meeting or being taken to a recovery house. Many of these stories defy belief. They sound like miracles and those who tell them often believe that's just what they are. A phrase that is often used to reassure a newcomer when they tell such a story is "as you continue with us, you will find that there are no coincidences." While ordinarily not defined, there is a belief in these programs that a higher power is at work in our lives. This reminds us again of the profound statement found over Dr. Jung's door: "BIDDEN OR NOT BIDDEN GOD IS PRESENT"

A book that stayed at the top of the best seller list for many months in the 1990s is James Redfield's, *THE CELESTINE PROPHESY*, a spiritual novel which over and over again makes use of the old adage "that when the student is ready the teacher will appear." Sometimes we are the recipients of the message and sometimes we are privileged to be the messenger.

The following are a few paragraphs from a small book, IS, written by Dennis Krum. Dennis was one of the leaders in my yearlong involvement with "A Course of Miracles" discussion group. One day, after that year was over, I felt the need to stop by his office while he was at work. I had never done this before. When I got there I told him that I did not know why I was there, but maybe there was a good reason. We chatted about things in general for about a half-hour and as I started to leave I asked, "Have you read *THE CELESTINE PROPHECY?*" He replied that he had not because he usually doesn't get into that kind of thing. "I stick pretty much to the "Course in Miracles," he said. I suggested, "I really feel you should read it" and with that I left. The following are excerpts from a story entitled "End Note" from Dennis Krum's book, *IS*.

"The evolution of this book has been, in and of itself, a wonderful learning experience for me. And as I read the preceding sentence, I realize nothing is 'in and of itself,' that ALL is part of the ongoing process of Life, of the evolution and growth and experience of Love, the I AM.

"This phrase of my learning, however, began with a lecture by Deepak Chopra in June, 1994, which lead me to read his *AGELESS BODY, TIMELESS MIND*. Shortly thereafter a dear friend suggested I read *THE CELESTINE PROPHECY* by James Redfield.

"As I read, I began to realize the Manuscript described the process of my life, my learning, and clarified the experiences I was having. And I began to understand more. From that inspiration, I began to pay more attention to my intuitions, to focus more clearly on my "insights," and to record them over the next few months.

"In December of 1994, I was pondering Christmas gifts for those closest to me, and a quote from *A COURSE IN MIRACLES* came to mind – 'the only gift worthy of the equal Sons of God is full appreciation.' What better way to show my full appreciation than to share my highest and best, most loving thoughts. And so I put together a little booklet, just a few pages, of those insights, called it *IS* and presented each with a personal letter conveying my appreciation. That, 'in and of itself' was another 'realization,' that 'giving and receiving are one,' for I knew their appreciation for me as I conveyed mine to them.

"I was encouraged to write more, to expand the booklet, and to expand its distribution to a wider circle of friends. A few months later I had two hundred copies printed, which were given away within a few weeks. The response was overwhelming, with more Love, more appreciation (on both sides) than I could imagine—And more encouragement to do MORE.

"And so a second expansion occurred, and the printing of a few hundred more, given to an even wider circle of friends, or 'strangers' who became friends through the giving of IS. And more Love, and more encouragement, and more growth, more 'insights.' And many people telling me that IS should be published, that these thoughts have value to many, and should be distributed as widely as possible.

"I have learned, as have many, to distinguish the fearful ideas of the limited self, ego, from the gentle guidance of the higher Self, which always provides the right answer. The ego ideas are always in a hurry, and full of questions. The higher Self is never in a hurry, and its ideas are effortless. It is gentle, but persistent. And so I have learned to listen, over time, and not rush to any quick ego decision.

"The Manuscript in *THE CELESTINE PROPHECY* talks about a new, emerging way of life, in which we will be paid for our insights and our value as a human being. As we appreciate our spiritual growth, we will be inspired to share our knowledge, knowing that we all are One, and thus we are helping ourselves to grow. And we will be inspired to give to those who give knowledge to us, who help us in that growth."

My point in quoting Dennis is that the supernatural ally or power that Campbell talks about may well come in the form of people and events in our lives. There are a number of stories told in twelve-step programs that also make this point.

Now, lets look at a partial list of methods that mankind has used to try to get beyond or overcome the gatekeeper - reason, concept and the five senses:

Prayer (The preferred technique for those who believe God is transcendent beyond the realm of experience.)
Meditation techniques
Initiations - Rituals
Sweat lodges (common to American Indians)
Hallucinatory drugs (such as Peyote, LSD, mushrooms)
Pain
Silence (Monastic Orders)
Breathing techniques
Dreaming (Analysis of)
Psychoanalysis
Sex (Hindu)
Alchemy
Alcohol
Dance
Whirling (the Whirling Dervish - Moslem)
Hypnosis
Stories
Asceticism (Self denial)
Koans (Zen Buddhism - Statements that blow or confuse the conceptual mind – example - "What is the sound of one hand clapping?")

STORIES

Now, lets look at one method of getting beyond the gatekeeper with which we are all familiar. The telling of stories is apparently almost as old as speech. We know from history that many stories have been told in order to convey something of the realm beyond the five senses. More specifically they are told in order that we might recall or remember something of the Divine integrity that lies buried deep beneath the layers of human learning - to awaken to an aspect of ourselves which identifies with this realm beyond thought and concept. But, before we say more about this method allow me to share with you a story taken from Vernon Howard's *PSYCHO-PICTOGRAPH* that beautifully illustrates what I am talking about.

"A Swiss shepherd boy was kidnapped by passing gypsies. As he was hustled away inside the wagon, he heard the ringing of the village bell. The sound became fainter and fainter as the wagon carried him away. But that bell's special tone made a permanent impression upon his mind.

"Years later, as he grew up, the memory of that bell stirred a restless urge within. It made him weary of the gypsy life. He longed to return to his rightful home. So he broke away from the gypsy camp and began his search. He wandered from country to country, village to village, listening intensely for the special ring of that single bell. He heard many peals as he journeyed along, but he always detected a false ring, and so refused to be lured away.

"Finally, while pausing by the roadside to rest, he heard a faintly familiar peal. He turned in its direction. The farther he walked the more swiftly he stepped. Something within him knew that he was hearing his village bell at last. And he followed it all the way home.

"Likewise, the ring of truth is inside every man. And this is not something merely mystical or philosophical. It is a practical fact. If a man learns to listen, if he refuses to be lured away by false sounds, he will find his way home. The man who listens will always recognize the ring of truth. And every man has the capacity to listen and to follow. (Mental Picture 1)"

I like this story because I think that almost everybody can relate to it. The feeling of being at home or searching for that place where we will be comfortable (at home) is one of the most common thoughts or pictures in the history of mankind. It is the picture of heaven, of nirvana, of peace. It is filling that hole in our gut. It is a story of Alice in Wonderland, of the Prodigal Son, etc., etc. It is a story of myth, fairy tale; real life passed on through centuries of oral tradition in books, through radio and stage, drama in musicals, opera, movies and television. In the stories of going home we are stirred and at times we get past the gatekeeper and we find peace.

MEDITATION

The practice of meditation is also, often described as coming home. In a videotape that introduces "The world Community for Christian Meditation" (one of two worldwide Christian meditation movements that have sprung up in the past twenty years) Father Laurence Freeman says:

> **"Like geese coming home, following their**
> **homing instinct, we have a homing instinct**
> **to God: the Spirit.**
> **Meditation is simply the way we get in touch**
> **with that basic sense of human direction**
> **and deep trust in the goodness of our nature"**

CARL JUNG 1865-1961

I don't know if Carl Jung ever used the term "gatekeeper" but he was very familiar with mythology. Indeed, it is quite possible that his greatest contribution to the understanding of man was his discovery of the relationship between the archetypes, that he found to be present in the unconscious, and their presence in religion, myth and art. He discovered the various archetypes while analyzing over 80,000 dreams during his lifetime.

It is quite evident that some of these archetypes are similar to the ogres, gatekeepers of myth, that Campbell calls the gatekeepers to the unconscious. However, it appears that the ego or false self is the true gatekeeper in Jung's understanding. I would compare Jung's ego to Nicolas' "highest spirit of reason." Although, I am sure they are in no way identical, it seems obvious that both concepts have at their core, the idea that there is in the mind of man that which constructs his world and his identity. And the material, out of which these constructions are made, is the world that can be felt, seen, heard, smelled and tasted. (experienced)

Jung, unlike Freud, came to believe that the unconscious was more than a kind of garbage dump for feelings with which we do not wish to deal; and that psychotherapy was more than bringing these repressed feelings to the surface. Jung not only recognized the value of dealing with repressed feelings but also came to an understanding of the unconscious that recognized a REALITY that was the true essence of man. He recognized in the archetype of the COSMIC MAN, the potential and true identity of man's nature. Because Freud did not recognize this, Jung separated from him in 1913, and until his death in 1961, Jung pursued research, which would allow humankind to more fully realize its potential.

In so doing, Jung looked into many of the techniques that we listed as ways to get beyond the gatekeeper. He particularly spent a great deal of time investigating an eastern form of Alchemy. A form he found was oriented towards the transformation of man, rather than base metals. Out of this exhaustive study, he designed a method of meditation that he felt would be more appropriate to Western culture.

Near the end of his life, Carl Jung wrote a book entitled, *THE UNDISCOVERED SELF*. (Copyright 1957) In this book the elderly author expressed his concern that the very survival of mankind may be in jeopardy. (This reflected the period known as "the cold war.") Today, although the cold war has subsided, I do not think Dr. Jung would be any less concerned. As I write, yet another schoolboy has opened fire on his classmates, killing two and wounding twenty-two.

It is my belief that Dr. Jung's assessment of the problem was and is essentially correct. His main thesis is that the health of society is dependent upon the health of its individuals. He, like Dr. Bateson and

Loren Eiseley, felt that there was something badly amiss in both. Dr. Jung contends that the modern individual is not psychologically healthy because the currents of modern life work against his/her healthy development. One of his major contentions is that both the church and the state look not at the individual but to the masses. The individual is seen as but a statistic and the masses are seen as what needs to be manipulated and controlled. He shows how the division between science and religion has become a significant part of the problem. Jung says, "The West cherishes the same 'scientific' and rationalistic world view, with its statistical leveling-down tendency and materialistic aims as the state religion of the Eastern bloc." (Page 50) "The result," says Jung, "is that we have, in effect, two social powers (the state and the church) vying for the allegiance of its adherence; both the church and state appealing to the adherence on the basis of reason." The effect of all this, according to Jung, is to reduce religion to a creed or doctrine and to effectively create a situation in which the unconscious aspect of man's nature is left unattended. Thus we live in a society that nurtures material and technological progress but not the growth of the psyche (soul).

Jung says that for man to truly be healthy, he/she must discover or uncover the unconscious (the undiscovered self) and unfortunately, very little attention is being paid to this area. In fact, he says, that "the worldly minded mass, man looks for the numinous (spiritual) in the mass meeting which provides an infinitely more imposing background than the individual soul. Even church Christians share this pernicious delusion." (Page 103-104) Jung sees the average person, whether a member of a church or not, as cut off from his SPIRIT.

MY STORY - OGRES AT THE GATE

For me, the ogres that stood at the gate and barred me from going beyond the wall of Paradise were numerous. I will take this opportunity to speak of some of them.

First, and probably foremost, was the ogre called Fear. I know now if one is going to pass beyond the gate one has to "let go."

During this period I went to several psychiatrists. I remember one saying to me, "You like to stay on top of things." I realize he was trying to let me know that if we want to be free we can't be on top of everything. It is just too big a job! It is playing God. It is trying to be something we are not. Trying to be on "top of everything" is to be trapped, not free. I was afraid to let go. What would happen if I let go? I didn't know and I was afraid to find out.

I was afraid because standing along side the ogre of Fear was the ogre of Anger. I think, subconsciously, I felt that if I let go, my anger would take control of me. I had experienced my anger and I had to keep a lid on it or it might destroy me or even worse, someone else. One of the reasons I was forced to resign from my first Parish was because some of the Parishioners told the Bishop that I had a bad temper. Sometimes I felt so uneasy and irritable, I just had to get away from everybody. When I did, I would often go to a bar and drink. I would wake up with a hangover and a bad case of guilt; however, I no longer felt so angry. I had let off some steam, so to speak. Consequently, I started thinking that it was good for me to go off and let off some steam.

What I didn't know was that I was addicted to alcohol. Thinking it was good for me was what they (in A.A.) call "stinking thinking." Alcoholism, along with my anger was the wild hair that I had feared for many years. One of the symptoms of alcoholism is denial. Denial says I don't have a problem with alcohol, I have a problem with those people and if I don't let off a little steam, God only knows what I will do!

Two other ogres standing at the gate were things called "please like me" and "principles." These two guys played tug-a-war with my ego mind. "Principles" was always telling me that I had to stand up for what was right, no matter what! "Please like me" would say that if you are going to stand up for your principles all the time, they're not going to like you. Principles would say, "You're not running a popularity contest here." Much of the time in the Parish, Principles would win out and I wasn't popular. Please Like Me would say, "I told you so." I would feel badly and think, "nobody understands me." I would end up with a bad case of P.M.S., Poor Me Syndrome. When this P.M.S. would get too bad I would start to get angry; then, it was time to let off a little steam.

With all of this going on in the background I met an ogre called Pride. I wanted to be liked, so I had to hide all of this from everybody. (even myself - there's that denial again!) Someone has said that an alcoholic is an "egotist with an inferiority complex." I can see that now. You can't help but feel some inferiority because down deep you know you're a phony - but you have to stay on top of things as long as you can, so you put up a big front. When we put on a big front, we just add to the layers of clay covering over our true nature just like the clay covered the Golden Buddha we saw in Thailand.

Now let's look at this subject from a slightly different perspective: Why couldn't I, a well-educated preacher get through the gate? That's a good question! You might recall that I'm not the only preacher to have problems. We have seen on television, evangelists crumble before our very eyes and heard the stories of hundreds of clergy who have faltered. In the early days of Christianity it is said that frequently people would say, "See how they love one another." Today the phrase I hear the most is, "See how hypocritical they are." Why do so many of us (people of faith) experience so little power?

The answer to the question is simply, "To what we are connected is by what we are directed" and we are essentially cut off from this power by the clay of our lives. I had lots of concepts. Let's take one important one and use it as an example. As a Lutheran, I was taught that we are "saved by grace through faith." This phrase is based on Romans 3:24 and is the passage that lead to Martin Luther's transformation. I believed in the concept of Grace (free gift of God), the concept of faith and the concept of salvation. I preached some very imaginative sermons on this topic over a period of ten years. For a long time, my attitude was enthusiastic but I continued to become a slave. Once again I asked, "Why?"

We have already covered some of the reasons why I was blocked at the gate. Let me add one more. The church in which I was an ordained minister did not encourage me to have an open mind. It said, "We have taught you what is true and you should be careful not to look for answers beyond this truth." When I became an ordained minister I was asked to take a vow to teach only the truth that they had taught me. (Now my church is not the only one which asks their ministers and lay people to take vows. Most do!) However, I found it interesting some years later to read what Jesus had said: "you have heard that it was said to the men of old, 'You shall not swear falsely, but shall perform to the Lord what you have sworn.' But I say to you, Do not swear at all, either by heaven, for it is the throne of God or by the earth, for it is his footstool" Matthew 6:33. This means we should not take vows that mortgage our future. I now know that Jesus said this because he didn't want our attitudes to become stifled, our concepts a burden and imaginations to become stagnant. He wanted us to continue the Vision Quest and to be open to newness. Now, why would the church ask us to make these vows in direct contradiction to Jesus words? Why would the Church become an ogre at the gate?

I wanted to be a good Lutheran, a good Christian. I wanted to be obedient and obey my vows but in the end I had to let go, I had to surrender to the wild hair, surrender to my powerlessness over everything. For Jesus in the same sermon said, "Resist not evil." Finally, I had to forsake my vows and surrender to the ogres, the monsters at the gate. I had to surrender to fear, pride, anger, alcoholism, lust and greed. Then and only then could I enter the gate and find freedom.

LESSON: We are powerless. Now I know that the world around us tells us differently, but the truth is, of ourselves we are powerless. The idea that in and of ourselves we have power is the real ogre at the gate. And until we give up the illusion that we have power, we are not open to the power that can usher us beyond the gate.

Surrender to the illusion that you have power and you will indeed know POWER. Surrender to the illusion that you are almighty and you will experience the Almighty. Even in this you will need help.

Chapter 20

REBIRTH

As the Hero continues his journey he enters into another world; an existence which is far different from the three dimensional world of ordinary existence. Joseph Campbell says that this aspect of the "Hero's" journey is depicted in many cultures by the imagery of being swallowed up by a large animal such as a whale or elephant. Having spent some time in Alaska I was particularly taken by the tale of trickster-hero, Raven. What Napi (old man) is to the Blackfeet and other tribes of the plains, Raven is to many of the tribes of the Northwest including the Eskimos of the Bering Strait.

One day Raven was drying his clothes on the beach when he saw a whale swimming close to the shore. "He called, 'Next time you come up for air, dear, open your mouth and shut your eyes.' Then he slipped quickly into his raven clothes, pulled on his raven mask, gathered his fire sticks under his arm, and flew out over the water. The whale came up. She did as she had been told. Raven darted through the open jaws and straight into her gullet. The shocked whale-cow snapped and sounded; Raven stood inside and looked around." (*THE HERO WITH A THOUSAND FACES*, Joseph Campbell, p. 90)

When the Scribes and Pharisees asked Jesus for a sign, he referred them to the sign of Jonah who spent three days in the belly of a whale. (Matthew: 12:38-39) On another occasion he dealt with the subject of rebirth quite directly. "Now there was a man of the Pharisees, named Nicodemus, a ruler of the Jews. This man came to Jesus by night and said to him, 'Rabbi, we know that you are a teacher come from God; for no one can do these signs that you do, unless God is with him.' Jesus answered him, 'Truly, truly, I say to you, unless one is born anew, he cannot see the kingdom of God.' Nicodemus said to him, 'How can a man be born when he is old? Can he enter a second time into his mother's womb and be born?' Jesus answered, 'Truly, truly, I say to you, unless one is born of water and the Spirit, he cannot enter the kingdom of God. That which is born of the flesh is flesh, and that which is born of the Spirit is spirit.'" (John: 3,1-6)

From this account we do not know exactly what Nicodemus was asking Jesus, but we can assume from Jesus' response that Nicodemus was inquiring either as to when God's Kingdom was going to be restored on earth, or how one gets to heaven. Whatever the case, it seems clear that Nicodemus' question was future-oriented. Jesus' response, however, was not future-oriented; it was here and now. He said, in effect, Nicodemus, the Kingdom of God is not about dying and not about control or power or government or authority; the Kingdom of God is about you. The Kingdom of God is about being fully human and being fully human involves two births. It involves the physical birth and a spiritual birth. He says when you experience the spiritual birth you will be born anew and at that time you will enter into a New World, you will see the Kingdom of God. The Kingdom of God is not something we wait for; it is something we can experience in the here and now.

It should be obvious by now that those people who have experienced a rebirth and/or have established a mystical relationship with God, are often at odds with and critical of established religion. This is true of the Jewish philosopher Spinoza, the Russian Christian Tolstoy and the poet Blake. It was also true of Jesus. He was highly critical of the established religion of his day. Nicodemus, you will note, was a member of that establishment and as such was a symbol of the recalcitrance (stuck in the mud long enough that mud turns to clay) that Jesus despised. As Jesus talks to him, he not only answers his question in a very direct manner but makes it clear to all those who are listening that the established religion of his day was hollow.

It should also be clear by now that the mystical experience about which Jesus was talking is a universal experience and not the property of any particular religion. Jesus, at that point, was a Jew talking to a Jew. He was not talking about baptism or an altar call or any kind of emotional release; he was talking about experiencing the Kingdom (a new consciousness).

Jesus obviously had something that Nicodemus, a leader of the Jews, wanted and he risked his reputation by going to Jesus. To minimize the risk he came by cover of darkness. I believe he was right in wanting what Jesus had, for it is the pearl of great price; it is that which one and all should covet. However, Nicodemus was apparently not willing to pay the price. Now, what is the price that must be paid for this universal experience? The Hasidic Jews discovered the answer to this question in the 18th century. Bill and Bob, the founders of the twelve-step programs found this same answer in the 20th century. The answer, however, was something Nicodemus was not ready to accept. The very fact that he came to Jesus by cover of darkness tells us why he and most of us cannot accept the answer. It also tells us why Judaism (Nicodemus, remember, was one of their leaders) was the way it was and why religion today is the way it is. The answer Jesus gave and the answer we do not want to hear is: "we must face reality." John 3:21 says, "He who does what is true comes to the light."

Most people coming into a twelve-step program are introduced to a prayer written by a 20th century Christian, Theologian Reihnhold Neibor. In effect, they are not taught to pray for that which can save them, but for that which can transform them. They are taught to pray for reality, the light.

"God grant me the serenity to accept
the things I cannot change: the courage
to change the things I can, and the
wisdom to know the difference."

In order to get a better handle on just what is meant by reality we need to go back and fill in some of the details. Like Iran today that is run by Moslem Clerics, Jewish religious leaders ran Israel, at the time of this discussion. Also like Iran, there were several different parties. In Israel the major parties at that time were the Pharisees, the ruling party; the Sadducees, the opposition party; and the Essenes who were so disgusted with the situation that many moved to the desert and formed a community known as Quaram. It is near Quaram that the Dead Sea Scrolls were found. These Scrolls, in turn, have helped to shed light on the political and religious situation in Israel at that time.

The fact that the Roman military was occupying Israel complicated the political situation. It may well have been this uncomfortable political situation that prompted Nicodemus to seek out Jesus. It may well be that what he was really seeking was an answer to the political situation. He may have wanted to know if Jesus had any insight into when God was going to restore his Kingdom and get these Roman soldiers out of Israel. If this was the case Nicodemus was, no doubt, surprised when Jesus turned the tables on him and in effect told him what is needed is <u>a change in you, not in your environment.</u>

As has already been stated, coming to Jesus was not without risk. This risk becomes even greater if we consider the fact that Jesus may have been considered an Essene. Although there is no evidence to conclude that he was, circumstantial evidence leads scholars to believe that John the Baptist was an Essene and that very fact could have led the Pharisees to conclude that Jesus was also associated with that enemy party. Such a move makes us wonder about the spiritual/psychological health of Nicademus at the time. The Pharisees prided themselves on having all the answers and were for the most part, a self-satisfied and self-righteous lot.

Was Nicademus like the Jews of 18th century Europe (that you can read about in the Appendix, TRANSITION II) having a "crisis of faith?" The account would lead us to believe that he was. The account would also lead us to believe that even though a "crisis of faith" was being experienced he had not reached bottom (to use a twelve-step expression). The pain connected with his crisis of faith, was not yet as great as the pain of self exposure, which would likely occur if he were to pursue Jesus' answer. An old Chinese Proverb says, "If one does not change the way he is headed, he will likely end up where he is going." Crisis of faith or not, Nicademus was not ready to risk giving up power and status, his way of life or way of thinking for this radical change. He was not ready to head in a new direction. Joseph Campbell says, "The myths and folk tales of the whole world make clear that the refusal is essentially a refusal to give up what one takes to be one's own interest." (*THE HERO WITH A THOUSAND FACES*; p59-60)

This then, is what facing reality means. It is facing the truth about ourselves here and now. It is the pain we are feeling; it is the "crisis of faith." It is facing up to our utter selfishness and self-concern. It is the situation in which we find ourselves and it is our willingness (or lack of willingness) to look at where we are heading and to take the responsibility for all of it.

One person in crisis said he had a "moment of clarity," a brief moment in which he saw himself for what he was. He said in that moment he realized he was not a good father, a good husband, a good son or a good brother. He also realized in that moment that he was an addict and that he needed help.

A "moment of clarity" is often a big dose of reality. It is the way it really is; not the way we want it to be. It is the way it is right now, not the way it can be or the way it was. A dose of reality can convince us that we are not as smart as we think we are, not as self-sufficient as we think we are, not as loving as we think we are. A dose of reality can convince us that we are selfish, self-righteous and self-centered. It can convince us that our ego/self isn't healthy and is leading us in a direction that we don't want to continue heading.

A dose of reality can be really good, but like Nicodemus, we may decide that reality will cost us too much. It will cost us our old ideas, our old familiar way of life and possibly some of our old friends. STOP! SLOW DOWN! TAKE A DEEP BREATH! If we want to see the Kingdom we have to face reality but we don't have to bite off more of reality than we can chew. It is at this point that the slogans of A.A. and the other recovery programs really begin to make sense. Listen to these and see that when it comes to biting off chunks of reality we really don't have to bite off more than we can handle.

Every new comer is encouraged to take these slogans to heart. (I have added a couple of my own.)

Easy does it.
First things first.
One day at a time.
Live and let live.
Life (reality) is a cinch by the inch
but it's hard by the yard.
<u>Live</u> your way into a new way of thinking, don't
think your way into a new way of living.
<u>Live</u> your way into reality; don't think your way
into reality.
<u>Live</u> your way into being human, don't think
your way into being human.
Keep coming back! It works! (It is pragmatic).

Jesus' discussion with Nicodemus suggests that there is a reality that many of us know nothing about. Many of us end up investigating it only in the midst of a "crisis of faith" and only when the bottle or drug or food or sex or people or places or things seem no longer to work and we have nowhere to turn. Nicodemus wasn't ready, things weren't bad enough <u>yet</u>.

Finally, let me suggest, the solution (rebirth) offered by Jesus has been discovered by many, including the Hasidic Jews in the eighteenth century and twelve-step people in the twentieth century. I believe this solution is not per se, a religious experience but a universal, spiritual experience. Rebirth can be a sudden displacement of old ego-orientation. However, more often, it is not a sudden experience but a process.

Aldus Huxley said that there appeared to be two kinds of religion. One encourages a direct relationship with the divine and the other requires a relationship with dogma and symbols. I don't believe one should assume that one is totally correct and the other wrong. I think the test is found in another of Jesus' teachings. One day Jesus saw an olive tree and there was no fruit on it. According to the story, he cursed it and it withered. The point of the lesson is, does it bear fruit?

In Jesus day the Jewish religion had become so involved in law, dogma and symbols that as Jesus suggested, it was not bearing fruit.

This appears to happen in all religions. In a book about Sufism I read that Sufism seems to come to the fore in Islam when Orthodox Islam loses its spontaneity and understanding of the unity of Islam. Sufism is the aspect of Islam that is concerned about the Inner Light and the direct contact with Allah. The author of the book, *THE ELEMENTS OF SUFISM*, Shaykh Fadhlalla Haeri suggests the ideal is that there should be a balance between the "inner knowing and the outer law" but often that balance is lost. It is in these times when the balance is lost that one group comes to the fore to correct the imbalance. In the midst of the Catholic Church Priest/pedophilia crisis, one Catholic leader proclaimed that he could see the crisis coming based on the kind of appointments that were being made by the Vatican in the last two decades. He said basically all of the Priests who were appointed to Bishop and Cardinal positions recently, tended to be protective of the Church as an institution. (Thus, the tendency to cover up its short-comings.)

If one puts all these thoughts together it seems to me that what we come up with is that there are not two different kinds of religions as Huxley says but two different aspects of religion: the exterior symbols and teachings and the interior experience. It seems quite clear to me the purpose of the symbols and teachings is to catapult one beyond the teachings and symbols themselves to the SOURCE. When a religion does not do this it is not bearing the fruit for which it is intended. Therefore, like the olive tree that Jesus cursed, it is of no value. The fruit of all creeds, initiations, symbols and ceremonies should serve as a midwife to bring about a new birth that in turn enables the Vision Quest Hero to enter the Kingdom.

As you might surmise from the above, this period of the Hero's journey is also referred to as a period of deep study and self-examination. In this regard we take this opportunity to correct a misunderstanding that may be forming in the mind of the reader. We have referred a number of times to people who have had a mystical experience that seemed to lead to a rather sudden transformation. This can and does happen but it is not necessarily the norm.

The norm is probably more in line with the person mentioned above who had a moment of lucidity or clarity. What was not mentioned was the fact that this person followed this brief moment with years of practical spirituality. This term, practical spirituality, which we will cover in detail later, means living life in such a way that builds on the moment of clarity; a brief moment of clarity, a spiritual breakthrough, the surfacing of some facets of the diamond but not a sudden and total transformational (spiritual) breakthrough.

William James, the author of *THE VARIETIES OF RELIGIOUS EXPERIENCES* referred to these slower transformations, as "of the educational variety." In the early days of A.A. a misunderstanding, similar to the one I fear I might have created in the minds of some readers, did occur in the early adherents to A.A. following the publication of the book, *ALCOHOLICS ANONYMOUS*, in 1939. Because of this misunderstanding an Appendix was added in later printings. This appendix entitled "Spiritual Experience," I believe, explains this as well as it can be explained. So it is, with appreciation for the pioneers of *ALCOHOLICS ANONYMOUS*, I include it here in its entirety.

SPIRITUAL EXPERIENCE

"The terms 'spiritual experience' and 'spiritual awakening' are used many times in this book which, upon careful reading, shows that the personality change sufficient to bring about recovery from alcoholism has manifested itself among us in many different forms.

"Yet it is true that our first printing gave many readers the impression that these personality changes, or religious experiences, must be in the nature of sudden and spectacular upheavals. Happily for everyone, this conclusion is erroneous.

"In the first few chapters a number of sudden revolutionary changes are described. Though it was not our intention to create such an impression, many alcoholics have nevertheless concluded that in order to recover they must acquire an immediate and overwhelming 'God-consciousness' followed at once by a vast change in feeling and outlook.

"Among our rapidly growing membership of thousands of alcoholics such transformations, though frequent, are by no means the rule. Most of our experiences are what the psychologist William James calls the 'educational variety' because they develop slowly over a period of time. Quite often friends of the newcomer are aware of the difference long before he is himself. He finally realizes that he has undergone a profound alteration in his reaction to life, that he could hardly have brought about such a change alone. What often takes place in a few months could seldom have been accomplished by years of self-discipline. With few exceptions our members find that they have tapped an unsuspected inner resource which they presently identify with their own conception of a Power greater than themselves.

"Most of us think this awareness of a Power greater than ourselves is the essence of spiritual experience. Our more religious members call it 'God-consciousness.'

'Most emphatically we wish to say that any alcoholic capable of honestly facing his problems in the light of our experience can recover, provided he does not close his mind to all spiritual concepts. He can only be defeated by an attitude of intolerance or belligerent denial.

'We find that no one need have difficulty with the spirituality of the program. Willingness, honesty and open mindedness are the essentials of recovery. But these are indispensable.

'There is a principle which is a bar against all information, which is proof against all arguments and which cannot fail to keep a man in everlasting ignorance—that principle is contempt prior to investigation.'"

-Herbert Spencer

LESSON: Rebirth is a radical change in self-identify. In rebirth, whether of the educational variety or of the sudden variety, our understanding of who we are shifts – shifts from being ego-centered to ESSENSE-centered or SELF-centered. To be SELF-centered is to become God conscious or conscious of the Divinity or Spirit of God within our own being. We are born anew!

Chapter 21

THE SPHERE OF REBIRTH

An eighty-five year old man and three children sat around his dining room table. The children were ten year old Rachel and two twelve year old boys, Jonathan and Benjamin. Each had an inquiring mind. They learned new things about triangles, squares and geodesic domes. They talked about mathematics, the earth, the universe and God. The man was R. Buckminster Fuller. The following quote seems to capture the essence of Bucky.

"Fuller was one of the most remarkable individuals who has ever lived. His wide-ranging mind, hauntingly free of the sense of limits that afflicts most of us, conceived poetry, architecture, automobiles, boats, furniture—and some of the most provocative and original mathematical, geometrical, and philosophical speculations ever written.

'There was something marvelous about Bucky (you couldn't think of him by any other name once you had met this elf disguised as an octogenarian). His most infectious quality was an unfettered sense of the immense potential of all humans. It was almost impossible to be around him without being caught up by it.

"He greeted all comers openly, with an evident love. You were his peer, whether you were a physicist, journalist, mail carrier, or child. The equality he offered was difficult to ignore."

The dialogue between these children and their new found friend, Bucky, as well as the quote above, can be found in the book, *FULLER'S EARTH; A DAY WITH BUCKY AND THE KIDS*, by Richard J. Brenneman. This is a delightful book based on the discussions between the children and Bucky that took place on three different occasions over a period of months. The discussions explore some possibilities for the future of education as well as showcasing, in a wonderfully warm setting, the mind and personality of the inventor of the geodesic dome.

So much has already been written about this amazing man. For our purposes I am going to share only one event from his life. Had it not been for this event, it is quite possible, that we would know nothing of R. Buckminster Fuller. This event, which took Bucky into the belly of the whale has proven to be significant in the lives of many thousands who have been impacted by this man and his ideas.

Bucky often referred to himself as the "world's most successful failure." By the time he was thirty-two years of age he had not only been forced out of Harvard (for five generations Fuller men had been Harvard graduates) but had also failed at business ventures. On top of this he had endured one of the greatest tragedies a person can experience, the death of a child. His daughter died on her fourth birthday while Bucky was at a football game. After the death of his daughter he entered into a period of self-deprecation and depression. One night he decided to commit suicide. He was a strong swimmer so that was the means by which he decided to end his life. He decided to go to Lake Michigan and swim out into the Lake until he could swim no more.

When he arrived at the lakeshore and just before he entered the water, a single thought entered his mind. "This is the last you'll ever have to use your mind, so you'd better use it. You'd better do your own thinking - see what you really think." According to Brenneman what followed was an "epiphany of overwhelming lucidity." Bucky suddenly realized that much of his pain had come from his sincere efforts to believe what others told him to believe, regardless of his own contrary feelings and <u>intuition</u>. He recalled that in the past what he had been thinking turned out to be true but that he hadn't had the courage of his convictions, that he continued to do what society had taught him even though he believed it to be false.

His second thought had to do with the realization of his own selfishness. He recalled thinking that selfishness was the root of his problem and the major cause of his pain was thinking and acting selfishly. At that point he said, "There has got to be a better way. What if I look at life differently." It is interesting that both of these conclusions are repeated almost word for word as the theme of two different books, each written some years after this event. The first, The Big Book of *ALCOHOLICS ANONYMOUS*, which says on, page 62 "Selfishness - self centeredness! That we think is the root of our troubles." And in the preface to the *COURSE IN MIRACLES* Helen Schueman, the one who received the material, writes:

"Psychologist, educator, conservative in theory and atheistic in belief, I was working in a prestigious and highly academic setting. And then something happened that triggered a chain of events I could never have predicted. The head of my department unexpectedly announced that he was tired of the angry and aggressive feelings our attitudes reflected, and concluded that 'there must be another way.' As if on cue, I agreed to help him find it. Apparently this Course is the other way."

These two books, one published in 1939 and the other in 1975 are considered by many to be inspired writings and have helped millions to see and live life differently. The different way is self-forgetting (not self-centered) and service to others, not selfish pursuit.

Brenneman says of Bucky, "A vast reformation was taking place in the young man's consciousness. Time seemed to have ceased, and he was aware only of the moment of his thoughts, coursing deeper and deeper toward some still unseen, but life-renewing center." From that time on Bucky resolved to see and live life differently. He resolved to quit asking what's in it for me? And he dedicated his life to the employment of all means to the "betterment of others." Every

185

time I see a geodesic dome I am reminded of this wonderful man and how symbolic he is of the transformation from self to SELF.

MY STORY

Without a doubt, the most important single event in my life happened in the summer of 1971. I was a thirty-seven year old professional, married with four children. If you didn't look beneath the surface, you probably would have thought that I was relatively content and successful. I was however, in deep emotional trouble and I did not know why. Within days after the event that I am going to relate I went to my supervisor and told him some of what I had been going through. I told him I either had a vocational problem, a family problem or a personal problem and I did not know for sure what it was but I was sure that I had a problem. I did not tell him that I had been to three different psychiatrists in the past five years. I did not tell him that I was in the midst of an affair and it was not the first one. I did not tell him that sometimes I drank too much and I was starting to use marijuana on occasion. I did tell him that I thought it was important that I resign from my position. My position was as the Senior Pastor of a relatively large Lutheran Church and he was my Bishop.

Among other things, I did not tell him the details of this story. During the summer I had taken a temporary assignment away from the Parish. The assignment was with the Chaplain's Clinical Training Program at McNeil Island Federal Penitentiary in Washington State. I took the assignment in part because of the problems I was having and thought that it might lead to a graceful exit from the Parish Ministry. As you already know, it did not.

One afternoon, several weeks after starting this assignment, we were scheduled to go down and visit "C" Block isolation (solitary confinement). Prison isolation areas are where prisoners are sent either for in-house punishment or to protect them from other prisoners. In some cases, they are sent to these areas to protect them from themselves. McNeil Island Penitentiary had three isolation areas. Besides "C" Block there were "A" and "B" Blocks.

"A" Block looked very much like an ordinary cellblock - just cells on one level with barred doors. There was one prisoner to a cell and the prisoners could not see each other. They could however, talk to each other and had devised clever ways to pass contraband when the guards were not looking.

"B" Block was very different. It looked like something out of science fiction. In the midst of a very large, well-lighted, antiseptically clean area was a row of solid steel compartments. Each compartment had a solid steel door that included a covered slot though which food could be passed. The compartments were quite small and could be totally darkened when the authorities felt that it was necessary. There was absolutely no noise. The prisoners were unable to communicate with each other and for days at a time the only human contact they had was when a guard slid their food through that slot.

"C" Block was an altogether different scene. I had heard about it; but when I finally saw it for myself, I could hardly believe my eyes. It was a dungeon right out of the thirteenth century. The only exception was the light that came from an occasional forty-watt bulb. The interior was made of gray stone. The cell doors were iron bars. The cells had nothing in them except a sink and a toilet. A few of the cells had mattresses, but many did not. The men, for the most part, looked like beaten lost souls. I suppose most were on Thorazine so any fight they had left in them was just not there.

Of all the men in "C" Block, Eddie stood out. There was still fight in Eddie. He stood with his hands on the bars of the door looking crazed and yelling insults at us as we passed by. His arms were a mass of scars belying his many attempts at suicide. I was told we were lucky that Eddie was standing in the door because when people came down to "C" Block, Eddie often took the opportunity to throw fecal material at them. Eddie was a notorious federal prisoner who was held in isolation not just for months but for years at a time. The authorities felt that he was not only a danger to himself, but to them and to his fellow prisoners. I had to believe that Eddie and the other prisoners I saw on "C" Block needed medical and psychiatric help, not a thirteenth century dungeon. (Some years later I saw Eddie on T.V. I think it was on "Sixty Minutes." He was out of prison and doing quite well. Apparently, somewhere along the way, he got the help he so desperately needed.)

Our group stayed in quarters on the prison grounds just outside the back gate of the main prison. That night I could not sleep. I thought about Eddie. I thought about my family, my parish and I thought about the other woman with whom I was involved. The next morning our Supervisor wanted us to talk about our experience in "C" Block. I was in a state of high anxiety and I tried to say as little as possible.

Toward the end of the meeting I was interrupted to take a telephone call. It was one of my parishioners. She was upset! My Assistant had been at her home the night before and told her that I was having an affair. The Assistant had apparently gotten this information from my wife. I had not told my wife about the other woman, but I had suggested to her that she should look for a job, as I believed that our marriage was in a lot of trouble. I lied to my parishioner about the affair but told her I was having some marriage problems. She understood as I had been counseling her regarding similar problems.

When I got off the phone, I was panic-stricken. I wondered whom else my assistant was telling and why was he trying to undermine me in this way? I knew if he was trying to help the parish, my wife, or even me, that there were better ways of doing so. I had to buy some time so I called the Bishop and told him what my assistant was doing. I admitted to the Bishop that I was having some problems. I also told him that I didn't think having my assistant undermine my ministry with the parishioners was the answer. He agreed and I felt a little better. I had bought some time.

That evening I called the other woman and told her what was happening. She said she had enough problems of her own and she was not going to take the chance of being dragged into a mess like the one I was describing. She said we had to end our relationship. I knew, for her sake, it was the right thing to do but it wasn't what I wanted. Frankly, I was really hung up on her. I was devastated!

The next day our group, along with some of the prisoners associated with the work of the prison chapel, watched the movie, "The Trial," an Orson Wells production based on the book written by the Austrian Existentialist, Franz Kafka.

The movie is the story of Joseph K. who was being accused of and tried for a crime. Strangely, he was never told what crime he had committed. Orson Wells portrays Joseph K. as continually going through door after door, and talking to sullen bureaucrats, trying to determine what the accusation was. The movie ends with K. running out into a large field and disappearing in a huge explosion. Halfway through this strange movie, I too wanted to run. However, I sat it out and when the movie ended, I thought I was the bomb that was going to explode.

As I passed by the prisoner who had requested this particular film, he asked, "How did you like it?" I said, with a stiff lip, "It got to me." His reply, "I thought it would." I knew I had to talk to someone. My best relationship in our clinical training group at the prison, was the youngest man involved. He was bright and seemed to have a natural ability to relate to people with problems. I got him aside by saying, "I need to talk to someone!" He said that he was aware that I was pretty uptight.

We found a place where we could be alone and I told him part of what was taking place in my life. I ended with telling him that I identified with much of Kafka's "The Trial" and that I felt like I was the bomb that was about ready to explode. The young man was not an ordained minister, but he was on the staff of a church. He told me his minister and he had been working with a new counseling technique, which he thought I ought to try. He said I should find a place where I could be alone. Then, I should close my eyes and get quiet - then feel all the pain and anxiety I was having. He said, "Just be with the pain for a few minutes and then slowly try to get beneath it. I don't know what you will find there; but whatever it is, it will be interesting." I was hurting so badly, I was willing to try anything.

I had recently learned a meditation technique and I was also reading and learning some Gestalt Therapy Techniques. With the use of these, I was able to do as the young man suggested, get quiet and then get beneath the pain. What emerged was an incredible feeling of loneliness. I had experienced lonely feelings before but this was something new. It seemed that at the core of my being I was a very, very lonely guy. I started recalling the songs I sang, usually while driving alone. They included, "Are You Lonesome Tonight," "I

189

Stepped Aside, After I Kissed the Bride" and my all time favorite tearjerker, "I'm Nobody's Child." The chorus:

"I'm nobody's child
I'm nobody's child
I'm like a flower
just growing wild.
No mammy's kisses and
no daddy's smile.
Nobody loves me,
I'm nobody's child."

I was surprised but grateful for this revelation. The pain and anxiety had substantially subsided and the deep sense of loneliness seemed like an incredible breakthrough that could lead to a new self-understanding. The next day at the prison when I could get my friend alone, I told him what had happened. He also felt I had made a breakthrough. He suggested that when I got a chance I should do the same thing and this time try to get below the loneliness. That evening I did some Gestalt exercises attempting to get beneath the loneliness feelings. After about a half-hour, I lay down exhausted and fell asleep. Several hours later I awoke with the most overpowering feeling I have ever experienced (before or since)!

It was unquestionably some kind of love, but it would be impossible to describe it as an emotion. I once described it as being like a warm gold brick that had been inserted in my chest cavity. It was warm, glowing and utterly solid. It wasn't like an emotion, it just sat there, never changing, solid as a brick. After daybreak, I got up and took a walk. The love brick was still there and I felt bliss in every cell of my body! When I looked around in the morning light, I saw a world I had never seen before. I was living in Washington State, nicknamed the Evergreen State. I had always enjoyed the lushness but on this particular morning, it wasn't just green, it was hundreds of greens! I never realized how many shades of green one could see. I couldn't believe my eyes. Everything had an aliveness that I had never seen before. Everything was Beautiful!

I didn't do much preaching that summer but the following Sunday was one of those weeks I was scheduled to come home and deliver the sermon. Considering what I had experienced during the week, I hadn't done much in the way of preparation. I turned to the 13th chapter of II Corinthians, verses 1-8 (The New Testament in Modern English)

"If I speak with the eloquence of men and of angels, but have no love, I become no more than blaring brass or crashing cymbal. If I have the gift of foretelling the future and hold in my mind not only all human knowledge but the very secrets of God, and if I also have that absolute faith which can move mountains, but have no love, I amount to nothing at all. If I dispose of all that I possess, yes, even if I give my own body to be burned, but have no love, I achieve precisely nothing.

"This love of which I speak is slow to lose patience - it looks for a way of being constructive. It is not possessive: it is neither anxious to impress nor does it cherish inflated ideas of its own importance.
"Love has good manners and does not pursue selfish advantage. It is not touchy. It does not keep account of evil or gloat over the wickedness of other people. On the contrary, it is glad with all good men when truth prevails.
"Love knows no limit to its endurance, no end to its trust, no fading of its hope; it can outlast anything. It is, in fact, the one thing that still stands when all else has fallen."

I had my sermon. This had always been one of my favorite passages in the Bible but I felt like I had just read it for the first time. The next day was Sunday. I preached on Love. I did little more than read a line from this text and comment, each time bringing forth my new experience and my new insights. I told the congregation that for the first time I understood this passage, that for the first time I had experienced this kind of love. I said, "For the first time I understand that without this love, I am nothing." I cried during the presentation; tears of relief and of joy. I was alive!

The congregation's reaction was very mixed. Many, including my wife and our physician who attended the church thought I was having an emotional breakdown. As I shook hands with him at the door, he said, "You need to come in and see me tomorrow." I didn't go in to see him. I believed then as I believe today, I wasn't experiencing an emotional breakdown but a spiritual breakthrough.

I knew in my heart it was the best sermon I had ever given but it was also the last sermon I ever delivered. The die had been cast. My days as a clergyman were over. For a few days I thought this might be the beginning of an all-new ministry and an all-new relationship with my wife. But that was not to be. It was just the beginning of an all new me. This gold brick of love-feeling in my chest lasted for days as did the heightened perception. I reveled in both the inner feeling and the beauty of the world around me. But all attempts to get my past relationships back on a new footing were in vain.

LESSON: Now in this lesson, let's focus on the term, "sphere of rebirth." Just what is this sphere, the environment, and the conditions conducive for rebirth? When Raven went into the belly of the cow whale and started looking around, what do you suppose he/she was thinking? I think it might have been something like, "This is nuts, really nuts. What on earth am I doing here?" What on <u>earth</u>, indeed, are <u>we</u> doing here? Bucky, on the shores of Lake Michigan, seems to be asking a similar question. This also is one of the haunting questions that Loren Eiseley's writings seem to continually ask.

Throughout this section we have talked about crisis; but not just any crisis; a crisis of faith. An external crisis, no matter how difficult, is not a crisis of faith until it begins to shake the foundations of beliefs; until it causes us to ask, "What on <u>earth</u> am <u>I</u> doing here?' A <u>crisis of faith</u>, caused by an external or internal event <u>is the sphere of rebirth</u>. Nicademus said, "Must I enter again into my Mother's womb?" Jesus replied, in effect, "No, not into your Mother's womb but into the womb of rebirth; into the realm of death." The Bible says we must die before we can be born again. The realm of rebirth is often a time of great stress when the old ego-self dies and you begin to experience a resurrection from the ashes of that death. The picture that we used to illustrate this in the second section of the book was the

Golden Buddha in Thailand. Only when the clay-covered Buddha was stressed and the clay started to crack, was its golden inner nature revealed.

Chapter 22

THE ROAD OF TRIALS

The road of trials in mythology is the place of danger, of dragons, dungeons, giants and shipwreck. All of these, of course, are familiar to us in our dream world. The world of dreams was the place in which Carl Jung discovered his archetypes - those aspects of mankind's psyche that typify both our <u>limitations</u> and our <u>possibilities</u>. It was, no doubt, these archetypes that drew Campbell and Jung to each other. For what Jung found in the thousands of dreams that he analyzed, Campbell found in the thousands of myths that he studied. Each man's findings confirmed the other's and conveyed to the world that the substance of mankind's subconscious is of one piece throughout history and cuts across all cultures.

One of the best known myths is that of King Midas from Greek Mythology. King Midas was given his wish that all he touched might turn to gold. At first, he was delighted when he touched a leaf and then an apple and sure enough each turned to gold. However, he was less delighted when the feast he ordered also turned to gold and finally, he was devastated when he went to his beautiful sleeping daughter and with a father's tender touch she turned into a pretty golden but lifeless statue. Midas wanted fulfillment but his human limitations (ego and greed) stood in the way.

Kae has a reoccurring dream, in which she is either playing tennis or bowling. If it is tennis, she absolutely cannot serve the ball over the net no matter how hard she tries. If it is bowling she cannot keep the ball on the lane, it gutters every time. She has asked me many times if I might have any idea what this dream means. When she read the following from Campbell's book, *THE HERO WITH A THOUSAND FACES*, (page 190) she began to understand.

"The agony of breaking through personal limitations is the agony of spiritual growth. Art, literature, myth and cult, philosophy, and ascetic disciplines are instruments to help the individual past his limiting horizons into spheres of ever-expanding realization."

After reading these sentences, Kae recalled this dream was occurring less often and that the last time this dream occurred she had actually gotten the ball across the net even though it was done with a great deal of struggle. She now feels that her continued use of breath therapy, meditation and the frequent use of the phrase, "You lead, I'll follow" is paying off.

In addition I would add, after listening to thousands of stories as a participant for many years in twelve-step groups and as a personal and group counselor, I have gained great respect for the integrity of the first step which identifies our powerlessness over the human condition. With the ego in charge, we cannot transcend the human condition, we cannot get beyond the net, our best intentions backfire (as they did with King Midas). The answer: (according to mythology, Dr. Jung and the perennial philosophy) is to <u>surrender</u> and align our own ego will with the will of the unseen one; the IN, WITH and UNDER. (See Appendix IV)

Kae's dream indicates an unconscious attempt to get past her human limitation by exerting effort. It <u>can't</u> be done by effort, only by becoming a channel. (The channel metaphor will be further discussed in chapter 24, THE RETURN) That is what Michelangelo captured in his magnificent David - surrender to the power of the covenant and the power that stood behind the covenant. The only effort necessary to align our ego wills with the will of the higher SELF are steps of willingness - willingness to accept our powerlessness and willingness to take the first steps towards surrender.

TOLSTOY (1828-1910)

Although most of Leo Tolstoy's years were lived in the 19th century, I include him among the 20th century lights that I feel Humankind must bring with us into the third millennium. This is true not only because he is regarded as one of history's greatest novelists widely translated and read in the 20th century but mainly because of the influence he has had on the 20th century through the likes of Mahatma Gandhi, Martin Luther King and Cesar Chavez. This influence has been powerful and widespread because TOLSTOY and those who followed in his footsteps learned to tap the power that is the essence of man.

Any attempt to capture the life of TOLSTOY in a few paragraphs is impossible for he was highly creative, deeply complex and often conflicted. It is not difficult to see his life in the various stages of the Vision Quest Hero. Like Buddha, he was born and raised in the midst of a noble family with means and position. Also like Buddha, he was deeply troubled by the suffering of the peasant masses. Although a military man in his youth, he became a pacifist in his later years. He despised tyrannical abuse by both the Church and State. Although, for many years, content in his marriage which produced a large family (thirteen children), he arrived at a point in his life when he felt he should be sexually abstinent.

After years of searching, he became a Christian, only to be excommunicated from the Russian Orthodox Church. One source says that TOLSTOY preached the Gospel of a living God within us, for which he was excommunicated. While this is true, it is an oversimplification of why he was excommunicated. In the process of his search for meaning he read much of the Church's theology. In his response to this he wrote, "I had intended to go to God and I found my way into a stinking bog, which evokes in me only those feelings of which I am most afraid; disgust, malice and indignation." In the end TOLSTOY experienced transformation by reading and embracing

197

Jesus' words in the Sermon on the Mount, especially the phrase, "resist not evil." He found these words of Jesus to be in direct opposition to the actions of the State which were carried on with the blessings of the Church. His reflections on this phrase led to the writing of the book, *THE KINGDOM OF GOD IS WITHIN YOU.* This book was banned in Russia but led to the nonviolent movement, sometimes referred to as Soulforce.

It appears to me that Tolstoy's understanding of Christianity is often misunderstood. For example, in the introduction to Emmet Fox's book, *THE SERMON ON THE MOUNT*, Fox says, "TOLSTOY endeavored to put forward The Sermon on the Mount as the practical guide to life, taking its precepts literally at their face value, and ignoring the spiritual interpretation of which he was unaware and excluding the Plane of the Spirit in which he did not believe." In an encyclopedia's reference to Tolstoy's conversion, it said he was converted to an ethical Christianity. Both of these interpretations I believe to be wrong. The last chapter of *THE KINGDOM OF GOD IS WITHIN YOU* clearly states the source of Tolstoy's beliefs and of his ethics. The following, from his diary recorded a few days before his death, captures the essence of his understanding. "We acknowledge God only when we are conscious of His manifestation in us. All conclusions and guidelines based on this consciousness should fully satisfy our desire to know God as such as well as our desire to live a life based on recognition."

TOLSTOY, the Vision Quest Hero, earlier in his life heard the Call and refused it. Later, when he was almost fifty years old, after a period of mental anguish, he heard the Call again and accepted. From that time on, he dedicated himself to aligning his ego will with God's will. In his writings he let the chips fall where they may and they fell hard both upon the Russian Church and their Russian Government, especially in regard to their treatment of the peasant masses. He battled with the dragons of his own guilt and he suffered the pains of his own hypocrisy. Not until the final weeks of his life, was he able to reconcile his beliefs about the masses and his own position of nobility and means. At that point, at the age of eighty-two, it seems he was no longer able to endure his hypocrisy and he left wife, family and estate to pursue the life of a simple peasant. It was a giant leap of faith and of love. It probably wasn't very practical because he didn't have the physical strength to get far. He made it only to the nearest railroad station where he contracted pneumonia and died within a few days.

If I could have counseled Count Leo TOLSTOY during his lifetime, I would have done the following: I would have had him turn to page 52 of his own book, *THE KINGDOM OF GOD IS WITHIN YOU,* where it says, "Blessedness consists in progress towards perfection." I would have had him read these words to himself and then I would have told him how important these words would become in the twelve-step movements of the 20th century where very often a recovering person is told by his or her sponsor, or another member of their group, to proceed with "Progress towards perfection." But they also remind them that the emphasis is on <u>progress,</u> not perfection."

MY STORY

Before I sat down to write about this period of my life, I spent a full day digging through old journals and legal pads looking for material on these years. I found five different versions of these years written at different times over a period of fifteen years. While "the road of trials" is a period that most of us never completely grow out of, there did come a time when I felt that I had reached a higher plateau; a time, as you will see, when the basic monsters of this period had been tamed if not destroyed. The following is a cut and paste compilation of those previous attempts to write about this period along with a few new insights and additions. I have selected this method in order to give the reader a feel for the struggles that I went through during this period of my life. In order to use these items as written there will be, once again, some duplication.

MY KAFKA PERIOD

"'I am dreaming that I have to go through endless corridors. Then I remain for a long time in a little room that looks like the

bathing pool in the public baths. They compel me to leave the pool, and I have to pass again through a moist, slippery shaft, until I come through a little latticed door into the open. I feel like one newly born, and I think: 'This means a spiritual rebirth for me, through my analysis.'" (*HERO WITH A THOUSAND FACES,* Campbell: page 104 Stekel, Die Sprache des Traumes, p.286)

I had to chuckle when I read this, because for those of you who have read Kafka's *THE TRIAL,* you know that the key figure K, has been accused of a crime and has no idea what the nature of the crime is for which he is being accused. Similar to the dream described above, Kafka's character goes through endless doors and hallways attempting to defend himself and to find out what indeed he is defending himself against. He enters and exits the doors of bureaucracy continually, and all the time being distracted in various ways from working on his case. Working on his case was both his obsession and that from which he was constantly distracted. As you read the following I hope you will see this dual theme in my Kafka period. (Both the obsession to work on my case and the continual distractions.)

During these years I often referred back to Kafka's, *THE TRIAL* with words like, "I'm working on my case," or "I am having difficulty working on my case." This repeated reference to "to working on my case" became a kind of joke between Kae and myself but both of us knew the seriousness of what I called, "my case." My case was to pursue the dignity within that I had discovered in the "love experience.' From the beginning I felt that this experience had something to do with my destiny.

However I tried to explain it, theologically or psychologically, one thing was clear - something new had been added to my life; something that could not be ignored and something that had power. Even though the great experience of love (solid agape) had faded, these things remained; the memory, which seemed to have a power all its own, the aliveness, the sense of being in touch with my feelings, the heightened sense of awareness and a being in touch with my dignity.

This new thing provided one side of a war that would rage within my life and psyche for the next twelve years. I can't really say that it was the classic war between good and evil or between God and the devil, but some aspects of such a war seemed evident. For me it was more specifically a war between what seemed to beckon to me from inside and what beckoned to me from the world around me.

Three years into this stage I started giving lectures at an alcoholic treatment center. The lectures mirrored what I was going through. The first lecture began, "There seems to be something about the nature of man that causes him to go outside of himself to look for meaning." I had become aware that meaning was found within but also aware that I was still seeking without. I wanted to be free but I was caught somewhere between the demands of my new inner world and the appeal of my new less restricted outer world.

Now, to be sure, I had been a Clergyman. I had been converted to Christianity and joined one of the mainstream protestant churches at the age of twenty. I finished college in a church-owned school, completed four years of seminary and did a year of advanced study. I served three different parishes in a ten-year period. I had faith - I felt that it was faith that I had caught as well as had been taught. It was faith based on feelings as well as an intellectual belief. But, it was not a faith that could draw on any power. When honest with myself, I didn't see much power in the faith of my fellow clergymen or in many of my parishioners. I didn't see much power manifesting in the parish or in the church as a whole. This assessment may have been exaggerated by my own soul sickness, my own blindness.

Now, what I was experiencing within was a new kind of power but I couldn't completely trust it. I couldn't rely on something within to provide me with goodies available in the world around me that at times looked ripe for plucking. In those twelve years, I not only had that battle raging but also, that battle kept me on an emotional roller coaster. No wonder there was recovery and relapse, marriage and separations, business success and business failure, investment gains and loses. I was baker, truck driver, counselor, school teacher, insurance salesman, real estate salesman, manager, owner, in jails, hospitals, psyche wards, emergency rooms, had back problems, depression, anxiety, skin cancer, broken bones, car accidents, and kidney stones. I attended many different churches, read books on self-help, Zen, Hinduism and mysticism. In the early part of this period I was sexually active, drank excessively and smoked some marijuana. I tried Psychiatry, Counseling, Transcendental Meditation, returning to the church, psycho-cybernetics, hypnosis, diets, fasting and exercise programs.

At the end of these twelve years things were pretty much as they were at the beginning. June 5, 1979 (eight years into this period) I wrote in a journal, "After reading all that precedes this page, I cannot but think the more things change the more things stay the same." I go on to mention marriage problems, vocational problems and self-image problems. When I went to the Bishop, eight years earlier, I mentioned the same three things.

Different wife, different job, different city - same problems. Other statements in the same journal entry indicated continued struggles with "trying to find ways to focus and be "single-minded", "spiritual experiences producing new insights" and "probing the mysteries, depth and promise of love." In the midst of all the distractions, I was still trying to work on my case. In the spring of 1981 I came to the end of my rope. I gave up the battle and surrendered.

KAFKA PERIOD - VERSION TWO
OLE CUT AND RUN

I was staying in a dingy little motel waiting for an out-of-town assignment from an Insurance Company that had just hired me as an Agent. I had a lot of time on my hands and naturally was doing a lot of thinking. Some of the time I was trying to figure out the future and a lot of the time was spent reflecting back on the events of the past month. I had resigned from the parish, the summer position at the penitentiary and had left my wife and family.

I found myself continually asking if that love experience was of God. I remembered people talking about God having a sense of humor and I thought if that love experience was of God then God does indeed have a sense of humor, a really weird sense of humor.

Here I sit, after ten years of the ministry and if this love experience is of God then I truly have a message to offer. For the first time in my life I have a basis from which to preach (love) but I have no base (pulpit) from which to preach. What am I doing? I'm heading out to sell insurance. Then, I recalled a phrase used by Dr. Warren Quanbeck, one of my Seminary Professors, "Let God be as original with the next person as he is with you." I thought, "boy this is really original." And a few weeks later some of the same thoughts went through my mind when I ran into one of my former parishioners. I was on my new assignment and we happened to be staying in the same hotel in Bellingham, Washington. As soon as he saw me, I was aware of the hurt look on his face. We chatted for a minute or so and then as we started to move on - I extended my hand in friendship. He turned around and walked away saying, "not today, not today, ole cut and run." That's what he called me, "ole cut and run." I sat down somewhat stunned and wondered, "Did I really have any other options?" I didn't know. (It didn't seem like it then.) The Psychiatrist that my wife urged me to go to said I was a "God-damn sick neurotic!" Is that what I am - a sick neurotic?

I thought to myself, I am a lot less sick now than I was a few weeks ago. Right or wrong, I have made some decisions and acted on them. I know I am not without problems. But, somehow I felt, in-spite of my confusion and as strange as it might sound, that I was on the right track. I started reviewing my session with the Bishop before I resigned. I told him that I was resigning because I either had a personal problem, a vocational problem or a family problem. I didn't know for sure just what it was but very possibly it was all three. I started thinking that it was all three. I guess I felt I couldn't begin to solve any of them without some time and space. I really didn't think I had any options. I felt that the die had been cast. I said to myself if they think of me as "ole cut and run" so be it. Didn't my efforts at reconciliation both with the congregation and with my wife blow up in my face? Didn't they—? I believe they did.

Just after I met Kae I started to meditate. I found my fellow meditators and the T.M. instructors to be very supportive of my call to grow, change and expand. In mythology this is the period that separates the wanna bes from the real thing. I call this time in my life the Kafkaesk period.

This period in my life lasted about twelve years. My case, as I understand it, was to pursue, develop and follow the new found inner integrity that had resulted from my peak experience. But, try as I might, with all of the allies that had come to support and assist me, I was continually being distracted from working on my case and the new found integrity or Self was constantly being overshadowed. Here are some words I wrote in a journal during that period:

"November 8, 1976 - The last three days have been hell and today has been more hell. I am sick. I need help. I have made an appointment with a medical doctor and a counselor. I don't want to lose Kae and yet my depression seems to be directed at punishing her. Even when I have tried to break through this I couldn't, it just got worse. Today I would have gladly died. I am feeling better now and I want to be with Kae. I know I can't blame her for my misery but things were so together for awhile and I keep asking why it couldn't be. I know she tried but where from here. I love her. My instability and inability to stay on top of my own emotions make it super difficult to work with other people. My depressions always cast great doubt on my ability and competency as a counselor. In depression I am always presented with a further problem. The problem is vocation. In some ways I am right back where I was five years ago with personal, family and vocational problems. I hope not total bankruptcy. HELP"

"November 9, 1976 - My instability is even clearer this morning than it was last night. I'm up and down like a roller coaster. Somehow I need to get stabilized and get my mind off of myself."

"April 12, 1977 - Kae and I are together on weekends. They have been filled with love and good feelings. I have been going to lots of A.A. meetings and my conscious contact with God remains. Two weeks ago I cried like a baby in a session with Bob (a counselor) and Kae - a great deal of anger was released as I poured out my feeling of being torn apart - wanting Kae and bombarded by non-monogamous feelings and thoughts. My priorities seem clear again - The absolute is ABSOLUTE!"

"September 7, 1981 - When I am one with my inner essence I am all I have ever wanted. When this inner essence is overshadowed I look without to <u>satisfy</u> my dissatisfaction. How ironic! Indeed, how insane! I can stir my cup of tea all day long but it won't taste sweet until I add the sugar. My sugar is my inner essence!"

In retrospect I was stuck because I was unwilling or unable to fully surrender to the new found divinity within. I was at the fork in the road and I wanted what both roads had to offer. I wanted it all and I was fearful that if I really became single-minded and took "the road less traveled" I would miss out on something.

One of the monsters that I had to struggle with was my obsession with women. When Kae and I got married I tried to be very honest with her about this. I knew that it had destroyed my first marriage and my profession. I told her I never wanted to live a double, dishonest life again. I also told her that I was willing to be monogamous but I didn't know if that was possible. I explained that for the last seven years of my marriage and ministry I had tried everything I knew (from prayer to therapy) to have this obsession lifted and nothing seemed to work. As I previously stated she says she entered the marriage with her eyes wide open. She also said that she honestly didn't know how she would react but that she would try to accept what happened.

During the early days of our marriage there was a minimum of involvement with other women but the mental obsession had a field day. What involvement there was gave a clear indication from Kae that the marriage was not going to be viable if monogamy was not the standard. By the same token, my very existence seemed to be tied to my attractions to the opposite sex and when I tried to suppress my desires I fell into depression. Finally it became clear I must make a choice. I faced the monster and said I am truly willing to pass you by. I got down on my knees and prayed that the obsession would be lifted and, miraculously, it was. I can't explain it but there has been no significant struggle with this problem from that day until now.

About a year later, I faced a second monster which finally allowed me to get by the fork in the road, allowed me to, in a sense, get off the roller coaster which went from emotional highs to emotional lows and enter into a period of stability. The monster of which I speak is that of self-righteous, self-serving pride. Again, the lesson was learned in relationship to Kae as you will see in the story that continues in the next section, MY STORY, the AT-ONE-MENT.

SELF TALK

Before leaving the ministry I became somewhat of an expert in Transactional Analysis; the system of psychoanalysis that uses the parent, child, adult construct. I found it to be a fascinating teaching tool and a fun way of reacting with others who were also familiar with the system. In the early 70's Dr. Eugene Harris, author of *I'M OK YOU'RE OK,* conducted twenty-four hour marathon group sessions in Sacramento, California. I attended one of these and found it to be good fun and I remember, at the time, I thought I had gotten some helpful insights into my own personality.

Even though I was able to identify certain feelings, thoughts and attitudes both in myself and in others and assign them their appropriate label I was never able to get in touch with or identify anything within myself that one would call "the inner child." In fact, I was no more successful in identifying inner parent, child or adult than I was able to identify the older constructs of Freud – i.e. Ego, Super Ego and Id. All this was after many hours of reading, group therapy, classes and thousands of dollars in Psychiatric sessions. I am not saying that I did not derive any value from all of this, but I am saying it is difficult for me to identify any value.

Likewise, there was a period of time in which I fastidiously read and practiced the *ART OF POSITIVE THINKING.* I read, studied and tried to practice the ideas contained in books such as *THINK AND GROW RICH, PSYCHO CYBERNETICS,* Jess Lair's *I AIN'T MUCH BABY, BUT I'M ALL I'VE GOT* and many others. Each time I tried a new idea, went to another seminar, read another book it was the same thing - a little rush of excitement, sometimes a feeling of eureka and then the disappointment. This isn't working either!

Do you know what despair is? I do. It's the feeling you get when you feel like you've tried everything and nothing works. You think about suicide and after you have set that thought aside another time, you either sink into acute depression or find relief and we all know there are many, many ways to find relief - some very destructive, others appear to be healthy, even constructive. But when you look at whatever it is, whether it be alcohol or Alka-Seltzer, robbing a bank or attending a baseball game, casual sex or caring sex, it is relief, release, not a solution, not a way out.

I don't know when it was for sure, but in the midst of all this searching, all this despair and all this seeking relief and release, it dawned on me that I was indeed lost, really lost! And, not necessarily at the same time, it dawned on me that virtually everybody around me was lost too! I recalled that this in part was the message of the churches and of the New Testament. The answer there was, "Believe in Jesus." But I tried that, I honestly tried that with everything I could muster. I **tried that**! And I ended up on the floor of a drunk tank. Yes, I was a preacher and teacher of the Church and I ended up in a drunk tank. But I knew I was not the only one who hadn't found an answer any place. In fact I began to wonder if I knew anybody who had really found the answer. Was there indeed an answer?

All these books and seminars, Gurus and preachers, teachers began to look to me like the lost leading the lost, the blind leading the blind. (Fredrick Neitche can enlighten you on the state of Nihilism if you care to read him.)

I still had one thing, I wasn't a complete Nihilist, and there was always in me a flicker of light, a flicker of hope. My experience, my love experience, what was it? What did it mean? And then there was my meditation practice, which seemed to put me in touch with that hope, that flicker of light, that flicker of life.

For years, I have spent hours and hours in bookstores and libraries just paging through books hoping to find an answer. Over the years I have found a few books which have pointed me in a positive direction and at the same time, found hundreds of books which had me going down another dead-end road.

For instance, Socrates said, "Know thyself." That is excellent advice. The best there is! It has been quoted by thousands of authors, used in classrooms by millions of teachers and heard from the pulpit around the world for ages. But, how many of these leaders of humanity knew, or know, themselves? How many were talking about egos and ids - Parent, Adult, Child? How many talked about our emotions, or our thoughts, or our bodies? How many talked about knowing our personalities? Virtually all of these people thought or think that knowing ourselves has something to do with these things and, the truth is, they just don't! Our true SELF is none of these things and that is just how lost we are. We don't have a clue, not a clue. Again, I've gotten nihilistic, haven't I. The following story by Vernon Howard gives us some insight into what I am saying.

"Picture a man lost in the woods, Dusk is descending and the dangers of the dark creep in. The man knows that a false step might drop him into a deep pit or treacherous marsh. Wild Animals lurk in the shadows. A storm threatens.

"Suddenly, the lost man sights another struggling wanderer. He asks for the way out. The stranger offers immediate and friendly help. After following the stranger for a while, the lost man realizes that his supposed guide is just as lost as he is. So he parts company, to set out once more on his own. Soon, he comes across a second stranger who confidently claims to possess an accurate map of the escape route. The lost man follows this new counselor, but again it becomes obvious that the man is self-deceived and that his map is a pathetic result of his self-deception. The lost man wanders on in deepening despair. He runs into others who claim knowledge of the way out, but he sees from the half-concealed distress in their eyes that they are just as lost as he.

"Then, as he stumbles about, the wanderer places his hand into his coat pocket for warmth. His fingers curl about something hard and reassuring. He withdraws a compass. He laughs with comfort and relief as he realizes that it was there all along. He had only to look within himself. He had been so busy inquiring of others, that he had failed to do the one necessary thing. But now he has found his salvation within himself."

My experience, my love experience and the regular practice of meditation that put me in touch with that quality, became my compass. With this as my compass, I began to make some progress. For instance, I started to make use of some old tools that were in my tool case. I started to acknowledge that this new life that was starting to emerge within me could be seen as a child. It is however, important to realize this child is not of my past, not feelings, not thoughts. But something new, something Holy!

It is in this regard I find myself able to use self-talk and affirmations - the following exemplifies how I have used this insight. Often, in the past and occasionally today, I have observed myself asking the question, "What do they think of me, do they like me, do they approve of what I just said or did?" If I don't check this, somehow my mind gives all kinds of negative answers to these questions and my true SELF can get overshadowed. The way I use self-talk is like this: As soon as I observe a question like what do they think of me, I say, quietly to myself, "What do you think of you?" I almost always respond with a feeling of love and I can say, "I love you, what's there not to love? I am God's son, I am light, I am peace." I had discovered within myself the IMAGO DEI (the image of God).

Somewhere, near the end of this twelve-year period I wrote this:

> There is nowhere to go,
> we are already here.
> There is nothing to seek,
> we already have it!
> There is nothing to conquer,
> we are already free.

LESSON: Once we have become conscious of having had a spiritual experience or even conscious of the need for one, it really becomes a matter of choice - choosing to yield the will of the little i (selfness), to the will of the big I (spirit). This, according to many sources, including the Big Book of Alcoholics Anonymous, is the proper use of the will.

Most of us find this process of turning it over is indeed a road of trials. But, rest assured, even a little willingness on a daily basis will prove to be successful. The ego does not give up easily. But on the "road of trials" the way gets narrower and little by little you will find yourself walking in the spirit of the Higher Power the INNER REALIY. The ABSOLUTE, not the relative, will become your joy.

EDITOR'S NOTE: One of the volunteer editors of this book asked several questions about this chapter. The questions were centered around the author's intent – questions such as, "Is it the author's intent that people follow his experience and start the practice of meditation? Also, "Is the author suggesting that even those who are not alcoholics should read the Big Book?" The author's response was: "Follow the guidance of the INNER TEACHER." (a concept that will be introduced in chapter 24)

Chapter 23

AT-ONE-MENT
PEACE

One of the universal pictures in myth is the hero's reconciliation with his father. (This picture is contained within the theme we discussed in a previous chapter, that of coming home). Reconciliation with the Father is of course one of the great themes in Christianity. But this theme is not restricted to Christianity. However, there is an aspect of this, that many in Christianity believe is unique. In Christianity, the Hero (Jesus) is able to effect an atonement on behalf of all and thus all are reconciled with the Father (God). However, today's mainline churches, especially the fundamentalists, would have us add (with scripture to back up their contention) "to all who believe." This qualifier then has the effect of setting Christianity apart from the perennial philosophy. It establishes <u>belief, rather than awareness,</u> as the essential ingredient for wholeness. Both the fundamentalists and the perennial philosophy would have us understand that Jesus came bearing the message of GOOD NEWS! (GOSPEL). But the two differ as to the content of that good news. The perennial philosophy says essentially that the good news is that the Kingdom of God is within us. If this is true, then separation from the Father is an illusion.

In the Sermon on the Mount Jesus said, "Blessed are the peacemakers for they shall be called the sons of God." (Matt 5:9) The peacemaker is none other than he or she who has discovered there is no real barrier between God and himself/herself. A peacemaker is one who turns within and makes the discovery that peace is within us. The peacemaker is one who, in discovering the peace within himself/herself also begins to realize that peace lives within everyone and everything. The peacemaker discovers at-one-ment with the ALL.

For those of you who are interested in pursuing this thought further, I suggest you read the account of the Prodigal Son in Luke 15. Read it, keeping in mind what has been said here. Look first at the context in which the story was told. (Luke 15: 1-2) "Now the tax collector and sinners were all drawing near to hear him and the Pharisees and Scribes murmured saying, 'This man receives sinners and eats with them.'" Now read the story and note that any notion of being cut off or separated from the Father is in the mind of the brothers, not the Father. Of course, the Father was glad to receive the younger son back from the far country where he had settled for pig slop. Likewise he assured the jealous older son that all he had, was his. Separation is an aspect of our lower nature or ego mind. At-one-ment is the nature of our higher SELF. The path of the Vision Quest Hero is to move from the sense of separation and abandonment to a sense of at-one-ment and peace.

You may also note that settling for pig slop caused the younger son to have a "crisis of faith" and the text says in that state he came to himself. The sphere of rebirth is the far country. He started to settle for pig slop and he said, "What on earth am I doing here?" The text says he came to himself and he started for home.

If one looks at the text from this perspective it would be easy to surmise that the older brother was just beginning to hear the call, to enter the sphere of rebirth, for his faith was being shaken by fear and jealousy. The story does not tell us if he answered the call. Who knows whether he came to himself. Who knows indeed! What we do know is that the Father remained very near. If Jesus was trying to tell his hearers something about God, it is clear to me that once again he was saying the Father is immanent (available to experience).

ALDUS HUXLEY

Aldus Huxley was one of those rather rare individuals who some feel had a sense of SELF throughout his life. If this is true, it seems quite probable that this experience became even clearer when as a child he was blind for a time. It was during this period that he started to write. His sight, after a period of total blindness, was partially restored and he lived out his life in this state.

Huxley, most noted for his novels, especially *BRAVE NEW WORLD, BRAVE NEW WORLD REVISITED* and *ISLAND,* was a student of many subjects and a keen observer of society. He was particularly insightful when it came to the subject of religion. In a lecture given at Santa Barbara, California in 1959 entitled "Man and Religion," he spelled out what he saw as two different kinds of religion. One, he suggested, was the religion of direct acquaintance and the other was the religion of dogma, creeds, symbols and liturgies.

In this lecture he divided the religion of dogma, creeds and symbols into two types, one of mythology and one of institutional religions. Huxley showed appreciation for two aspects of mythology. One is the fact that the nature of myth is amorphous and makes less of a claim to being true than creedal and doctrinal religions. Secondly, mythological religions often involve the body in dance and ceremony. Huxley says movement of the body often opens up the individual to direct contact. He notes that western religion has been refined by "bourgeoisie attitudes" and the body has become less a part of worship. He mentions two exceptions, the Quakers and the Shakers because their bodies spontaneously express themselves due to direct contact. In fact their very names come from the spontaneous responses. The Quakers quake and the Shakers shake. Both Kae and I have experienced some of this spontaneous reaction of the body when practicing specialized meditation techniques. We understand this as the release of stress and tension that is needed in order to have a clearer experience of the ABSOLUTE. In other words, we are ridding ourselves of the static (stress from the nervous system) which interferes with direct contact.

Huxley did not make a direct historical connection between mythological and modern institutional religions in the same way that Campbell did although his statement about bourgeoisie attitudes refining religion seems to make an indirect connection. The main thrust of his Santa Barbara lecture was to point out the relationship and the differences between creedal, doctrinal religion and that of the religion of "direct acquaintance."

Huxley says it is the difference between <u>knowing about God</u> and <u>knowing God</u>. He notes in the history of western religions there has always been an uneasy relationship between these two traditions - the mystical tradition and doctrinal, creedal, liturgical whether the tradition be Moslem, Christianity or Judaism.

Huxley intimates that institutional religions have downplayed the mystical experience, because it was considered only a few were capable of the sublime spiritual experience of direct acquaintance with the Godhead. It also seems that those with direct acquaintance have often constituted a threat to the institutions; because they are seen as undermining the control of institutions which have based their authority not on conscious contact but on dogma, doctrine and creed. Huxley felt that the idea that direct acquaintance was only for the few was not true and stated his belief - "practically everybody is capable - if he sets about it in the right way." In his book, *THE PERENNIAL PHILOSOPHY,* which was published in 1944, he includes the following quotes, which support this contention.

"God does not reserve such a lofty vocation (that of mystical contemplation) to certain souls only; on the contrary, He is willing that all should embrace it. But He finds few who permit Him to work such sublime things for them. There are many who, when He sends them trials, shrink from the labor and refuse to bear with the dryness and mortification, instead of submitting, as they must, with perfect patience." - St. John of the Cross

Huxley felt that belief itself is a neutral thing and could be either good or bad depending on the circumstances. Certainly it doesn't take much thought to realize this is true. We know strongly held beliefs can and do result in prejudice, false judgment, division and war. In order to illustrate the problem, even the dangers of belief systems, Huxley discussed the various atonement doctrines that have found favor in the history of the Christian Church. He used as the basis of his discussion a thesis by Dr. Adams Brown who had been a professor of Union Theological Seminary in New York.

As Huxley spoke I was taken back to my own seminary days, listening to Dr. Warren Quanbeck talk about the history of Atonement doctrines. I found it interesting that Dr. Quanbeck's presentation of this subject had been very similar to Dr. Brown's. As previously mentioned, atonement was a common theme in mythology. (The reunification of the hero son, with his father) The question Christian theology has asked is how did Jesus restore mankind to the heavenly Father? This question played a part in the first major split in Christendom. The split that resulted in the Roman Catholic Church and the Greek Orthodox Church that took place in 1054. One prominent difference between these two institutions was the question: what was important about Jesus? The Greeks thought that Jesus life was the most important thing and the Romans felt that it was his death. Each of the various views of the atonement depends on one's view of the Father. As you will remember, in our short look at the prodigal son story, I said the father did not change. He loved his sons and he assured them both of his love. The atonement was based merely on their understanding that they could never be separated from his love. But that is not the kind of God pictured in many of the atonement doctrines.

1. Jesus as the Pascal lamb. Following the Jewish custom of sacrificing animals to God, Jesus is seen as a sacrifice provided by God the Father himself for all who will accept the sacrifice. The Father is seen as one who demands that sacrifices be made to him and if you do not accept his sacrifice your sins cannot be forgiven and thus you are damned.

2. Jesus, a substitute - Here, God the Father is seen as governor and lawgiver. Mankind has broken the law and someone must pay the penalty. Justice must be served. Jesus, the righteous one, bears the

punishment that was due to man. All who accept Jesus as their substitute will be saved.

3. Jesus as ransom - A ransom must be paid for the sin of Adam and Eve and all who followed. Someone righteous had to die to pay the ransom; but, to whom was the ransom to be paid? Some said it had to be paid to the devil to get man back and others said it had to be paid to God in order to satisfy God's honor. Once again belief is important, for salvation is only to those who accept that Jesus paid the ransom for them. The idea that the ransom was paid to God the Father in time led to another great division in Christianity.

It was theorized by some in the Roman Catholic Church that this ransom was held in a storehouse and could be added to by other righteous individuals such as Saints who had passed on. This super abundant merit could be handed out to those who needed it for the forgiveness of sins. This practice was called indulgences. In the 16th Century these indulgences became available for a price. Some like Martin Luther saw this as a scandal. Martin Luther's opposition to the selling of indulgences ultimately led to the Protestant reformation and further divisions within the Christian community.

Huxley went on to say that this example could be carried through in virtually every doctrine of the church. The point is that each picture of atonement reflects a different view of the Father and illustrates the problem of transferring experience into conceptual and symbolic terms.

THE PERENNIAL PHILOSOPHY, on the other hand, is Huxley's attempt to show the universality of the religion of direct acquaintance. In it's purest form he shows it to be inclusive rather than devisive. German philosopher and mathematician Gottfried Leibniz, (1646-1716) first coined the term itself (Perennial Philosophy). But, as Huxley points out, the rudiments of this philosophy may be found among the traditional lore of primitive peoples in every region of the world and in its fully developed forms it has a place in every one of the higher religions.

In *THE PERENNIAL PHILOSOPHY* you will find essentially what Campbell discovered in his study of myth and what Jung discovered in his study of the psyche of man. That discovery is mankind's ability to have direct contact with the Higher SELF (the

IMAGO DEI, the image of God). The perennial philosophy shows that giving an accurate expression in word concerning this direct acquaintance is virtually impossible, yet the sameness of the experiences can be recognized.

Following are a few of the passages that Huxley quotes and comments on in this remarkable anthology. These quotes are by those who have had a direct contact, who have gone beyond the gatekeeper, who have traveled the road of trials and have found at-one-ment with the ONE.

"Behold but One in all things, it is the second that leads you astray."- Kabir

"In those respects in which the soul is unlike God, it is also unlike it self." -St. Bernard

"The knower and the known are one." - Echart

Huxley comments on Echart's quote saying, "'I live, yet not I, but Christ in me.' Or perhaps it might be more accurate to use the verb transitively and say, 'I live, yet not I; for it is the Logos who lives me.'"

Luther is said to have loved the passages of the *THELOGIA GERMANICA*, which says, "Goodness needeth not to enter into the soul, for it is there already only it is unperceived".

Near the end of the Santa Barbara speech, Huxley had a few words to say about the mystical experience and its fruits.

J.J. Olier was a devout French Roman Catholic. He was a participant in what was called the counter-reformation. He says:

"The holy light of faith is so pure that, compared with it, particular lights are but impurities and even ideas of the saints of the Blessed Virgin and the sight of Jesus Christ in his humanity are impediments in the way of the sight of God in His purity."

Olier here describes the mystical experience, the direct contact and says that it is <u>so</u> <u>pure</u>; that all else are impurities. Here we see in one individual a picture of that uneasiness that exists between the conceptual and direct experience in religious institutions.

"The seed of God is in us. Given an intelligent and hardworking farmer, it will thrive and grow up to God, whose seed it is; and accordingly its fruits will be God-nature. Pear seeds grow into pear trees, nut seeds into nut trees, and God seed into God." - Eckhart

"A man has many skins in himself, covering the depths of his heart. Man knows so many things; he does not know himself. Why, thirty or forty skins or hides, just like an ox's or a bear's, so thick and hard, cover the soul. Go into your own ground and learn to know yourself there." - Eckhart

When Meister Eckhart talks of layers of skin covering the SELF I was reminded again of the beautiful Golden Buddha we saw in Thailand that was once covered with layers of clay.

"In other living creatures ignorance of Self is nature; in man it is a vice" - Boethius 480-525, a Roman Philosopher and contemplative.

Huxley ends his book *THE PERENNIAL PHILOSOPHY* with the words of Philo. Philo of Judaeus 30 BC - 50 AD. Philo, a Jew said the only conceptual approach to God was to say what God was not. He did, however, talk about an intermediary of God, which he called the Logos. Language that the writer of the Gospel of John borrowed to describe Jesus in the beginning of his Gospel. We will likewise end this section with the quote from Philo.

"Households, cities, countries and nations have enjoyed great happiness, when a single individual has taken heed of the Good and Beautiful...Such men not only liberate themselves; they fill those they meet with a free mind. – Philo

MY STORY

"It is a spiritual axiom that every time we are disturbed, no matter what the cause, there is something wrong *with us*. If somebody hurts us and we are sore, we are in the wrong also." (Step 10, p. 90, *TWELVE STEPS AND TWELVE TRADITIONS)*

The following event marks my transition from the road of trials stage to the at-one-ment stage. One night, like Jacob of the Bible, I wrestled with God. I was having one of my all too frequent battles with Kae. I don't remember what it was about but I do remember that it had been going on for a couple of days and now I was ready to make peace. (Kae seemed to have learned over the years that our fights were not going to end until I had run my course.) It was my habit to think things through to get a handle on where I had been wrong and to save face I would also diplomatically indicate where I thought she had been wrong. I tried to be objective, fair and conciliatory. Most of the time, it took some time and discussion for Kae to accept her culpability as I saw it.

On this particular occasion I had my presentation together but I couldn't get myself to go to Kae and ask for a meeting. I had learned something new in my twelve-step meetings and it stuck in my craw. It basically said that when you have a problem with another person, you only take your own inventory, not theirs. If I were to take that seriously, it would mean that I couldn't outline our latest problem. I could only take my own inventory. I could only outline the ways in which I had contributed to the problem. I found that very distasteful. I felt that Kae would take advantage of my vulnerability. However, I finally decided I would try it. I waited for Kae to get home from work. When she got home I couldn't break the ice, I continued my coolness.

Then, the debate started within my head again, should I go back to the old way or should I try this radical new method. Several times during the evening I thought I had made my decision to go with the new approach only to lose courage. We went to bed. I couldn't sleep. I tossed and turned, obsessed with my right to share with her where I

219

thought she also was wrong. I got out of bed and paced the floor in the living room. I lay down on the couch, tossed, turned, obsessed some more and broke out in a sweat. Towards morning, I started dozing off only to have the struggle continue in the dream state.

Finally, in twilight sleep, something resolved within me and I found some peace. I remember thinking, "I wrestled with God just like Jacob of old." Then I thought it to be a rather humorous thought. Today, I believe that is exactly what happened. My SELF was starting to have its way with me (ego). My wife was in a hurry the next morning, she didn't have time for a discussion. During the day I remained at peace and started reviewing my relationship with Kae. I came to the conclusion that I had not really been all that easy to live with in the past years, that she had to put up with quite a lot and that I had been unwilling to face up to this until now. When she came home, I told her just that. I didn't take her inventory, just my own. I could see on her face a surprised look of relief; she stood there with her mouth open in silence. She didn't take advantage of my vulnerability as I feared she would. From that day forward our relationship started to change for the better. Today our relationship is mutually satisfying, loving and democratic. We really enjoy each other's company and are best friends as well as lovers. We still, on occasion, have disagreements; most of them very minor because we both tend to take care of our own side of the street and are not quick to take the other's inventory.

Recently we learned an acronym for f.u.n. which is "finding unlimited newness." After discussing this with each other we agreed that this was one of the reasons our relationship was so good; it is because we do continue to find newness in our life together. At one point we added to this acronym saying our relationship is not only fun but also it gets f.u.n.i.o.r. for we continue to Find Unlimited Newness In Our Relationship.

ONLY ONE

Sitting on the second level of the Kingdom in the midst of 40,000 other recovering alcoholics at the ninth International Convention in

Seattle (1990) was an emotional experience I will never forget. It was the first International Convention after the toppling of the Berlin Wall and the change in the Soviet Union. For the first time recovering alcoholics from the Balkans, East Germany and Russia were represented at a convention. When the flags from these countries were introduced there was wild applause and many tears. (At smaller meetings, men and women from these countries told of how A.A. saved their lives and that A.A. was beginning to take hold in their lands. All these stories were very reminiscent of early days of A.A. in the United States.)

After the flag ceremony ended my emotions settled some and for a few moments, I started to daydream. I began to think about the power that had wrought 40,000 miracles and turned 40,000 drunks into beautiful people. As I listened to the speakers' stories of jails, accidents, divorce, hospitalizations and etc. I thought how different these 40,000 people are from what they were a few years ago. I had kind of a strange thought. What if, after this meeting let out, these 40,000 people filled the streets of Seattle and the power that had transformed them was cut off. I mused that if that were to happen, it is conceivable that before sunrise, the LA Watts riots would seem like child's play in comparison. I quickly gave thanks to my higher power because I knew that in truth there was no chance of a divine power shortage. In fact, during that convention, which was the largest convention to that date in Seattle, according to police reports, it was a very peaceful time.

Five years later, I sat on the third level of Jack Murphy Stadium in San Diego, California in the midst of 60,000 miracles. I tried to capture the same feeling I had in Seattle. For whatever reason, it didn't happen.

It was a beautiful evening - the flag ceremony was nice; eighty-seven countries represented this time. Wow! - A.A. in eighty-seven countries, many different languages, customs, sexual preferences and religions. The speakers were good. All spoke of their love for A.A. and their newfound relationship with their higher power. The speakers that evening included a French-Canadian man, a lady from California with a Catholic upbringing and a Hindu gentleman from South Africa. After the presentations the meeting was near its conclusion. We all stood up, joined hands and 60,000 recited the Lord's Prayer. During the prayer, a wonderful peace came over me. I was no longer aware of my voice or my body and it was then that I realized that all of the stories, all the countries, all the different religions did not divide us. At that moment our differences were not important for I sensed that beneath it all there was just one of us. Once again, I had experienced the unity of the mystical experience - AT-ONE-MENT!

LESSON: You have heard the Herald's call. You have made the decision to walk the "Road less traveled." You have surrendered your illusion of power at the wall of Paradise. You have discovered a power greater than yourself. You have walked the road of trials and learned to conform your will to the Higher will. You have started to experience the At-one-ment. You are starting to know serenity and peace. You are finding that your intuition really works. You are beginning to understand the heart of the perennial philosophy, which says, "I am That." To your surprise you find yourself saying, in awe and with gratitude, I am something else, "I'm not this, I'm That!"

Chapter 24

THE RETURN

"The two worlds, the divine and the human, can be pictured only as distinct from each other—different as life and death, as day and night—Nevertheless—and here is a great key to the understanding of myth and symbol - the two kingdoms are actually one. The realm of the gods is a forgotten dimension of the world we know." (*THE HERO WITH A THOUSAND FACES*, Joseph Campbell; page 217)

Thus, in Campbell's words, we get a hint of the meaning of the words (that I once considered using as the title of this book), **WHAT YOU ARE LOOKING FOR IS WHAT IS LOOKING.** It's a metaphor, not a concept, for these words came forth from the intuition of St. Francis of Assisi (1182-1226) not from his ego-mind. For St. Francis, the two kingdoms had become one. He had entered into the silence of the other world and returned with a new vision. Having done this, he knew that what he had been looking for was not **apart from,** but **one with** his true SELF.

Much better known to most of us is the prayer of St. Francis, which gives us further insight into St. Francis himself, and Also to Campbell's understanding of myth. The prayer reads as follows:

"Lord, make me a channel of thy peace—that where there is hatred, I may bring love—that where there is wrong, I may bring the spirit of forgiveness—that where there is discord, I may bring harmony—that where there is error, I may bring truth—that where there is doubt, I may bring faith—that where there is despair, I may bring hope—that where there are shadows, I may bring light—that where there is sadness, I may bring joy. Lord, grant that I may seek rather to comfort than to be comforted—to understand, than to be understood—to love, than to be loved. For it is by self-forgetting that one finds. It is by forgiving that one is forgiven. It is by dying that one awakens to Eternal Life. Amen."

Now note specifically the words, "make me a channel," and "for it is by self-forgetting that one finds," and "It is by dying that one awakens to Eternal Life." These are metaphors. They are not concepts, for they are meant to catapult us into the ultimate destiny of "the vision quest hero." For the final destiny of the vision quest hero is to find the "boon" (the gift of enlightenment or spiritual understanding) and return with it showing himself or herself to be the master of two kingdoms.

St. Francis' story (although he lived over eight hundred years ago) is not all that different from the stories of some of our more modern vision quest heroes. St. Francis was the son of a wealthy cloth merchant. His early life was of a normal well-to-do rich kid. His social life was active; he served in the military. When he was twenty-one years old he was stricken with a very serious ailment. His life was changed and for six years he spent long periods in silence and prayer. He started ministering to lepers and to the poor and finally, at the end of this period he disinherited himself from his Father's fortune and, with the blessing of the Pope, started the Order that now bears his name. Two things stand out about his transformed life - his love of nature and his love for the less fortunate.

Unlike some vision quest heroes of his day he did not choose to remain behind cloistered walls. St. Francis became the master of two worlds. He returned with the boon, he did not seek to remain in the bliss of silence. His Order did not wall off the world, but served in the streets. Like Buckminster Fuller, Mother Teresa and others, he tried to bring the message he had found to the world that was still searching for an answer. He said, "Make me a channel of this forgotten realm."

Now let's turn again to his words, "What you are looking for is what is looking." This is a metaphor meant to catapult us beyond the mind, beyond concepts, beyond the dragons and monsters of thought into the void of mystery. May we, like St. Francis enter the void of mystery and like him return with the prayer on our lips? "Make me a channel of thy peace and where there is hatred may I bring love and where there is sadness may I bring joy." One thing we know about the void of mystery is that all those who do return, do so with a new found experience of love and a new found realization of joy.

NEW AGE HEROINES

On a number of occasions I have been asked, "What is new-age religion?" My answer has never satisfied me and I doubt that it satisfied the questioner. One reason for this is that until today, I haven't given it much thought or study. As I sat down to write, the first thought that came to my mind was a phrase in a commentary on the Book of Romans, that I last read well over thirty years ago. (The name of the author of this commentary has long been forgotten.) It said, "There is a being lost, a being torn apart, a being rent asunder in the peace of God."

As I think about it, this seems like a good place to start because new-age religion is about the peace of God. It is also about both institutions and individuals being torn apart and being rent asunder. New-age religion is facing the truth about the past and the future while trying to live in the peace of God, the NOW. It is searching, it is change, it is excessive, it is experimentation, and it is getting lost. It is sometimes throwing the baby out with the bath water, but it is good.

At its best and at its center it is a recalling of St. Francis' words about self-forgetting and of being a channel, of getting in harmony with the perennial philosophy and of discovering the Internal Teacher, the Kingdom of God within. New-age spirituality is, among other things, about women.

The emergence of women in the workplace, in the church and in leadership is an apt example of the meaning of the phrase, "There is a being lost, a being torn apart, a being rent asunder in the peace of God." In no small way, the women's movement has been a spiritual movement. It has also been a movement that has changed and tested every social institution, not the least of which has been the family.

It is not accidental that new age spirituality has emerged in a time of growing women's rights and liberation. They are one and the same. Up until now we have given no examples of vision quest heroines. Certainly there have been contributions by women to the perennial philosophy down through history but the best examples of what I have been trying to bring forth have been men. However, in the last twenty-five years, that also has changed.

Some of the best examples of new age spirituality and the revival of the perennial philosophy are women. I have the feeling that in the last twenty five years women have been the leaders in the discovery of the Kingdom that is IN, WITH and UNDER (See: Appendix IV). I have chosen to highlight five of them - women who have become channels of HER peace.

HELEN SCHUCMAN

Earlier we referred to Einstein's "My Credo" in which he talks about mystery being at the core of life, of science and of religion. Helen Schucman came smack-dab up against that mystery when she and her colleague, William Thetford (both professors of Medical Psychology at Columbia University's College of Physicians and Surgeons in New York City) said, "There must be a better way."

This was an outcry by two people who, with all the study of human psychology and with the responsibility of teaching courses in the field to future medical professionals, could not themselves get along. Their relationship was strained to the point of pain and they said, "There must be a better way." Neither was spiritually inclined and they were not looking for a spiritual answer, but they did mutually decide to look for a better way.

The task was difficult at the start, but they remained <u>willing</u> to continue their search. After some time, Schucman started having unusual dreams. Her colleague encouraged her to write down a description of the images that were coming to her. When she did, she wrote, "This is a course in miracles," and what followed was well over a thousand pages of material that was recorded over a period of seven years. Helen and Bill became a channel of the mystery and they found the better way. Since then thousands of people, by studying *A COURSE IN MIRACLES* have also found "a better way". A quote from the preface of the book, *A COURSE IN MIRACLES*, explains that better way.

"It (referring to the course) is not intended to become the basis for another cult. Its only purpose is to provide a way in which some people will be able to find their own <u>Internal Teacher</u>." (underline added)

MARIANNE WILLIAMSON

Among those who have championed *A COURSE IN MIRACLES* since its publication is Marianne Williamson. Marianne tells her story of transformation in her book, *A RETURN TO LOVE.* She was born in the fifties and, although a bit older than my daughters, her story reminds me of my daughters' stories. It is the story of growing up in a world where the message of what it means to be a woman, is unclear. It is the world of "I am woman" but it is also the world of "Stand by your man." It is the world of "be your own person" but don't neglect your responsibilities to your man, your children, your parents, your community and your church.

In this world, Marianne and thousands like her have tried to fight their way through this maze of conflicting information and pressures.

She was not alone in her search that included serial relationships, alcohol, drugs, eating disorders, religion and addiction.

Addiction led Marianne to a twelve-step program and then to "A Course in Miracles." At first, as a Jewish woman, she was put off by the Christian terminology of the Course; but, in spite of this, she found herself pursuing it in depth. She experienced the Internal Teacher to which the Course refers. Within time she started teaching, lecturing and writing with the Internal Teacher as her guide and the Course as the foundation of her understanding.

In 1993 she published a book entitled, *A WOMAN'S WORTH.* This book, specifically addressed to women, brings forth the same essential message as the book that you are now reading. She refers to this as discovering and embracing the Goddess within. She makes it quite clear that women (and men) have to discover something within themselves before they can really find what they are looking for in another. She also indicates in all of her recent books that there is much to be done in this world, but before you can do something, you have to discover something. Before you can do something really constructive, you have to know who you really are. In the case of women, you have to meet and embrace the Goddess that is you. Literally, you <u>must</u> get in touch with your own divinity.

In the introduction to her latest book, *HEALING THE SOUL OF AMERICA,* Marianne sets forth her analysis of the spiritual condition of America as we enter a new century. She uses the Eastern Teaching of the Tao to set forth her thesis explaining that America has become overbalanced in yang and deficient in yin. She states that our founding fathers set forth a plan based upon the ideas of the European age of enlightenment that they hoped would create a balance between these two principles. However, the pursuit of money and all that it represents has caused us to lose contact with the yin (the spiritual).

Recently, Marianne has affiliated herself as a minister of a Unity Church. The Unity Church is a metaphysical church that believes that Jesus is divine but by the same token believes that each of us is divine as well. Charles and Myrtle Fillmore established the Unity Church in the 1890s. Marianne continues to actively teach "A Course in Miracles" and to lecture throughout the world. She frequently appears on TV programs such as "Oprah" and "Larry King Live."

She is an example of a "New Age Heroine" who has returned with the boon and a message for the world. (SEE: Appendix III – WEBSITES)

THE RECOVERY OF RELIGIOUS IMAGINATION

While browsing in the library, looking for additional material on Mother Teresa, my eye was drawn to a book entitled *THE CELTIC WAY OF PRAYER* by Esther De Waal I opened the book and read these words in the preface:

"Coming from the farthest fringes of the Western world, Celtic Christianity keeps alive what is ancient Christian usage, usage which like that of the East comes from a deep central point before the Papacy began to tidy up and to rationalize. This was more difficult in Ireland, Scotland, and Wales, the Isle of Man, Cornwall and Brittany, the main Celtic areas, simply because of geographical distance and the lack of towns. This point is of more than antiquarian interest. It also speaks to me symbolically, taking me back to the ancient, the early, both in my own self, and in the experience of Christendom, where I encounter something basic, primal, fundamental, universal. I am taken back beyond the party labels and the denominational divisions of the church today, beyond the divides of the Reformation or the schism of East and West. I am also taken beyond the split of intellect and feeling, of mind and heart, that came with the growth of the rational and analytical approach that the development of the universities brought to the European mind in the twelfth century. Here is something very profound. This deep point within the Christian tradition touches also some deep point in my own consciousness, my own deepest inner self."

After reading this I knew I had not only found another vision quest heroine but a great summary to this section. Esther De Waal was a student and teacher of history at Cambridge University. After marriage she moved to Canterbury where she raised four sons and began an encounter with the monastic past. Today she leads retreats and lectures on the Celtic and Benedictine traditions.

A few facts about the Celtic tradition to which Esther De Waal refers will give you ample evidence that she rightly deserves the title of "New Age Heroine." What Esther discovered was a tradition which had been transported from the Continent of Africa and not from Europe. It was the tradition of the Desert Fathers. The Desert Fathers of Egypt was one of the sources that Aldus Huxley used to develop his thesis concerning the Perennial Philosophy. Recent research on the Desert Fathers also indicates that they used a mantra-based meditation, which is not unlike that which is taught in the East. A Benedictine monk, Father John Main, started a revival of this meditation technique. Father Lawrence Freeman now heads the movement. (SEE: Appendix III – WEBSITES, also see Appendix V - MEDITATION).

In addition, Esther recognized that Celtic Christianity had merged with or adopted some of the elements of that religion that existed before Christianity's arrival; a naturalistic religion not different from that of the aboriginal peoples' throughout the world. These people in their lives acted out and expressed the archetypes that both Jung and Campbell would later discover. Esther's reaction to this was not negative as she came to realize that this had added richness and imagination to their prayer life and devotion and, in her discovery, was adding riches and imagination to her own life.

Esther realized these people were in touch with their own dark side, or as Jung would say, "their shadow." It seems that they lived their lives in the present moment and in a sense of constant prayer. It seems that their adoption of Christianity might well have come from an already present knowledge of the God within. Esther shares that St. Patrick's breastplate said, "Christ within me" - something that I had not previously known, but of great interest to me.

MOTHER TERESA, 1910-1997

When I first thought about this section, Mother Teresa was the first person to come into my mind. However having only heard about her in the news, I was not sure she would further the development of our theme. I had no doubt that she was a remarkable woman but I did not know for sure, what motivated her. I proceeded to read three books. One, a biography and another, a compilation of her own words and prayers and the third, a description of the work done by Mother Teresa and her Sisters.

I was pleased to learn that much of what Mother Teresa taught and lived is a confirmation of the ideas that are being presented in this book. The language is different but the teachings are the same. Before I attempt to illustrate this, let me give you a brief description of the mission carried out by the "Missionaries of Charity."

Prem Nivas, a railroad dump in Calcutta was given to the Missionaries of Charity in 1974. It has been converted into a virtual community to serve those afflicted with leprosy. The community, built by the lepers themselves, has workshops, dormitories, clinics, schools and outpatient facilities. It regularly serves 1,400 cases per month.

Shshu Bhwan is a children's home in Calcutta that houses three hundred sick and hungry children along with a clinic that sees from 1000 to 2000 children a week. It feeds up to 1000 people per day.

Nirmal Hriday is a home in Calcutta for the dying. Like all of their facilities, the ministry is open to Muslims, Hindus and Christians alike. There are a hundred beds for the dying. During the day a school for street children is conducted on the roof of the facility.

The Missionaries of Charity serve over 9000 meals each day in their main facility in Calcutta. They have facilities in over one hundred and twenty countries serving the poorest of the poor, the sickest of the sick and the loneliest of the lonely; street people with aids, drug problems, alcoholism, mental illness and malnutrition. Mother Teresa started serving the poor on the streets of Calcutta in 1946. Today there are over 4000 Sisters and Brothers serving the poor, sick and dying worldwide.

In India, where Mother Teresa first established the Missionaries of Charity, a common greeting of the people is "Namaste" (usually spoken with the palms together and while bowing). It quite literally means, "the divinity within me greets the divinity within you." There is no doubt that the greeting for many is routine and a part of custom but Mother Teresa, along with the Sisters and Brothers of her order carry out their work allowing the divinity within themselves to minister to the divinity within each person for whom they care; whether it is a maggot-infested dying person or someone sick and fecal-covered. Whether the person being served is Hindu, Moslem or Christian, the ministry is always and simply the divinity serving the divinity.

The Order's concept of this divinity may differ from the largely Moslem and Hindu people they serve but their love is not based on understanding, but experience. Mother Teresa established her Order, not on the teachings of the theologians, but on her own experience and her understanding of the Saints of the Church such as St. Francis, St. Benedict and St. Teresa of Avila from whom she took her name. In the silence of her own heart, Mother Teresa discovered the divinity. Being true to her own background, she knew that divinity as Jesus. She not only recognized Jesus in her own consciousness, but in the world around her, especially recognizing the divinity in the poor and suffering. In the midst of the poorest of the poor, she often recalled the words of the suffering Jesus on the cross, "I thirst."

Mother Teresa and her Sisters and Brothers maintain a constant and conscious contact with their divinity by being what she called, "contemplatives in the world." This contemplation begins in the morning by praying as they put on each garment, by saying their rosary as they walk the streets of Calcutta (or wherever), by seeing the face of Jesus in every one they meet or care for, by partaking of the Eucharist each evening and by spending time with the silence that can only be found within.

Some additional facts about Mother Teresa and those who serve with her:

-They dedicate themselves to the same poverty as they find in the people they serve.
- They eat the same food they serve.
-Like St. Francis, they let their deeds do their preaching both to those to whom they minister and to the Church.

-Where do they get their strength? By practicing Silence "We cannot put ourselves directly in the presence of God if we do not practice internal and external silence."

One of the things that we have seen repeatedly is that those who practice inner-silence and experience a conscious contact with God also begin to have this external experience. "Silence of the heart is necessary so you can hear God everywhere - in the closing of a door, in the person who needs you, in the birds that sing, in the flowers, in the animals."

These words and many others like them have led me to believe that Mother Teresa and the Missionaries of Charity have found through their way of life "a simple Path" that has enabled them to get beyond the gate of the mind and to experience the Kingdom of God which is at hand. They call their higher power Christ, Jesus and Mary but they will tell you to call him what you want; but find HIM/HER in the Silence of your heart.

Service in itself can be a benefit in getting beyond the gate of self. It can aid us in self-forgetting but Mother Teresa teaches us that we cannot give what we do not have. The compassion that her Sisters and Brothers express is a love born in the silence. Mother Teresa has a deep understanding of the importance of silence as well as its' relationship to the Eucharist. Her understanding of the Eucharist was unique as well. (See: Appendix IV- IN WITH AND UNDER)

I am especially excited about Mother Teresa, (as a vision-quest heroine) because we have identified so many that have been disparaging of institutional religion. Mother Teresa, on the contrary, was a Roman Catholic through and through and worked within the framework of the Institution. Her work both honored the institution and gave witness to the contemplative tradition within the history of the institution. She was a witness of the Church and to the Church.

A television news report showed a young woman (one of the Sisters of Charity) bathing the open sores of a leper. She wore no rubber gloves or protection of any kind. The reporter said to her, "I wouldn't do that for a million dollars." She turned to him and said, "neither would I."

SUMMARY

In the past, from time to time when I would hear about Mother Theresa I would ask myself how could anyone do what she is doing; how could anyone be so selfless, so loving? It is now clear to me that the extent of Mother Teresa's love is another of those great mysteries. But, I believe it is no less or no more a mystery than the writing of *A COURSE IN MIRACLES*; no more a mystery than a Jewish woman using the language of Christianity to bring thousands to an awareness of their own <u>Internal</u> <u>Teacher</u>. *All became channels*!

LETTER TO KAE

Dear Kae,   May 26, 2000

With, but a few exceptions, the first draft of our book is complete. As you will remember, I shared with you on that summer we met (almost thirty years ago) that I wanted to write a book. The central theme that I shared with you then has not changed, but many details have. Without you these details would have been quite different. I can't imagine that they could have been so rich had we not lived out these details together. I view you as a co-author, not just because of all your help, nor because of your poetry that has added so much depth, beauty and insight, but also because of these details. (Our life together) It's been fun (<u>f</u>inding <u>u</u>nlimited <u>n</u>ewness) together.

I now want to ask you for one more favor in regard to the book. I would like you to write a conclusion to the "Vision Quest Hero." I extend this invitation for several reasons. First and foremost, you are the most significant "vision quest heroine" in my life. Secondly, you bring a perspective different from mine to the subject. You bring the prospective of one who has always had a sense of SELF, one whose spiritual growth has been of the educational variety, one whose early childhood years were quite normal and whose adult life has been relatively trauma-free. In addition, you do not have an addictive personality and you have not experienced any addictions in the usual sense of the word.

If you consent to this, I would like you to relate to your life as a "Vision Quest Heroine" in the light of the above comments.

Love, Richard

MY RESPONSE TO RICHARD

As I look back at my life it seems that the things that Rich said about me are true. When I look at my childhood I do see that I was one of those fortunate people who had some conscious contact with my inner essence. Yet, here it is a year later and I have not yet responded to Richard's request. My reticence, I am sure, is ego orientated. I feel embarrassed to be mentioned in the same category as Mother Teresa and the others. I am also aware that the concept itself is foreign to my twenty-first century western mind. When I think about it I realize, as Richard has been pointing out, that this modern western mind is my problem.

And yet, when I stop and say, "You lead, I'll follow" and I get my ego out of the way I realize that I am a vision quest heroine in a similar way that Rich sees himself as a vision quest hero. I feel that I have conquered the ogre at the gate by simply recognizing my ego and the role it plays in my life. It is such a freeing feeling to look to my VICTOR to lead. I have found something within me that is so humbling. In one of my poems I describe it as, "the inner ESSENCE, the depth of the soul, the source of all life, the infinite whole." It is that very real part of me that has overcome and will continue to overcome all true obstacles.

Even though I have had some contact with this essence from childhood on, there was a time in my life when I was struggling at the gate, hanging on to the cliff by my very finger tips. My ESSENCE was over-shadowed. I felt trapped in a failed marriage and my mind couldn't let go. At one point, during this time, I remember my four year old son coming to me at I was sitting huddled and crying; he asked, "Mommy, should I bring you Jesus' book?" I'm sure he said

235

that because I had spent a lot of time searching for answers in the Bible. I finally did what I needed to do and got out of the marriage. It wasn't long after that when, in the words of myth, a "Herald" entered my life.

I knew that Richard was early in his recovery and I was aware of the ramifications of that but he had something that reminded me, once again, of that ESSENCE in me. I often wonder where I would be if I hadn't met Richard. The poem that I have written describes his impact on my life. He is the Herald that helps me remember to go to the inner teacher.

YOU ARE

You are the light of my love
that beams from my Soul,
that glistens and listens
at your feet - the whole of the
universe exposed from your mind.
Knowing - you are my love
my one-of-a-kind.
YOU ARE MY MENTOR

You are the man that rides me to grow
puts thorns in my nest, then goads me to go -
into the unknown, unleashing my fear.
Kicking and screaming I move,
with you always near.
YOU ARE MY TORMENTOR

I dare not resist too long or too strong
because it's with you at my side
the place I belong.
YOU ARE

LESSON: In a discussion of how easy it is for us to wallow in our own personalities or selfness Huxley says, "It is for this reason that all the masters of the spiritual life insist so strongly upon the importance of the little things." Mother Teresa makes this point as well and in the following story she shows how important these small things can be in the lives of others.

REMEMBER THE SMALL THINGS

"Some of my sisters work in Australia. On a reservation, among the Aborigines, there was an elderly man. I can assure you that you have never seen a situation as difficult as that poor old man's. He was completely ignored by everyone. His home was disordered and dirty.

I told him, "Please let me clean your house, wash your clothes, and make your bed." He answered, "I'm okay like this. Let it be. "I said again, "You will be still better if you allow me to do it."

He finally agreed. So I was able to clean his house and wash his clothes. I discovered a beautiful lamp, covered with dust. Only God knows how many years had passed since he last lit it.

I said to him, "Don't you light your lamp? Don't you ever use it?" He replied, "Of course.'"

From that day on the sisters committed themselves to visiting him every evening. We cleaned the lamp, and the sisters would light it every evening.

Two years passed. I had completely forgotten that man. He sent this message: "Tell my friend that the light she lit in my life continues to shine still."

I thought it was a very small thing. We often neglect small things." *(IN THE HEART OF THE WORLD.* Mother Teresa, pp. 53,54.)

Chapter 25

MASTER OF TWO WORLDS

In mythology, when the Hero returns from the sphere of rebirth and the road of trials, he or she returns as the master of two worlds. Both the religions of the East and the West speak of this fact. Paul said, "be in the world but not of the world." Ramakrisna said, "It is a joy to merge the mind in Indivisible Brahman through contemplation. And it is also a joy to keep the mind on the Lala, the Relative without dissolving it in the ABSOLUTE." The Hero returns to live in both worlds.

Recovery in twelve-step programs amounts to living life on an all new basis. Having had a spiritual awakening, one returns to daily life with a new outlook. After giving instructions concerning the first nine steps of A.A., the Big Book – *ALCOHOLICS ANONYMOUS*, records these words:

"If we are painstaking about this phase of our development, we will be amazed before we are halfway through. We are going to know a new freedom and a new happiness. We will not regret the past nor wish to shut the door on it. We will comprehend the word serenity and we will know peace. No matter how far down the scale we have gone, we will see how our experience can benefit others.

That feeling of uselessness and self-pity will disappear. We will lose interest in selfish things and gain interest in our fellows. Self-seeking will slip away. Our whole attitude and outlook upon life will change. Fear of people and of economic insecurity will leave us. We will intuitively know how to handle situations, which used to baffle us. We will suddenly realize that God is doing for us what we could not do for ourselves." (pages 83-84)

I once heard a Christian preacher say that he has known religious people who were so heavenly-minded that they were no earthly good. That is not the way of the returned Hero and it is not the way of a twelve-stepper in recovery. The following writings are examples from my life that deal with this reality.

LIVING 200% OF LIFE

As we near the end of our journey, I want to pull together the various paths we have traveled. I wish we could make all of them converge at a single point. In order to do this, I would have to fall back on mystic visionaries who have experienced a glimpse of the future; someone like Pierre Tielhard de Chardin. He took the "long view" of history, evolution, religion and personal experience and saw in some future time all the paths converging into a unity, a oneness, something he called the Omega Point.

I am not that visionary. I am not that mystic. However, at times, times when I have come the closest to living 200% of life, I share the vision. I not only share the vision, but I have, for the most part, sought to make it a present reality. I believe in some degree this has been done. This is possible because as Einstein taught us at the beginning of the twentieth century, time is relative. Thus it seems that when our human apparatus is properly tuned, we can poke our consciousness into timelessness while still existing in time. When we do poke our consciousness into timelessness, while still living in time, we approach living 200% of life. We know the ABSOLUTE in the midst of the relative.

It is by living 200% of life that we answer the questions posed in the early pages of this book. The two questions are: "How can we move toward a concept of SELF which is more viable for this new millennium?" That question was posed by University of Chicago Professor, Csikszentmihalyi in his book, *THE EVOLVING SELF.* The second question was found in one of Kae's poems where she asks, "Where do I set my center post for stability?" I hope the following will clarify what it means to be the Master of two worlds and further answer the questions that were posed by Kae and Csikszentmihalyi.

PRACTICAL SPIRITUALITY
ONE DAY AT A TIME

Kae and I had just seen a matinee presentation of Noel Coward's *Relative Values.* This is a fine, though seldom produced stage production. The setting is early twentieth century England. The plot exploits the often petty, but well entrenched differences between the classes. During our ride home from Cedar City, Utah where a Shakespearean Festival is held each summer, the words of Shakespeare kept running through my mind. "All the world's a stage and all the men and women merely players." (*The Merchant of Venus*) All at once, a sense that has been constant in my life in the last few years, (at different levels of clarity) became incredibly clear! The sense I am talking about is the central theme of this book: Higher Consciousness. I was simultaneously aware of both the unchanging and changing values of life. It was clear to me that Shakespeare was exactly right - that all the world is a stage and all of humanity is involved in a great drama, played out against the backdrop of the eternal non-changing. I was keenly aware of the world's drama, of my own personal drama and at the same time, I was just as keenly aware of THAT which is absolute - THAT which does not change - THAT which is eternal.

The analogy of the movie and the screen came into my mind on that day as well and on that particular occasion, it seemed to be an absolutely perfect analogy. On that day, I clearly experienced being

241

both the screen and the movie. The drama of my life with all of its surprises, heartaches, excitement, pleasure and meaning, passed through my mind. I could see that my life was but a movie. I could see that my life was always changing and, at the same time, I was aware of that part of me and that part of the world that never changes. It was clear. I am both the screen and the movie. I am living in both the relative and the ABSOLUTE.

At that moment I was living 200% of life, 100% of the ABSOLUTE unchanging value of life and 100% of the changing aspect of life. These peak experiences tend to pass. However each time I have one, the impression of the ABSOLUTE seems more deeply imbedded in my consciousness. Also, the more I become consciously aware of the ABSOLUTE value of life, the better I seem to handle and relate to the changing aspects of life.

RAGS AND OLD IRON

One night years ago, when I was Pastor of two congregations in rural South Dakota, I came home after an evening of meetings, turned on television and settled in to watch The Tonight Show. One of the guests was Oscar Brown Jr. He sang two songs that in at least a small way changed my life. Those two songs were "Brown Baby" and "Rags and Ole Iron," I believe both were written by Oscar Brown Jr.

I had never been around Afro-Americans to any significant extent. I was raised not to be prejudiced and I tried not to be, but I was ignorant. The time was early in the sixties and news of civil rights activities was of real interest to me, but I was living in rural South Dakota and the only people of color I ever saw were Native Americans. That night on television I saw a black man sing about looking down at his little brown baby in a crib and he had the same feelings, the same hopes and the same aspirations that I had for my four very young children. My reaction was - he is just like me. I have never forgotten that reaction.

The second song, "Rags and Ole Iron," is about a junk man, wheeling a small cart through a Chicago neighborhood calling out, "rags and ole iron, rags and ole iron." He was collecting mostly junk, the stuff others wanted to throw away. Again in this song, I saw the humanity of black people and consequently, I began to take a more active role in the Civil Rights Movement.

Today as I go about my part-time job that I have in order to augment our income, I often think about the rag man going down the street calling out, "rags and ole iron." For today, I am a ragman. My job consists of searching in thrift stores and flea markets for used clothing to sell to an exporter. The storyteller in the song is a man with a broken heart. He lost his love and as the old ragman passes by he wishes he could give him his poor broken heart. I also identify with this part of the song. I have identified something in my heart that I would like to give to the old ragman. I'm not sure if you would call it a broken heart, a bruised ego or what, but there is a place within me that's broken and as of yet, it hasn't healed.

When I made the decision to go into the ministry, I attended Pacific Lutheran University after having completed two years of junior college in my hometown. While at P.L.U. I established close relationships with other young men who were studying for the ministry. After graduation many of us headed to the Midwest and four years of Seminary. A number of us married and started families in those four years. Because most of us were far away from our families of origin, we became like family to each other. After the four years of seminary and graduation, we set out for our new assignments as church Pastors. Many of us were from the West and eventually we ended up back there. Our group continued to see each other on a fairly regular basis at Church Conventions, Pastoral Conferences and at vacation time. Over the years those close ties continued.

When I left the ministry, I was disenfranchised from that family. I made some attempts to stay connected but I was no longer a member and I missed them. At times I was downright lonely.

Over the years my spiritual and emotional health improved. In the process of recovery I tried to share these improvements with my old family - most attempts have been futile. I am now an outsider, my theology is not orthodox and my faith is suspect. The irony of this is that today I am the kind of human being I always hoped and prayed that I could be. I am a healthy wholesome person. I am more moral and a more loving person than I was as a minister. Today I am the best Richard I have ever been. But today I have no pulpit. I don't really want a pulpit, but sometimes I really do get the yen to share the new me and the foundation upon which this new me has been built.

In the midst of writing what I have just shared, I went into a kind of Walter Mitty fantasy - I started thinking about being invited back to some place like the Seminary or maybe a Pastoral Retreat to give a presentation. At this event many of my old friends would be in attendance. I'd let them know that although I am just a ragman, with daily help from my Higher Power, I am "happy, joyous and free." I went so far as to prepare my presentation. But, this ole ragman will never be invited back to the Seminary, so I'll share it with you.

I DID GO FURTHER WEST OR
MAYBE IT WAS EAST

Thirty-nine years ago the Seminary I attended and the church it represented sent me out and told me to help people build their spiritual houses. I said, "Wait a minute. I haven't finished building mine." They assured me that they had given me all the blueprints I would ever need and that the great builder would always by near by. So I accepted their word and went out to build spiritual houses.

I immediately ran into some problems. There were people out there that had been working on their houses for years and they weren't so sure they wanted some young man, just fresh out of school, telling them how to build their houses. Besides, they said, the fellow who just left was a better teacher, knew more about spiritual houses and was more fun to boot. Well, I stayed three years and few people said, "Thanks, you have made a real contribution to our house." Some of them suggested that I should think about another kind of work. "Well," I said to myself, "I like building spiritual houses. I am going to try it again." I did, fifteen hundred miles further west. (I knew somebody once said, "Go West, young man, go West." So I did)

I liked the little town and the people, but they said, "He's not like the last guy, not as energetic, not as involved in the community and not as much fun." I stayed two years and then moved three hundred miles further west. At my new location there were lots of people to work with and lots of opportunities. Some of the people seemed to like me right from the git-go but a bunch of them said, "He's not like the last guy, not as good a builder, doesn't seem to be as bright and not as much fun. I stayed there five years and my own house toppled over and I ended up trapped inside.

After some time I managed to free myself from the old house that had me pinned down and I decided to start over again building my own spiritual house. This time I vowed I would not assist anybody in building his/her house until I had mine up on a good firm foundation.

Well, that was twenty-five years ago. But I got my house up and it has taken pretty much the whole twenty-five years, but it is a mighty fine house. Now I am ready to help you with yours if you feel you need a little help. You must understand that this business of building a spiritual house is unlike any other undertaking you have ever attempted. Others can give you ideas and encouragement, but the business of actually building is 100% up to you. You will find that every time you try to rely on anyone else for the next step without having it verified by your own sense of integrity you will have to redo that step. "Work out your own salvation with fear and trembling." (Philippians 2: 12-13)

The first decision you have to make in building a spiritual house is whether it is going to be built on rock or sand. (Matthew 7: 24-27) Now you may say, "that's easy, rock of course." But wait a minute, not so fast. If you build on rock you have to consider the cost. Number one, you have to have a rock architect and in order to find him you have to go to his kingdom. This kingdom is very near but, to many of us, hidden. There is only one rock architect but he's never too busy to work with each of us. Now the easier, softer way, at least on the surface, is to build on sand and the sand architect is easy to find and cheap too. His name is Ego. I'm sure you know him/her. Now, let me tell you that if you build your house with Ego it will probably be exciting, but in the end the house will probably fall. I know mine did and with a thud!

Now, let's assume that you do decide to build on rock. Here's what you will need to do, and as you'll see, there are some other considerations. Seek first the Kingdom. Now almost everybody has tried to build with Ego first and they are so filled with his ideas that even though they haven't worked very well, they are not able to accept rock concepts at face value. Now the first rock concept you must work with is that there is a Kingdom very near you that has everything needed for building a spiritual house on rock. I said the Kingdom is near you, you can't see it, but it is near you and you do have access to it if you have the right key. Now I am willing to give you the key but it is of no value unless you use it. You must use it regularly in order to dwell in the Kingdom, on a daily basis. The key is simply this, "go within." The kingdom is everywhere but your access to it is in the SILENCE within.

Now, entering the Kingdom is like entering a new realm and it will take time to adjust and get acquainted. That's why it must be done on a regular basis.

BE STILL AND KNOW THAT I AM GOD
(PSALMS 46: 10)

At some point, maybe after days, weeks or months of going to the Kingdom, you will get a message. It may be a feeling, a sense, an intuition, but however it comes it will say, "Be still, be still, I am the rock architect" and you will know that it is so. Your job at this point in time, is just to spend time on a daily basis with the architect. You will learn. Much of the time, unbeknown to you, you will be learning how to build your spiritual house.

CHOOSE YOU THIS DAY
(Joshua 24: 15)

Now, sometime after you have experienced the presence of the architect, you will begin to notice a kind of push-pull conflict in your life. Well that's your old architect (Ego) trying to win you back as a client, trying to convince you that he is still capable of doing the job. He will even try to convince you that there is no problem building on sand. It is at this point that you must not only be aware that there are two voices, two architects in your life, but you must begin to say "no" consistently to one and "yes" consistently to the other. Many years ago there was a carpenter who was extremely well acquainted with the architect and he made it clear that we can not serve or listen to both. We must make a decision once again, do we want to build on rock or sand.

LET YOUR EYE BE SINGLE
(Matthew 6: 22-24)

If you make the decision to go with the rock architect, you must keep your focus. This really involves continuing to do what you have already learned to do - going to the Kingdom on a daily basis and spending time with the architect. It also means getting rid of old ideas. If you are going with the rock concept, you will need to get rid of all sandy notions. This will be done with regular self-examinations with someone you trust. It's like taking inventory. Get rid of old useless stock to make room for the new. The more one-pointed or focused you get, the faster your spiritual house will come together.

GO INTO YOUR CLOSET
(Matthew 6: 6)

A short while ago I mentioned a carpenter who knows a thing or two about building spiritual houses. It turns out that he really is as good an authority on this subject as there is. One of the things he stressed was frequent consultation with the architect. Interestingly enough, he not only said they should be frequent, but secret. He himself claimed to be in constant contact with the architect. He said on one occasion that he had such good rapport with the architect that he indeed felt that he and the architect were one.

BE YE TRANSFORMED
(Romans 12: 1-2)

Now one of the things that I learned was that the difference between sand dwelling and rock dwelling is so vast that it just doesn't call for a radical change or thinking but it calls for a transformation. Now, a fellow named Paul, who was a latter day disciple of the carpenter said, "Be ye transformed by the renewal of your minds."

HAVE THIS MIND IN YOU
(Philippians 2: 5-6)

Some years after the carpenter died, this fellow Paul said if you really want to build a spiritual house you need to have the same mind that was in the carpenter who, he said, emptied himself and lived the life of the rock architect. I assume that the mind-set that the carpenter talked about when he referred to himself as being one with the rock architect and the mind that Paul talked about were one and the same. Now friends, having built a house with the ego as the architect and one with the rock architect I can tell you that having this mind that was in the carpenter is essential to the job of building a spiritual house.

Now, you ask how does one go about getting this mind that the carpenter had. Well, you just continue to do what we have already outlined. You spend at least twenty minutes a day morning and evening, in the secret place and in the presence of the architect. (Many say the carpenter is there too.) As you do this, little by little, your mind is transformed. It takes on the quality of the rock architect. Your attitude toward the outside world will change. The world will have less and less influence over you and at the same time it will become friendlier, more beautiful, more loving and more charming.

ALL THINGS WORK TOGETHER FOR GOOD
(Romans 8: 28)

Now, as the outside world begins to take on this new charm, you will begin to see that things that once looked like tragedies can be seen in a different light. Indeed, you will see that the very things that you once felt harmed you are now being used by the rock architect to help you build your spiritual house.

Consider for a moment how the eagle builds its nest. First it builds the outer structure by intertwining twigs. Then it finds and places into the twig structure briars of thorn and then plenty of soft grass and fiber to provide comfort. It is into this place of comfort that the eggs are laid and hatched. As the eaglets begin to grow, little by little the soft material is removed to make room for the growing babies. Soon the thorns are exposed and what was once comfortable is now becoming increasingly uncomfortable, until on one magic day the eaglets are encouraged to leave their miserable nest and experience their first flight.

This is nature's way, and a lot of what we see as evil is nature's way as well. Discomfort is built into the self-serving ego life in order to help us make our leap of faith and take a real chance on the rock architect.

The carpenter used to say, "Resist not evil" and almost no one could figure out what he was talking about. He knew and understood nature's way. He knew about eagles' nests and thousands of other ways in which nature encourages growth by using discomfort. Today millions of people who claim to follow the carpenter do not understand "resist not evil." Yes, we all know that trials and tribulations can be character building but the carpenter was talking about more than character building. He was talking about moving out of the realm of suffering and building your home in a whole new neighborhood.

AND IRON WILL SWIM
(2nd Kings 6: 1-7KJV)

Not only will things once thought harmful become useful but also things once thought impossible will become the stuff of everyday life. The uncommon will become common.

If you persist in this pursuit, one day, without hardly realizing that it has been happening, you will have built a spiritual house and what a magnificent house it is. From time to time you will hear the carpenter's voice saying, "You are the light of the world." You will rejoice because you know he means you. You know that your light is no longer under a bushel basket (ego, clay) but has been liberated by contact with the rock architect. You know deep within, that indeed, you are the light of the world.

And you hear him say, "You are the salt of the earth" and you know it is true. Today you are not salt that has lost its savor. You are LIFE itself and that is what it means to be the salt of the earth. You are LIFE in the midst of decay.

And you will hear him say, "You are the image and likeness of the architect" and you will rejoice because, deep within, you will know that it is true and you will look at your spiritual house and you will say, "It is good, I am the master of two worlds. I live on the ROCK and I work and play in the sand."

Note: Before you move forward to the fourth section of this book, some of you may have a decision to make. The decision is whether or not to read Transition II, called "Spiritual Psychology." Transition II, now found in APPENDIX II represents a continuation of my three years of concentrated study. It is a little heavy and somewhat detailed. The content includes one of my experiences as a hospital Chaplain. It also includes a discussion of Jewish mysticism in the European communities of the eighteenth and nineteenth century. It ends with a discussion of "facing reality," a concept central to Jewish mysticism, transcendental meditation and twelve-step programs. The piece ends with an introduction to Practical Spirituality.

PRACTICAL SPIRITUALITY

UNCOVERING AND DISCOVERING

SECTION IV

INTRODUCTION

TO PRACTICAL SPIRITUALITY

It was a beautiful morning in June. Kae and I were visiting two of our children and their families who live in the beautiful wooded area between Tacoma and Olympia, Washington. We were making a trip to the grocery store. Jazz was playing on the radio. The station was KPLU, a public radio station run by my alma mater, Pacific Lutheran University. Hymns, not jazz would have been the style when I graduated almost a half century ago. The jazz stopped and the news began. Topping the news was the report of a meeting taking place among the Bishops of the American Catholic Church. The goal of the meeting was to adopt a policy regarding Priests who sexually abuse children. This scandal was threatening the very fiber of the Catholic Church.

Just as the news was ending we passed an old church. It was now an antique shop. A quarter of a mile later we passed another church. It too was an antique shop. The news was over and the beautiful old jazz classic, *Moon Beams*, was playing. Kae started to sing along. Suddenly majestic Mt. Rainier stood tall and breathtaking between the trees. As we turned the corner we started passing the walls of the palatial estate of J.C. Knight, the new-age channeler of the spirit teacher, Ramptha. Then, the sign – CAUTION – MILITARY TANK

CROSSING. I wondered for a moment. Had I been transported to another time and place – perhaps the future? No, it was the present, June 13, 2002, 10:45 A.M.

This convergence of sight and sound took place in less then ten minutes. I tried to make sense of it all. I tried to get my mind around it all and to make it fit. For a moment I was frustrated by my mind's inability to rap it all up in a neat package and then I remembered the words, "there is a mystery about it all." Later, as I recalled this event, I thought to myself - this is the world in which I live, a world of rapid change, of great diversity. Nevertheless we still have a need to connect the dots (to be connected). Practical Spirituality is about connecting the dots of our lives in the context of the MYSTERY.

In spite of times when we feel isolated and lonely most of us have known something of our connectedness here on Planet Earth. Our deepest connection is unknown to our five senses. We have reserved a word for our deepest connection. We call it spirituality. Indeed, these very words, "our deepest connection" may well serve as a definition of the word spirituality. In other words, spirituality is our deepest level of connection. In fact, we have gone so far (in this book) to suggest that our spiritual connection is so deep and so complete that we are literally, not many, but ONE.

You may ask then, what is practical spirituality? The answer – Practical spirituality is doing those things which make the mystery of oneness show its face. It involves uncovering and discovering and much of this is an inward journey, uncovering and discovering - excavating the psyche or soul. We have previously referred to this excavation metaphorically as experiencing the nut beyond the nutshell and seeing the gold beneath the clay.

Getting the MYSTERY to show its face is not an easy task. Over the years, I have watched hundreds of people in twelve-step programs struggle with the second step that says, "Came to believe a power greater than ourselves could restore us to sanity." Some, sadly, were never able to make the leap or, as we previously described it, were never able to get past the ogre at the gate.

I remind you again of the Apostle Paul's words, "Work out your own salvation with fear and trembling." Now, what does this mean? I'll tell you what I think it means. It means, take these steps towards wholeness and connectedness with a certain amount of caution. It also means that you are the one who is going to have to take these steps. But, you are not alone. Check often for the still small voice of the inner teacher. It means, seek the guidance of the inner teacher even if you don't believe you have an inner teacher. As you read the next eleven chapters, which are intended to give you some framework for the task of uncovering and discovering, I strongly suggest that you frequently ask of your inner teacher, "Is there something here that I need to do or learn?"

Some who have read this manuscript feel I should have been more specific in my instructions. My answer to them is: I can't do that because my purpose is to help you find your INNER TEACHER. who will show you personally the way of synchronicity. I also remind them of the words of one of my professors who said, "let the Holy Spirit be as creative with the next guy as he was with you." As you have read, the SPIRIT was very creative with me and I dare not forget this as I speak (write) to you.

Because music is an instrument of the MYSTERY that helps us connect the dots, I have chosen to use it as a theme for this section. Also in this day when there seems to be so much animosity and suspicion between the people of Moslem faith and the people of other religions I have decided to introduce this section with one verse written by a man who many consider to be humankind's greatest mystical poet. His name is Rumi. He was a Sufi Moslem, born in Afghanistan in 1207.

"Love, the supreme musician is
always playing in our souls."
by Rumi

DISCLAIMER

In this section we frequently refer to Twelve-Step Programs. We believe that in the last sixty-five years Twelve-Step Programs have proven themselves to be a virtual laboratory for the testing of age-old spiritual principles and values. The growth of these programs is, in our opinion, the best proof of the effectiveness of these spiritual principles. We do not consider ourselves to be authorities on these programs nor do we in anyway speak <u>for</u> Alcoholics Anonymous, Emotions Anonymous or any of the many Twelve-Step Programs.

One of the main reasons for writing this book under a pen name was to protect Richard's anonymity and to honor the tradition of Twelve-Step Programs which states in Tradition Eleven, "We need always maintain personal anonymity at the level of press, radio, and films." We ask that this be honored by all in the media.

POINT OF VIEW

Even though many of the illustrations and references in this section reflect our experience in A.A. Al-Anon and Emotions Anonymous, we think you need not be put off by this fact. As noted above, the principles embodied in these programs transcend the organizations themselves and can be helpful to anyone who wants to apply them to their lives. Two Twelve-Step Organizations that have broad appeal are Al-Anon (for those who have been affected by alcoholism) and Emotions Anonymous. Jerry Hirschfield, M.A., a licensed therapist in California and author of *MY EGO MY HIGHER POWER, AND I,* was positively affected when he became involved in a twelve-step program. He concluded that everyone could benefit from practicing the twelve steps. This conclusion gave birth to a book which he authored; *THE TWELVE STEPS FOR EVERYONE...*He added a sub-title, for everyone "who really wants them."

Chapter 26

THE MUSIC

**Sings the silent soul
in harmony and accord with itself,
the entire whole.
Sings the silent soul.
Integrity set free -
teeming with "simply to be."
Silence abounds
making harmonious sounds.
Sings the silent soul.**
by Kae

Before my triple bypass heart surgery in March of 1997, I went to a Sports Club about three times a week for a light workout on the treadmill and stair-master. After my surgery, on Doctor's orders, I was told to walk every day and increase the walk as I got stronger. A two-mile walking path in our complex goes by the back yards of many homes and also passes designated green belts. Most of the yards are nicely landscaped with grass, trees, flowers and cactus. I live in the southwest part of the United States and consequently almost every day provides delightful walking weather. To my surprise, I started to enjoy my walk so much that I have not returned to the health spa. I walk two miles a day and to get a little more total body workout I carry some weight in each hand.

From the beginning I have tried to make my walk a "now" experience and to be aware of the sights and sounds. In the summer of 1997 I read a book by Rabbi Zalman Schachter-Shalomi entitled, *FROM AGE-ING TO SAGE-ING.* As the title of this delightful book suggests, it is about fostering wisdom in the retirement years. The book contains many of the ideas that I am sharing with you. Like Kae and I, the Rabbi believes in the universality of spiritual truth. He has studied with masters of various religions including Sufi, Buddhist, Native American and Roman Catholic. In his workshops, which he conducts under the auspices of the Spiritual Eldering Institute (which he founded), some physical exercises are practiced. I quote from his book:

"At our workshops we practice gentle stretching exercises and massage to promote flexibility and relaxation.—We exercise as sages in training, performing our regimes in a relaxed, focused, and sensible way to restore the body to limberness and vitality.—It also gives us more energy for carrying out the work of spiritual eldering.

"On the physical level, then, respect and reverence for the body serve as the foundation for our spiritual journeys. In our workshops, we teach a prayer that expresses the gratitude we feel for the exquisite service performed by our bodies each day. When walking in the morning, we make a mental survey of the body, blessing and giving thanks to our dear old friends; the limbs; the organs of perception, such as eyes and ears; the organs of digestion and elimination, such as the kidneys and the bladder; the heart and the brain; and the pulse. We end the prayer by saying, 'Thank you, body, vehicle of my spirit, for taking me for a wonderful ride one more day.' Such a prayerful and grateful attitude goes a long way in enlisting the body support in eldering work."

I started using this idea with some modifications. As I start my walk I look around and take in everything. After forty or fifty seconds I say, "thank you for my eyes." Then I shift to my hearing, taking in the sounds of the birds, the rustle of the breeze blowing in the trees, the traffic and so on and I say: "Thank you for my ears." I then turn my attention to my skin. I notice the warmth of the sun, the feel of the cool air and again I say, "thank you." I repeat this with the sense of smell and the sense of taste. The taste I encounter is usually the coffee or orange juice that I had just before starting my walk. To pick up on the sense of smell, I spend time in deep breathing. Then, as suggested by the Rabbi, I turn to my body parts and body functions that support my senses and my walk.

At times, I am more detailed than others thinking about the tiniest cell and how it is supplied with nutrition. Unless I am exceptionally preoccupied by the time I finish this routine, I find that I feel wonderfully alive and in a heightened state of perception. In this state it is easy to feel one with my surroundings and to have gratitude for all. Kae has participated in this exercise with me from time to time. Her poem, "I Am" expresses her response to feeling one with nature.

I AM

I am the wind that awakens the sea
drinking the energy that pulses in me.

I feed on the greens of the forest near by.
We are the forest that catches the eye,
that feeds the soul; once empty, now whole.

I dance on the rock, taste the crust of the earth.
I sip on the sunset and relish this birth.
Lifted by wings, I'm learning to fly.
I am the bird that soars in the sky.

This beautiful oak, I talk to the tree.
"I am you and you are me."

> My mouth waters from drinking
> what nature provides.
> I am drinking, not thinking.
> I AM
> by Kae

I shared this program with some friends of many years who were visiting us from out-of-town. While here, they joined me on my walk. When they returned home we received a thank you note that included the following: "We are working on the thank you God series on our walks. Makes it so much more enjoyable! It's hard to have a bad day after that."

Having followed this routine several years I find that I can often just open up all my senses of awareness without going through the details. When this happens, I say quietly to myself, "Thank you."

Not long ago I had a new and unexpected experience on my walk. I was feeling exceptionally good and at one with my surroundings and in the process of saying, "thank you." At that moment I noticed that the sun was rising in the East and that a full moon was hovering over the mountains in the West. Both looked large and bright. A phrase from a hymn went through my mind, for I was for a moment indeed tuned in to the "music of the spheres."*

Occasionally I find it difficult to be in the moment especially when my mind is preoccupied. When I am in such a state I remind myself of the following story - Two monks pass by each other several times each day on their rounds. One morning, the first monk said to the other, "You lost your smile." The second monk shrugged and passed on by. In the afternoon, as they met again, the first monk said, "I see you found your smile." The second monk said, "Yes, a flower had it and I got it back." I too, on my daily walks, have often had a flower return my smile.

---

* Before turning the page to read the next chapter, pause for a moment and ask yourself, "What is the key to such an experience?"

262

LESSON: Always try to maintain an attitude of gratitude. (See: APPENDIX III– WEBSITES)

Chapter 27

THE KEY

I was shopping in a local supermarket. I had just left the pharmacy area where I had checked my blood pressure (it was good) and I was passing the Bank. At that moment I became aware of a fracas which was growing ever louder by the second. What at first appeared like a minor misunderstanding was now turning into a racial war and a shouting match. I quickly left the scene thinking how easily it is in our society to be distracted, to be drawn into the negative.

At the same moment I turned the switch - turning off thoughts about this ugly scene and all the negative thoughts about our society and started to listen to the music of the spheres. At once I was filled with love and gratitude.

Having read most of this book, you know that my ability to turn this switch has taken me a long time to achieve. But the important thing is that I have indeed gotten to this point. The important thing for you, is that this book shares the ingredients necessary to enjoy this same success.

I have already shared "my story" with you. However, let's return to it one more time and ask two specific questions: What was the **key** to my turnaround? And what was the **key** to my spiritual growth over time? The short answer to the first question is that I went within and the short answer to the second question is that I continued to go within.

Now I hope that after reading to this point these answers do not sound altogether strange. But, if they do, I believe the material in this section will bring some clarity to these answers.

If you have the time and a dictionary handy, I would like you to look up the word **key.** Then, read the definition. Most importantly, note how much space is taken to define the word. Now flip through the pages of the dictionary and note that very few words occupy as much space as this little three-letter word – **key.**

While all of us carry **keys,** most of us take them for granted. That is until we lose one. When that happens we are locked out of something: our car, our home, our office, our safety deposit box. When that happens we often feel panic or frustration. We ask, "What am I going to do now?"

Just for a moment let's return to our musical analogy. What would happen if the Conductor of a band handed out a piece of music to the members and there was no key signature on the music. I can assure you that the first question would be, "What **key** is this music in?" Let's imagine that the Conductor doesn't know and he says, "Play it in whatever **key** you like." Well, those of you who know music know what a disaster that would be. It would be pure chaos! We would experience panic and frustration.

To a great extent this illustrates why our world is in such a chaotic condition. We are all trying to play the music of life and we do not know what **key** it's in. We have lost the **key! We are locked out!** We often experience panic and frustration and we frequently ask, why?

Rumi, the great Sufi Poet, knew this when he said, "Love, the supreme musician, is always playing in our souls." He also knew that most people in his day were not in tune with their **INNER ESSENCE** – their souls. The Author of the Bhagavad-Gita knew this when he said, "Still your mind in me, still yourself in me, and without doubt you shall be united with me. Better indeed is knowledge than mechanical practice. Better than knowledge is meditation." Jesus knew this. One day he was having a discussion with Pharisees and the discussion got quite heated. One lawyer stood up and said, "You have insulted us." Jesus spent a few moments trying to explain himself and then he said **"Woe unto Lawyers! For you have taken away the <u>key</u> of knowledge; ye entered not in yourselves, and them that were entering in, ye hindered."** Luke 11; 52.

It appears that Jesus was saying to the religious leaders of his day, "You have lost the **key!** You are locked out! You are separated from the knowledge that can make you whole and what is worse as people of influence, you are keeping others from finding that knowledge!"

Today, many people pursue spiritual growth without success! The reason is simple. They are not in possession of the **key.** Today many leaders – religious, political, educational, do not have the **key.** They hinder rather than help solve the chaos of our world.

I spent ten years as a Pastor. I did substantially what I was trained to do but I did not possess the **key.** I am afraid that those who came to me were hindered rather than helped. It is sad to say but if people found the **key** in my church it was probably in spite of me not because of me.

The material in the following chapters should be read with one thought in mind, that ideas are presented in order that you might discover the **INNER TEACHER,** the **INNER HEALER,** the **INNER GUIDE.** I am not an authority. Kae and I are just people who have, by grace, been granted the **key.** Over the years we have been taught by the **INNER TEACHER,** healed by the **INNER HEALER,** and been led by the **INNER GUIDE.** The discovery of this **INNER ESSENCE** (whatever you may call it) is the **key** to understanding.[*]

LESSON: Psalm 46:10, "BE STILL AND KNOW THAT I AM GOD."

---

[*] In the next chapter you will read about some modern day clerics. Ask yourself, as you read, to what extent do they seem to possess the **key?**

Chapter 28

TALK SHOW

I was watching a local television talk show hosted by one of our community's well-known attorneys. His guests were three clergymen from the community: a Christian, a Jewish Rabbi and a Moslem Cleric. The discussion was lively and informative. The three guests interacted with compassion and good humor although their differences were apparent. As the host guided the discussion it became obvious that he was attempting to lead the guests to talk about and recognize what the three religions had in common.

At one point the host said, "Today it seems that many young people have forsaken your churches and become a part of the 'New Age movements'." He continued interjecting some of his own thoughts that might account for this move. He said, "It seems to me that many of these young people are seeking something that is part of each of your traditions but something that has little emphasis in your programs at this time." Then, turning it back over to the guests, he said, "What I am talking about is meditation."

Each of the guests in turn, talked about the history of meditation in his particular tradition. The Priest spoke of the history of the Christian Church emphasizing how important meditation had been. He explained that a number of meditation techniques had been developed in the Monasteries by different orders of Monks and Nuns. The Jewish Rabbi talked about the tradition of the Kabbalah and how it reemerges with renewed interest from time to time. It was noted that certain celebrities at this time seem to be rediscovering the value and teachings of the Kabbalah. The Moslem Cleric spoke of the long tradition of the Sufis who are the caretakers of the meditation tradition in the Moslem community.

The Host then inquired regarding what each was doing in his own congregation to teach meditation. The guests all squirmed a bit as they tried to give some kind of answer. Essentially, the answer to a man was "not much." The Host then asked, "Why not, if people are seeking this, why not?" The only answer I heard was that today people are too busy; too busy to listen to the "Music of the Spheres." To busy to "Be still, and know that I am God:" (Psalms 46:10)

****

If the premise of this book is correct, then the conclusion of these three clerics could well be tragic! In order to make it clear how tragic this might be we need to return to the words of Mahatma Gandhi (*WORDS OF GANDHI,* page 146): "It is because we have at the present moment everybody claiming the right of conscience without going through any discipline whatsoever that there is so much untruth delivered to a bewildered world." The lack of discipline—"Ah, there's the rub."

Thirty years ago I took a course designed by Maharishi Mahesh Yogi. It was called "The Science of Creative Intelligence". At that time many of the concepts were foreign to me and I was somewhat skeptical. One concept that I was skeptical about was what Maharishi called the "Home of all Knowledge." He said that such a realm existed but it was transcendent, beyond the realm of the five senses. Even though transcendent, this realm can be accessed by ordinary men and women according to Maharishi. He said the technique for accessing this realm is meditation. Today I am no longer a skeptic.

Today I believe that Plato and Socrates, in their own way, talked about this realm. I believe that when Jesus spoke of the Kingdom of God he was talking about this realm. When Leo Tolstoy found that truth was something that could be verified within his own consciousness he had discovered this realm. When the Apostle Paul said "it is no longer I who lives but Christ who lives in me," he had discovered this realm. When Einstein spent much of his life trying to scientifically verify the "Unified Field Theory" he was trying to verify the existence of such a realm—a realm he intuitively experienced on a frequent basis.

In Section III of this book we described in some detail the journey of the Vision Quest Heroes of mythology. These heroes from every land and every culture depicted the journey that every man and woman must take in order to enter the "HOME OF ALL KNOWLEDGE;" to know the truth that makes us free.

Gandhi said, "I am a Christian and a Hindu and a Moslem and a Jew". It is abundantly clear that he did not say this because he embraced all four belief systems but, because he had experienced the realm from which the truth of each had come. He had discovered the LOVE, which is at the heart of their teachings. He had accessed the HOME OF ALL KNOWLEDGE. Because Gandhi manifested such great love many Christians including Dr. E. Stanley Jones (an American missionary who knew Gandhi intimately for years) called Gandhi "one of the most Christ-like men in history." Now the question is, "Why did he consider him Christ-like?" He was Christ-like because he had exercised the discipline necessary to access the Kingdom of God, the HOME OF ALL KNOWLEDGE.

We are a bewildered world and we need to recover the discipline of SELF-discovery that can return us to the TRUTH that Gandhi knew. We need to recover the discipline of going within (meditation). I will not be so presumptuous as to say that the techniques that I use are the ones that you should use. Neither will I say that there is only one right way to meditate. However, I intend to spend the rest of my life encouraging the world to rediscover this important discipline so that more and more individuals might hear the SILENCE and listen to the "Music of the Spheres." (See: Appendix III —WEBSITES)

LESSON: As we have noted previously, "Bidden or not Bidden, God is present." Also, we have noted that the fact of His presence is a

tragedy unless we <u>consciously</u> become aware of this presence. Thus –
the importance of the admonition like the one below:

"Still your mind in me, still yourself in me,
And without doubt you shall be united with me
Better indeed is knowledge than mechanical practice
Better than knowledge is meditation."
(From the Bhagavad Gita)

■■

Chapter 29

PRACTICAL SPIRITUALITY

Entering the realm beyond concept and thought through meditation, the realm beyond the "Gatekeeper," is both practical and spiritual. It is spiritual because the motivating force is unseen, beyond comprehension and mysterious (mystical). It is practical because it makes a difference in everyday life. It is embracing the TRUTH instead of being duped by the lie. Practical spirituality turns the cup that is half-empty into the one that is half full. It changes a bad attitude into an attitude of gratitude. It gives one an unchanging foundation in the midst of change and trial.

Practical spirituality is that which enables one to do as the old popular song expressed, "accentuate the positive and eliminate the negative." Practical spirituality does not make people so heavenly-minded that they are no earthly good. That kind of religion is not practical and it is doubtful that it is even spiritual. Over the years I have read numerous surveys taken that attempt to ascertain the everyday practicality of attending church. For all too many people, Sunday morning church attendance has very little carry-over into their daily or practical life. For most of these people it seems that church going is a kind of insurance policy based on the future; a hopeful guarantee that as the early American revivalists used to say, "they will have pie in the sky when they die by and by."

When an alcoholic or an addict of any kind, for whatever reason, starts practicing the twelve steps and the obsession is lifted, that is spirituality and that makes a difference here and now. It makes a difference in his or her life and all persons with whom they associate. When a hopeless gambling addict has his or her obsession removed when practicing the same twelve steps; this is practical. It means bills will be paid, promises kept, relationships restored, children will eat and trust will once again be established.

When through spiritual means (uncovering and discovering) the obsession of the sex addict, or the food addict, or the drug addict, or the workaholic (and so on) is lifted; that is practical. Practical spirituality as we discovered in previous chapters is often born in times of "spiritual crisis."

Before we get into the nitty-gritty of practical spirituality, let me remind you once again of the thoughts of Chicago University Professor, Csikszentmihalyi who said that in order to survive in the new millennium mankind will have to come to a new understanding of himself. We believe that practical spirituality is the Key to this new understanding.

The spiritual crisis that Martin Buber described (See: Appendix II, TRANSITION II.) which took place in the eighteenth century Jewish communities of Eastern Europe was the result of those people pinning their hopes on false messiahs only to have them exposed. This is the nature of every spiritual crisis. The examples that we have just used of the alcoholic, drug addict and so on are examples of people whose savior has been exposed as a fraud. Then he cries out for another way. For at that moment he is left with a vacuum, a void to be filled. At that moment he is ready for the discovery that life is not lived from the outside in, but rather from the inside out. Life is not a matter of taking in, of filling up, of seeking from without. Life in its purest sense is first and foremost a discovery of what we already are - (SELF).

Now, lest you think this does not apply to you, let me refer to a familiar Bible passage that says, "All have sinned and fallen short of the glory of God." It's true; we all do miss the mark! This is the message of every major religion. We are missing the mark! And we are missing the mark because we are more than we think we are. I know that for some of you that sounds like a contradiction, but it is true. We do have a HIGHER SELF. The emphasis of the Bible passage should not be that we are sinners, but that we have within us the glory of God (IMAGO DEI) and that like an arrow that has fallen short of it's target we are falling short of our true potential. Practical Spirituality enables us to wake up to who we are.

When Kae and I lived in Seattle we had season tickets for the Seahawks. (Professional football team) As they were a new franchise, they were not very good but they were lots of fun. We followed them very closely and we were always eager to hear what the head coach had to say about the upcoming game. One of the phrases we learned to expect from him was, "You have to play the hand that's dealt ya." It didn't matter what the question from the reporters might be; the answer was often the same. He might be asked about injuries to key players, players in trouble with the law, difficult travel or schedule problems. His answer was, "You have to play the hand that's dealt you." Practical Spirituality is facing reality and playing the hand that's dealt you. I have tried to make it clear that one of the realities we have to face is our spiritual nature. If we don't face this fact we are not playing the hand that's dealt us. Let me illustrate!

Life is a game in which each of us has been dealt two cards and many of us, in one way or another, have refused to play the hand that has been dealt us; we have only picked up one card. When we do this we are not only shortchanging ourselves but also society and the future of humankind. There is a sense in which each of us has been dealt a joker and a Queen or King. The Joker is wild and the King and Queen are of equal value. Each of us has an opportunity to win or be successful at the game called life but if we just pick up the joker, even though it is wild, it has no value. It is a wild card and gets its value by being matched with another card. Those who play life with just the human or ego nature are playing with a wild card, a joker and life finds little true value.

Those who try to be Godlike, who permanently confine themselves to monasteries, or who go into the desert into silence and

275

meditation in order to cut themselves off from worldly life, also are attempting to pick up only one card. For a few this may be the right thing to do, it may also be beneficial to society. For others it may be running away and a refusal to play the hand that's dealt them.

Some people pick up one card and they kind of peek at the other but they never really play with both cards. We obviously could carry this analogy further describing in some detail the Royal SELF and how it transforms and gives value to the wild card, the joker self. The important point is that we do have two natures and if we are not in touch with both we are not just selling ourselves short, we are literally selling out.

The following chapters about prayer, meditation, starting our day in the right position and etc. are all things we need to know and practice if we are going play harmoniously in the symphony of life; if we are going to play the game of life with the hand that has been dealt us. The hand that has been dealt us is both relative and ABSOLUTE. We need to face the truth and realize that we didn't come to earth to play solo; we came to play in the symphony that is directed by the UNSEEN ONE. When we do, we will find that life is not - "a tale told by an idiot full of sound and fury signifying nothing." (Macbeth by Shakespeare) We will find that life is a beautiful symphony conducted by the Composer Himself.

LESSON: Live life on life's terms and remember you are not the director.

Chapter 30

GOOD ORDERLY DIRECTION

Hmmm - Howard Hansen. That's the man the radio announcer said would be directing "The Norwegian Symphony," the next piece - Howard Hansen - the composer. I was traveling down the road to Flagstaff, Arizona listening to a classical station. Howard Hansen's name was mentioned and my mind drifted off to a scene over forty years ago. I was attending Pacific Lutheran College in Tacoma, Washington. Pacific Lutheran had about a thousand students. It was known for its choir that toured the United States and Europe frequently, but its band was another story. It wasn't a good band and I wasn't a good trombone player. I had played trombone in high school, switched to baritone, and now after four years, I was playing trombone again. There were some excellent musicians in the band but there were far too many members just like me for this group to be a quality band.

However, all that was different for just one day and one piece of music. It was the day that Howard Hansen, Director, Composer and President of the Eastman School of Music came to direct our band playing one of his compositions.

The occasion was a Naturalization Ceremony in which several hundred people of various nationalities were accepting citizenship and pledging loyalty to the United States. There were many dignitaries present including the Mayor of Tacoma, the Governor of Washington and the featured speaker, Alvin Barclay, Vice President of the United States.

We started practicing the piece several weeks before the occasion. The day before the actual ceremony Howard Hansen came and directed our rehearsal. By the time the rehearsal was over we were all encouraged. The next morning we practiced again and Dr. Hansen convinced us that we really sounded good. Something new was stirring in every one of the musicians and we couldn't wait for the ceremony. The time finally arrived along with a parade of speakers. Then it was our turn. The master of ceremonies simply said "Dr. Howard Hansen, Composer, Conductor and President of the Eastman School of Music will be conducting the Pacific Lutheran College Band in one of his own compositions."

Even the sound of the introduction made us sit taller. Dr. Hansen conducted and we played. We played as we had never played before. In fact, I believe that on that one occasion, directed by the Composer himself, we, both individually and collectively, played superbly. We were in the **FLOW**! It seemed like a miracle. We were all amazed at what we had just accomplished!

I had not recalled that day for years but since recalling it I have thought about it frequently. That one day now stands out for me as a living parable of my life today. A more recent occasion also illustrates the harmony I am now experiencing.

In a previous chapter I told about my attendance at the 1990 International Alcoholics Anonymous Convention in Seattle. I lived in the Seattle area for a number of years and had the opportunity to see the Kingdome built from the ground up and had attended many sports events there over the years. One thing I had never done was to sit in the Press Box. The night of the first mass meeting I sat in the Press Box and for some reason I started to think like a reporter.

There were forty thousand people in the Kingdom and virtually all of them were alcoholics - that's forty thousand stories! I began to think in terms of statistics - how many gallons of booze had been consumed by these forty thousand people during their drinking days; how many days of jail time; how many broken dreams, broken marriages, broken promises; how many drunk-driving charges; how many battered wives, abused children, deserted husbands. Forty thousand stories, forty thousand men and women who had literally been to hell and back.

But why? Why do these twelve-step programs work so well? For me, the best answer I can come up with is found in my little parable, of that "not so good band" that played like the Marine Band on that one day. That day they were directed by the Composer himself.

Each of these forty thousand people and all the millions that they represented back home in both A.A. and other twelve-step programs had come to a point where their particular disease or obsession coupled with self will, became so humiliating and so painful, that they begrudgingly accepted the idea that there must be a better way. When they opened that door ever so slightly and ask to be shown the other way, if there was one, they were once again (or possibly for the first time) opening up to the Composer of life.

With that opening, they came to see that life was composed as a symphony and not as a solo. We had all been playing our life like it was a solo, insisting on our own will, our own way and our own interpretation. As a soloist we played a lot of sour notes in the symphony of life and we embarrassed and alienated ourselves. Slowly, through the twelve steps of recovery we started to have some direct contact with the Composer, who most of us found deep down within our own nature. Through conscious contact with the Composer who obviously knows more about the symphony than anyone else, we started to learn more about it, both as individuals and as a group. We found out, sometimes the hard way, that the Composer of life wanted to direct His own symphony. This was a hard pill for us to swallow but our experience tells us that things did get better.

When we don't allow the Composer to direct, we go back to our solo life and once again we create discord in the symphony, and interestingly enough, within ourselves. In fact it seems that we need the symphony more than it needs us and the symphony is not a harmonious symphony if it is not directed and who better to direct it than the one who knows it completely, who gave it birth, the Composer.

On Sunday morning of that same week, forty thousand people once again filled the Kingdom for the final session of the Convention. Three speakers told their stories - stories of how they had played solo and created disharmony and how today, they were grateful to be playing in the symphony - how grateful they were to get daily direction from the Conductor/ Composer.

LESSON: "To what you are connected is by what you are directed." (Guy Finley) If we have uncovered and discovered enough to be connected to the INNER ESSENCE then we will be directed by the SUPREME MUSICIAN of whom Rumi speaks.

Chapter 31

GOD'S WILL IS FOR US TO PLAY IN THE SYMPHONY - NOT SOLO

Many years ago, towards the end of my Lutheran ministry, the President of the congregation, who also happened to be my medical Doctor, asked me to prepare a study on the question, "What is God's will?" I said that I would. I never did. The more I thought about the subject, the more I knew I was not ready to talk about it. As you already know, at that time, I didn't know my "head" from a hole in the ground, so I certainly didn't know the will of God.

Today I am ready. Today I have something to say about the subject. You probably realize by now that what I know or what I think I know is based on experience. Everything I believe today, no matter where the idea may have come from to begin with, is mine by virtue of confirming internal experience.

Mine is not the intellectual approach but the approach of allowing life itself to confirm or deny. In short; does it work? And, does it feel right? My program is now, and has been for many years based on the eleventh step - "sought through prayer and meditation to improve our conscious contact with God as we understand him, praying only for knowledge of His will for us and the power to carry that out."

The first thing I would emphasize to my Doctor friend and his associates is that understanding God's will is an individual thing born out of prayer and meditation with a God with which you (the individual) have conscious contact. I would emphasize that my experience tells me it is possible to have a conscious contact with something that is bigger and more important and more intelligent than my selfness (my ego self).

Today, God's will, to me, means: Getting in touch with and staying in conscious contact with a power greater than myself. Again, the meaning of the twelve-step program slogan, "first things first," (according to A.A.'s co-founder, Dr. Bob) simply means, seek first the Kingdom of God. This means uncovering and discovering, excavating the psychic until you start getting glimpses of the key of knowledge (the Kingdom of God). It means taking seriously Plato's words, **"THE LIFE WHICH IS UNEXAMINED IS NOT WORTH LIVING."**

This means praying to this power (even if you are not sure what this power is) on a daily basis <u>only</u> for knowledge of his will and the power to carry that out. This has been a powerful tool for me on the road to greater humility. It is asking a power greater than my self for direction and guidance. In addition, it is asking for the necessary will to follow that guidance. It means I am turning my entire life over on a daily basis to something that is much bigger than the "little general," my ego-self.

As you do this, I suggest that you consider three words - three qualities that my Higher Power has convinced me are His will for me. They are the desire to be willing, honest and open. These three words are often linked together in the opposite order. But lets now consider them, one at a time, in the order that I have listed creating the acronym WHO, rather than in the order creating the acronym HOW. Based on my own experience these are some of the questions I would ask you to consider.

WILLING - Question # 1: Are you willing to accept that there may be a higher power, something that might even be worthy of the term, God?

When I reached the end of my rope, in spite of being a clergyman with a fair degree of education, I no longer believed in God. My belief system was bankrupt. I was spiritually, morally and to some extent both mentally and physically bankrupt. Although unknown to me I was having a "spiritual crisis." In spite of my disappointment with the God of my belief system, in spite of my disillusionment with the church and its teachings, I found in the midst of this crisis the need for a higher power; a power greater than me who could get me out of the mess I was in.

Question # 2: Are you willing to accept that you might have been looking for God in the wrong places?

Question # 3: Are you willing to explore the possibility that God is found deep down within your own self?

Question # 4: Are you willing to consider that your present ideas or concepts of God, no matter how ingrained (sophisticated or infantile) may be getting in the way of a real conscious contact?

Question # 5: Are you willing to set aside your old (present) ideas about yourself, your world, your God and be open to something new?

Question # 6: Are you willing to be honest with yourself about these and other questions?

HONEST - Question # 1: Are you willing to question your ability to be honest with yourself?

I found out that, even though along with others I considered myself to be a frank and honest guy, I was literally incapable of being honest with myself. However, I did put up a good front by being frankly open in areas that were not a threat to me.

Question # 2: Can you honestly say you know who you are?

(I thought I knew but I didn't have a clue. All I knew about myself was what the "little general" wanted me to know.)

Question # 3: Are you being <u>honest</u> with yourself when you say, "I am <u>willing</u> to be <u>open</u>." Before you answer, read this question again very slowly. Many of us find that the first thing we have to do is pray for the willingness to be willing.

OPEN - Question # 1: Are you <u>willing</u> to be open?

This is one of the great benefits of the twelve-step groups. It gives you the opportunity to explore in a safe setting the meaning of openness. I am convinced that for most of us openness has to be learned.

Question # 2: Are you willing to be vulnerable?

Again, the safe setting of people with the same problems you have is the place you can experiment with your vulnerability. In group settings you will hear your story in the story of others and in so doing you will begin to share your own story. As you continue to share your story over weeks, months and years you will become less vulnerable and more open.

Question # 3: Are you willing to become transparent?

This is a state where the ego-self no longer needs to be protected. I no longer identify with my ego (most of the time) so I no longer need to protect it. These three concepts and questions can be very valuable in the pursuit of God's will for you. It is my feeling that this must be done in the context of praying only for his will and the power to carry that out. Praying for our own selfish needs only delays our progress.

In the past sixty years twelve-step groups have literally been a laboratory in which millions of people have experimented with the question that the Doctor asked me to study, "What is God's will?" In these laboratories it is my personal observation and experience that God's will has been revealed. (For more information on 12-step programs – (See Appendix III - WEBSITES)

It appears to me that man was meant to live in fellowship; for it is in the context of fellowship that I have seen and experienced the metamorphosis (positive spiritual change) talked about in this book. In fellowship, millions of hopeless drunks, addicts, gamblers, neurotics, etc. have not only been restored to health but have gone on to lead lives they never dreamed possible.

It also appears to me, based on these same experiences, that God would have man live in conscious contact with his higher SELF. The point of this book is that the higher SELF is God or of God. Either way it is our point of conscious contact. In such contact man experiences and learns eternal values like love which leads to service and peace, which leads to serenity.

Furthermore, it appears to me that this fellowship with both God and man produces a caring community in which all people, regardless of religion, race or station can come and be loved until they are able to love them SELVES. With this new found love and in <u>continued</u> fellowship with both man and the higher power individuals will <u>continue</u> on a daily basis to seek and know His will and the power to carry that out.

The final thought I would like to leave with you in this Chapter is that addiction can be a gift. There is something about the nature of man that causes him to go outside of himself to find fulfillment. Now what that "something" is has been the subject of many books. Buber called it the "evil urge." For our purpose, at this moment, let us just call it man's alienation from his SELF.

Addiction is a soul sickness, the result of seeking a false solution to this alienation. As Dr. Jung stated in his letter to Bill Wilson, (mentioned in Chapter 18) "The craving for alcohol was the equivalent, on a low level, of the spiritual thirst of our being for wholeness." When this seeking turns to ruin or bankruptcy it may produce a state in which a person is <u>willing</u> to seek to know his or her SELF. It is at this point that spiritual bankruptcy becomes a spiritual gift. It is at this point that the "evil urge," the "wild hair" can be turned around and used by the Divine to alter our ego system, which, as Campbell points out, has become a monster.

This is, as I understand it, the will of God: To come to the understanding that with the help of the DIVINE and our willingness the "evil urge," the "wild hair" can become the blessing that brings us to the realization that WE ARE SOMETHING ELSE!

Well Doctor K. I know it's long overdue, but here is the study on God's will I promised you so many years ago. In regard to your question, after many years I realize that it is not "what" but "WHO." "What is the will of God?" First and foremost the will of God is that we find out "WHO" we are - that we each discover our TRUE SELF. I am totally convinced that this TRUE SELF is either GOD or OF GOD. God's will is that we all seek HIS/HER direction in the symphony of life on a daily basis.

The will of God is that we find our true SELF, the Kingdom Within. The first step in this process is that we have the necessary willingness, the honesty and openness that we see the "little general" for what he or she is, "a phony!" At this point we must also come to the realization that "life is a cinch by the inch but hard by the yard." We can only demote the "little general" on a daily basis, "one day at a time."

Note: There is a Twelve-step program or support group for almost every problem. (Again, see Appendix III – WEBSITES) You might also look in the announcement section of your local newspaper.

LESSON: Step 4 - Made a searching and fearless inventory of ourselves. When we live life on life's terms like any business we need to take a frequent inventory. Our goal however is always "progress not perfection." Plato certainly knew the importance of this lesson. **"THE LIFE WHICH IS UNEXAMINED IS NOT WORTH LIVING."**

Chapter 32

TUNING UP

The harmony of an instrument in tune
The soothing summer breeze in June
The soaring seagull's swoop and sway
The glistening shimmer of a moonlit bay
Each enters the being, invades the soul
adds joy to the spirit and comforts the whole.
By Kae

In TRANSITION I (found in the Appendix I) we note the influence of the Pathagorians on Socrates and Plato. For the Pathagorians, philosophy, spirituality, mathematics, music and the health of the body are all related and fit together. We have also made the point that the social evolution of the Western mind over the past 2500 years has done a good job of dividing all these into very separate disciplines. We have gone so far as to call this separation a sickness, a problem that some feel must be corrected if our species is to survive. In the following we look for ways to regain or remind ourselves of our forgotten unity. As we do, we will continue to use music and the symphony as our metaphor. Aldus Huxley said next to silence, music is the greatest expression of the divine.

We are aware of music and sound being used in sacred ceremony. Chants, hymns, mantras (like aum or om) have all been used for thousands of years. Sound is vibration and vibration relates to math (the higher the pitch, the more frequent the vibration) Just think of all the different vibrations taking place in a large symphony. In the moments before the "big bang" there was vibration and thus began "the music of the spheres." The New Testament says, "in the beginning was the word (logos)" (sound, vibration, energy, waves).

In the West we are once again recognizing the relationship of sound to both spiritual and physical health. Alternative medicine practitioners are having positive results using therapeutic methods that involve music, sound, energy and vibration. Neuroscientists are discovering that the molecules in the body are the basis of our emotion. They are discovering how these emotions effect our body, mind and consequently, our health. They are also discovering how these molecules respond to various stimuli such as sound and music. (These discoveries are closing the door on the Descartian notion that the body and mind are separate.)

When I think of the relationship between sound and spirituality I am reminded of two things. One is my experience when I listen to music, especially string quartets. When the music starts I close my eyes and before long I am beginning to hear the silence between the notes. Listening to music was my first experience of being in touch with the SILENCE outside of meditation.

Kae and I both like to go to Classical Jazz Festivals. One time in Sun Valley, Idaho I heard a group from Connecticut and I had the same experience as I frequently have when listening to classical music. After hearing this group I got on a bus to go to another venue. I was sitting next to one of the musicians from the Connecticut group. I told him I thought his group was one of the best I had heard because I could hear the silence between the notes. I had forgotten myself! He had no earthly idea what I was talking about. For those of you who are familiar with Dixieland or Classical Jazz, you know why. It is a very full sound! I chuckle to myself every time I think about this incident. Evidently Kae has the experience too. She writes:

Onerous beginnings
with time bound endings
sandwiched in between—SILENCE—
without beginning or ending

Secondly, in a Science of Mind Church I attended, a Tibetan Bell was used as a call to meditation. As soon as I would hear the bell my nervous system would start to settle down and I would ultimately enter into a deep meditative state.

PRAYER

"As long as you believe that God is only in heaven and does not fill the earth let your words be few. Only when you come to know that you too contain His presence - only then can you begin to pray." (Hasidic saying)

I feel that I am qualified to comment on these words from Hasidic literature. I have experienced both sides of the coin. I have experienced the sublime silence of the DIVINE within and the noise of my own desperate prayers. For as it has been noted, I once was paid to pray, I was a professional pray-er - something with which I became increasingly uncomfortable. During those years as a paid pray-er, I prayed to a God in heaven. It wasn't until the last days of my ministry that I started to recognize the Divinity within.

Throughout this book we have tried to make the distinction between <u>concept</u> and <u>experience</u>. Some call this the difference between the head and the heart. When it comes to prayer this becomes a very practical issue. Is that to which you are praying the Divinity within yourself – the IMAGO DEI, or is your God in some far off heaven? Look back at the line from Hasidic Literature. As this text indicates, it makes a difference whether or not you have established a conscious contact, whether or not you know the God of direct experience or whether your God is a teaching from a book, church or parent.

289

Many who come into twelve-step programs are not sure whether they believe there is a God. Many say, "I believe there is one but I don't think he/she cares about me." The group will then tell them to act as if there is one. They might also tell them that if they don't have a God to pray to, borrow theirs. The following words are for those who do not yet know a God of direct contact - a God within! For those who have established direct experience (a conscious contact), maybe these words will be a refresher course or reminder.

My friend, if you have gotten this far in this book and are one of those who does not yet know the God of direct contact it would seem to me that you are ready for this KNOWLEDGE. In order to gain this KNOWLEDGE my best advice is: act as if it's true and if need be, borrow my God. My God is in me but He/She is <u>also, in you!</u> If you don't want to borrow my God, then borrow one of the following.

The Hindu says, "I am THAT." - "All that is, is THAT"
The Christian says, "The Kingdom of God is within."
The Jews talk about the Shekhinah, (divine eminence, the light within)
The Moslem Sufis say, "The outer law is my action
        The path of purification is my way
        And the inner reality is my state."
        (attributed to) Muhammad

Act as if God is in you and pray, "Thy will be done" in the morning when you awaken and as often as you need to or want to during the day. At night, before you go to sleep, simply say, "Thank you" or "Thank you God."

A longer version of, "thy will be done" is contained in the eleventh-step. It says, "I pray only for God's will for me and the power to carry that out." For me, the word <u>only</u> is very important. It is an ego-deflator. I am praying for God's will, not mine, not what my ego wants and desires. God wants my ego deflated so I can experience the inner presence; so I can be my SELF.

If you find that you cannot borrow my God, who is in you too, and pray "thy will be done" then simply pray everyday for the willingness to realize or experience the TRUTH. If you can't do that, simply pray for the willingness to be willing.

In twelve-step programs we say to the newcomer, "do ninety meetings in ninety days." It takes some time for new habits to form and old habits to die; it takes time for the ego to be pierced; so try praying to my God, who is also in you, for ninety days. You can even use my name if you want to. Using my name may sound silly, even blasphemous to some, but it is neither, if it helps you get started. Say: "Rich says he has a God, he says his God is also in me. If this is true, please help me to know you." Try this on your knees for ninety days. "Why on my knees?" you ask - because your ego hates to get down on its knees. It hates more than anything to acknowledge its enemy, the SELF within. And believe it or not, it is just old habits that keep you from knowing the Kingdom within, the Shekhinah; for what the ego is - are old ideas and old habits that overshadow and cut us off from our inner essence. When we say, "thy will be done," we are asking the God within to take control and to demote the "little general."

WHAT THE EGO LOVES

Now let me talk a bit about what the ego loves. I said the ego hates to physically bow down to the TRUE SELF but it absolutely loves to erect false gods or idols for us to bow down to. As you know, one of the Ten Commandments says we should not have any false gods or bow down to any idols. That however, is the delight of the ego. Its self-assigned job is to erect idols to which we can bow down. In most of us it appears the ego feels this is its job. In most of us it does its job very, very well.

Now nothing in this world has real meaning apart from our TRUE SELF and anything to which we give meaning will keep us from our TRUE SELF. That sounds like a "catch 22" and it really is. Another way of looking at this is in terms of direction. Anything we find meaningful outside of ourselves is by its nature an idol because it draws us away from our TRUE SELF. In fact, it causes us to go in the opposite direction. As I said, this can be anything. The big three categories are the pursuit of wealth, pleasure and fame. Now almost everyone will tell you these are not evil or wrong in and of themselves but how on <u>earth</u> do we pursue these and follow the command to seek first the Kingdom of God. These pursuits appear to be <u>without</u> and the Kingdom of God is <u>within</u> - another "catch 22."

The more we pursue stuff on the outside the further we get from the truth and thus from our TRUE SELF. The further we get from our TRUE SELF the emptier we feel, the more pain we have and thus the more we need something to fill the void. Once again, it can be anything - church, alcohol, the Bible, a Guru, Jesus, activity, sex, success, money, prayer, golf, television, Internet etc., etc. It can be anything outside of our SELF that we look to for relief and consequently it becomes an idol.

When we find that something that really makes us feel alive we often times turn it into an obsession. Many of us literally pursue it to the gates of hell. We pursue it until it kills us or takes us into some kind of personal bankruptcy - financial, physical or emotional. It is at the point of bankruptcy that many of us have cried out, "If there is a God, please help me." And many of us can testify that at this point, something within us responded to the cry of desperation, offered us a flicker of hope and we grasp hold of it like a line thrown to a drowning man. The "catch 22" is solved and in spite of appearances, the process probably proceeds quite naturally until full liberation is achieved; interestingly enough, including those things that are on the sideline. They take on a new meaning that no longer detracts or gets between us and our real SELF. Jesus said it best when he said, "seek ye first the Kingdom of God and all <u>these</u> <u>things</u> will be added unto you." Incidentally Dr. Bob (the cofounder of A.A.) was once ask what the slogan "first things first" meant. He replied: "it means to seek first the Kingdom of God."

Now, what about the people who are more civil, more refined, more in control than the ones we have just described. I see two groups. One group somehow learns from those around them. They don't have to go to the gates of hell to get the picture. They pick up the same set of tools that the desperate do and seek the SILENCE within. The second group, apparently quite large, seems to be characterized by Henry Thoreau's quote: "The mass of men lead lives of quiet desperation." They know nothing of the UNITY that is our heritage and they play quietly off-key in the symphony of life.

LESSON: Learn the lesson of *Deep Ecology;* HUMILITY.

Chapter 33

HOW DO YOU START YOUR DAY?

Back in the early 1990s my youngest Daughter was involved in the 501 Levi craze. She would buy a pair of 501s in a thrift store or yard sale for a dollar or two and ship them overseas and resell them for as much as $50.00 a pair. During one period she was selling in Sydney, Australia and while setting up her business there she invited me to visit her and enjoy the Country.

On the first morning there I experienced one of those moments that Carl Jung calls synchronicity - moments that have become more common in my life as the years go by. These are moments when one experiences the concurrence of events in time that seem to defy all odds.

I arose before my Daughter awoke and was strolling from the upscale area of Potts Point to the nearby commercial area of Kings Cross. As I walked along, the thought came into my mind that I should find an A.A. meeting that I could attend during my three-week stay. When I came to the library near the square in Kings Cross I decided to check and see if they had a bulletin board listing community events such as twelve-step meetings. As I did, I noticed an open door with a couple of people standing by it. As I approached them, one asked if he could help me. I said I was looking for a calendar of events. One of the men responded, "What in particular are you looking for?" I said, "an A.A. meeting." The man said, "Come on in" and as he did, he looked at his watch and said, "it starts in one minute."

There were about thirty people at the meeting. They met two days a week, Wednesday and Saturday mornings at 8:00 A.M. The name of the meeting was, "How Do You Start Your Day" which at the time was of particular interest to me. It was a great meeting with a mixture of solid A.A. and good humor. I also experienced something at that A.A. meeting that I had not experienced before or since.

Every once in a while someone would be asked, "How do you start your day?" and the person would stand up and sing a little ditty about how they personally "start their day in the A.A. way." The words and tune varied from person to person but usually included something about prayer, meditation and reading from the A.A. literature. The way I found the meeting, the name of the meeting and the good fellowship, has all served to sear this experience in my mind. As I said, this idea had become particularly important to me because for many years I have started my day with my meditation technique which takes about twenty minutes. Then I read some spiritual literature. In the year prior to my trip to Australia I had been reading on a daily basis the following words from the *Big Book of Alcoholics Anonymous:*

"On awakening let us think about the twenty-four hours ahead. We consider our plans for the day. Before we begin, we ask God to direct our thinking, especially asking that it be divorced from self-pity, dishonest or self-seeking motives. Under these conditions we can employ our mental faculties with assurance, for after all God gave us brains to use. Our thought life will be placed on a much higher plane when our thinking is cleared of wrong motives."

"In thinking about our day we may face indecision. We may not be able to determine which course to take. Here we ask God for inspiration, an intuitive thought or a decision. We relax and take it easy. We don't struggle. We are often surprised how the right answers come after we have tried this for a while. What used to be the hunch or the occasional inspiration gradually becomes a working part of the mind. Being still inexperienced and having just made conscious contact with God, it is not probable that we are going to be inspired at all times. We might pay for this presumption in all sorts of absurd actions and ideas. Nevertheless, we find that our thinking will, as time passes, be more and more on the plane of inspiration. We come to rely upon it."

"We usually conclude the period of meditation with a prayer that we be shown all through the day what our next step is to be, that we be given whatever we need to take care of such problems. We ask especially for freedom from self-will, and are careful to make no request for ourselves only. We may ask for ourselves, however, if others will be helped. We are careful never to pray for our own selfish ends. Many of us have wasted a lot of time doing that and it doesn't work. You can easily see why."

"If circumstances warrant, we ask our wives or friends to join us in morning meditation. If we belong to a religious denomination, which requires a definite morning devotion, we attend to that also. If not members of religious bodies, we sometimes select and memorize a few set prayers, which emphasize the principles we have been discussing. There are many helpful books also. Suggestions about these may be obtained from one's priest, minister, or rabbi. Be quick to see where religious people are right. Make use of what they offer."

"As we go through the day we pause, when agitated or doubtful, and ask for the right thought or action. We constantly remind ourselves we are no longer running the show, humbly saying to ourselves many times each day "Thy will be done." We are then in much less danger of excitement, fear, anger, worry, self-pity, or foolish decisions. We become much more efficient. We do not tire so easily, for we are not burning up energy foolishly as we did when we were trying to arrange life to suit ourselves."

"It works—it really does."

"We alcoholics are undisciplined. So we let God discipline us in the simple way we have just outlined."

After reading these words, I would spend a few moments contemplating and praying about my day. I had started this particular procedure upon the recommendation of my sponsor. I was very pleased even somewhat fascinated with the difference it had made in my day. At the same time I started to become aware of just how many twelve-step people had some sort of procedure for getting their day off to a good start. My first sponsor used to say; "Every morning I have to speak with God before my ego wakes up." Sometimes he would add that on days when his ego woke up before he did, the day usually didn't go so well. His practice was to get up, put on his jogging clothes and run a few miles. While he was running, he said he would talk with God.

Another friend of mine gets up, hops in the shower and writes, "Hi God" in the condensation on the shower door. Over the years, I have heard many different ways in which twelve-step people start their day including going to mass, church, mosque and temple. Invariably those who stick around find a way to start their day in the A.A. way (a way that works for them as an individual A.A. member).

At the present time my own personal procedure is to arise around 4:00 A.M., do some stretching exercises, a breathing program and my meditation technique. After that I take my two-mile gratitude walk. This is a fairly extensive program for starting one's day. But for me, doing these exercises is the difference between a day lived in the now, and one lived in either the past or future. (Over the years since this was written I have modified this schedule quite a bit. I no longer get up at 4:00 A.M. and I don't do all aspects of the program every day.)

Many people in twelve-step programs find getting down on their knees for prayer is an important part of starting and ending their day. The importance of this act is found in the definition of an alcoholic, that is "self-will run riot." Because most addictive people in recovery recognize the truth of this statement they find, at first, getting down on their knees is difficult. It's difficult because it flies in the face of that self-will. I don't know that Vernon Howard was talking about kneeling, but he says, "Living in the present begins by starting our day in the right position." That right position is not self-will.

A final point which is often mentioned in twelve-step programs, is the concept of starting your day over again. It is said if your day isn't going well you can start it over again as many times as you need to. This is often done by saying something like "Thy will be done" or as Kae says, "You lead, I'll follow."

In the spirit of Vernon Howard's "starting the day in the right position" I conclude this piece with the words of Pablo Casals, (1876-1973) perhaps the greatest Cellist ever:

"For the past eighty years I have started each day in the same manner. It is not a mechanical routine but something essential to my daily life. I go to the piano and I play two preludes and fugues of Bach. I cannot think of doing otherwise. It is a sort of benediction on the house. But that is not its only meaning for me. It is a rediscovery of the world of which I have the joy of being a part. It fills me with awareness of the wonder of life and with a feeling of the incredible marvel of being a human being."

LESSON: The closest thing to eternity in this life, is NOW. NOW, in the deepest sense, is that sublime state of consciousness that is <u>beyond thought</u>. Starting the day in the NOW, we think, is the supreme way of starting your day in the right position. Here we see the connection between practical spirituality and the **key** of knowledge and that they are in essence, one and the same. Kae met a lovely lady while we were visiting friends in Mexico that reminded us of this <u>Truth</u>. Kae was invited to play bridge with a group. While so doing she met Pamela Pollard. At almost the same moment both Kae and Pamela realized they had something in common – a connection.

That connection turned out to be the fact that they both regularly start their day by seeking the realm beyond thought in meditation. Later, Pamela gave Kae a book of her poetry. It is entitled, *BEYOND THOUGHT. (*See Appendix VI for one of Pamela Pollard's poems on meditation)

Chapter 34

IN ORDER TO PLAY THE RIGHT NOTES IN THE SYMPHONY WE MAY NEED A TUTOR

Shortly after Kae and I met we talked about starting a company which would develop and present seminars. Among the subjects we considered for such seminars were personal growth and the fundamentals of financial success. At that time *I AIN'T MUCH BABY BUT I'M ALL I'VE GOT*, a book by Jess Lair, was very popular and it caught our eye.

Jess was a Professor of psychology at the University of Montana at Bozeman. His book was an outgrowth of his class presentations. Much of the material in these presentations was based on his own personal growth following a heart attack. Jess concluded that stress, and emotional buildup may well have had something to do with his heart condition. The heart attack led to an evaluation of his goals, values and interests. **He began in earnest to examine his life**. As the book title would indicate his presentations were folksy and included down-to-earth ideas for growth and wholeness.

Kae and I felt that Jess would be an ideal person to kick off our seminar endeavor. Consequently, we negotiated with Jess to come to Tacoma, Washington for "A Day with Jess Lair" seminar. The seminar itself was a success but did little to help us develop our

301

business. However the opportunity to rub shoulders with Jess helped us to ingrain some of the ideas that had first attracted us to his book. One of those ideas was the concept of transparency, of learning to be real and open. Jess said that in order to be real and not phony, you need to develop five friends to whom you can tell your secrets, with whom you can learn to be real. This same concept is emphasized in twelve-step programs. It is at least one of the reasons for group meetings and is the particular emphasis of having a sponsor.

After a meeting a few years ago a fellow named Jim walked up to me and said, "got time for a cup of coffee?" I said, "no, I've got stuff to do." Two weeks later he did the same thing and I told him "no" again. Several days later we were both at another meeting and he insisted that we go for coffee and this time I relented.

At coffee Jim proceeded to tell me how his Sponsor, John, had helped him. He told me an interesting story about how John had buttonholed him, and this is what he was doing with me. He said, "John knew that something was bothering me before I realized it myself." He shared with me that over the years, John had confronted him in a similar way on numerous occasions. The way he talked about John was almost spooky. And then Jim opened the big book of A.A. and started showing me different passages. One of those passages was: "we are sure God wants us to be happy, joyous and free." (Page 133) He said, "I know that you have been around quite awhile but I am having trouble seeing happy, joyous and free in you." I was stunned.

At that time I had about ten years of continuous sobriety and later I found out that he had about eight. To make a long story short, Jim told me that he would like to do for me what John had done for him. He said, in effect, "You have stopped enlarging your spiritual life and it is starting to kill you. When you talk at meetings it just tears me up because you are crying out for help." I said, "I don't think so." He then said, "Believe me, it's true."

The next time I saw Jim he said, "John gave me a message for you." Now that was curious! We went to coffee and he told me (that without compromising my anonymity) he had discussed my situation with John. John said, "Rich needs to remember something." In order to do that, John suggested I once again read Emmett Fox's *SERMON*

ON THE MOUNT and *ILLUSIONS* by Richard Bach. He also suggested that each morning I read pages 87-89 in *THE BIG BOOK*. (quoted in part in the last Chapter) I don't exactly know why, but I did just as Jim said and things have not been the same since!

Apparently I had started to rest on my laurels. I had become complacent and was literally "not enlarging my spiritual life." Oh, I was going to a few meetings a week and working with a newcomer now and again, but apparently I wasn't growing. The phrase "not enlarging my spiritual life" was a reference from a story in *THE BIG BOOK*. It tells of a man in the early days of the program who, after some time, went out and got drunk and it concludes the story with the words, "because he failed to enlarge his spiritual life." Jim, (over a period of weeks) helped me to see that I <u>was</u> hurting and that I needed to pick up my set of spiritual tools and get to work. With Jim as my Sponsor, that is exactly what I have been doing, and I thank my Higher Power for sending people like John and Jim into my life. One of the reasons for writing this book is the feeling that I might be able to do for someone else, what Jim did for me and what John did for him.

I am now convinced no one, in or out of the Program, can be "happy, joyous and free" unless they are enlarging their spiritual life. And it is quite possible that most people need a sponsor to help them see the truth that they must confront. I realize that sticking with a spiritual program is not always easy and continued expansion can be trying, but "don't quit before the miracle happens." And in the spirit of "Easy does it, but do it" begin to explore ways of enlarging your spiritual life.

One suggestion made to new comers in Twelve-step programs is not to make any radical changes in the first year. This is good advice because, after a year, a person will usually be in better physical and emotional condition to make sound decisions. One generally gains perspective regarding problems after some time on the program. This advice may also apply to other spiritual programs. The following suggestions are given in the spirit of "Easy Does It!"

If you haven't gone to church for a long time, maybe you should consider giving it another try. If you do not feel that your church points you to that authority deep down within, then maybe, it's time to find a church that talks about the Divinity Within. Consider learning a meditation technique. Marty Mann, the first woman A.A. member and the founder of the Council on Alcoholism started practicing Transcendental Meditation after being in the A.A. Program for more than thirty years. In an audiotape that was being distributed within the Transcendental Meditation movement, Marty Mann not only shared her own positive experience with the technique; she also encouraged others to investigate. She specifically felt that it could be beneficial to people with addictive personalities.

LESSON: If you are in a twelve-step program and you don't have a sponsor - get one! Get one who will pull your sheets (tell it like it is) when that's what you need.

NOTE: Today, ten years after John told Jim, "Rich has something to remember," I can tell you that he was right! I had to remember who I am. I had to remember that "I AM SOMETHING ELSE!" In order to remember who I am I had to become transparent, I had to have someone with whom I could share my secrets.

Chapter 35

I STARTED PLAYING SOUR NOTES

On April 20, 2001 I got out of bed and started playing sour notes. I had a bad day. It certainly wasn't the first and it most likely won't be the last. In the parlance of 12-step programs I had a slip. A slip means falling back into old patterns of thinking and behavior. For an alcoholic it can mean drinking, but it can also mean participating in the kind of thinking and behavior that, if not checked, can ultimately lead to the first drink. These periods of participating in thinking and behaving in an alcoholic manner, but not drinking, are often called "dry drunks" or "emotional benders." It is a period in which the person reverts back to his old personality. He or she reverts back to the mind of a "chronic alcoholic." "Still childish, emotionally sensitive and grandiose" page 123, *TWELVE STEPS AND TWELVE TRADITIONS*. Fortunately my emotional bender did not last long because I was reminded in a meeting of both my condition and the solution.

At the time of this slip I had written, but not found a place for the following articles. They soon came to mind because they include some of the truths that I needed to remember in order to recover from this emotional bender. The first article explores the need to become <u>aware</u> of the nature of our own particular "ego-mind." The second

305

article further explores the nature of the ego-mind and contrasts it with the transformed mind. It also suggests that there is a proper use of the human will in both choosing between these two minds and maintaining a relationship with the higher mind. As you read these let me suggest that the minds of an addict, chronic alcoholic and other problem people differ from more normal people <u>only</u> <u>in</u> <u>degree.</u> A high degree of abnormality is often a blessing because the contrast between the sick condition and true wholeness becomes more obvious. Relative health often permits one the dubious luxury of continued denial.

THE MIND OF—

Like other animals, human beings are born with natural drives and instincts. Unlike the other animals in creation we seem to have developed or have been given more freedom in the use of these drives and instincts. This freedom is usually called self-will and is coupled with our ability to think and to make individual decisions.

It also appears that this freedom is the source of much, if not all, of our problems. We have not, as a specie, become totally responsible. By our own admission we often act irresponsibly. We seemingly have the opportunity to be the master of our own fate, to have control over our drives and instincts. However, we often allow these drives and instincts to become our Master. It seems the freedom of will, that makes decisions possible, acts as a catalyst which increases the power of these drives and instincts. In other words, when we stand back and look at the animal kingdom that appears to be without free will, we see the continuity of natural law without abuse on one hand and without creativity on the other.

If we look at ourselves with some objectivity, we find each of us is an experiment in the use of free will. This experiment is to demonstrate the effective use of drives and instincts in the hands of freedom. Some of us seem to be handicapped from the beginning by heredity, family of origin and environment. If this is an experiment, you may say some have the deck stacked against them while others seem to be privileged. This, of course, is a matter of perspective.

Some people believe we come into this life having pre-set the conditions that will give us the maximum spiritual benefit for this lifetime. They believe we choose our own mothers and fathers and the various trials we will face. This is not an experiment set up to fail, but one that has the potential to strengthen us on our ongoing spiritual path. When we come into this life the pre-planned scenario is forgotten. As we reenter the spirit world, we will be once again reminded of it. When this happens, and if one more time the lesson is not learned, we will probably say something like, "Oh sh—, I did it again!" On the other hand we may be pleased to find out that we passed the test. This idea is often associated with the belief in reincarnation. From my point of view, whether or not we believe in reincarnation is not important.

However, I do believe we must come to an understanding which allows us to "act as if" we participated in setting up our life's plan. This idea of setting up our own test has been extremely valuable to me. It is a construct that makes it clear that I am responsible for my own life. It, in effect, says that I am ultra-responsible for all that happens to me and that I am not a victim. If I play the role of a victim blaming parents, poverty or schools for my present situation, I get what one of my friends calls P.M.S. (Poor Me Syndrome). This syndrome is the very opposite of taking ultra-responsibility. In fact, taking ultra-responsibility for my life has been the cure for the "Poor Me's."

A passage from the *I CHING* says, "Nor must our own passions and shortcomings be glossed over." Ultra-responsibility looks at our passions and shortcomings squarely in the eye and calls a spade a spade. It says, "I claim my passions and shortcomings, they are mine. Somewhere, someplace I have chosen them for my self."

This is precisely the lesson and the meaning of Steps one, four and five in the twelve-step programs. In the twelve-step programs people say things like, "I have the mind of a chronic alcoholic, I have the mind of a compulsive gambler, or I have the mind of a people-pleaser," etc. By the time people grow to the point where they have the awareness of their particular ego-mind and can say, "I have the mind of_____" (chronic alcoholic, hostile individual and so on), they have become aware of the nature and characteristics of such a mind. It is an indication that they have not glossed over their shortcomings; they have embraced them admirably. By the same token, they are admitting a kind of defeat and have surrendered for they know that such a mind cannot save, redeem or transform itself. By this time they know they need help from a higher mind or power. This is the nature of Steps Three, Six and Eleven. (See Appendix IX – Twelve Steps)

Ultra-responsibility demands finding out what kind of ego-mind you have. It means knowing whether you have grown beyond this ego-mind to become consciously aware of another mind, a mind that is not ego - a mind that does have the power to save, redeem and transform. It is a mind that goes by many names but it is not many, it is One. The Apostle Paul said, "Have this mind in you that was in Christ Jesus." The *I CHING* says, "Man has received from heaven a nature that is innately good, to guide him in all his movements." To be ultra-responsible is to accept that the ego-mind is not the mind that can guide us in all of our movements. Being ultra-responsible is ego accepting its limitations; ego turning over its will to a higher will and ego finding a power greater than itself. The following poem reflects Kae's personal work in this area:

You Lead - I'll Follow

When my ego wants to take command
I have to stop and think - too easy to
topple - to reach the brink - to become
self-involved selfishly and then suffer
because - nature doesn't allow the ego
much ground without a painful turn around.

So - just remain innocent and wait for
the call and life evolves from the soul
satisfying and stable and full of surprise
and leads you on paths where you'd
never arrive with the ego in command.

So I try to identify my ego and keep
it in line by repeating with meaning
addressed to my soul, "You lead -
I'll follow," and then I feel wholesomely whole.

If this life is in any way a self-prescribed test as was suggested, then the test is exactly this—to find out the nature of our particular ego-mind, its character and limitations.   Once that is done, the acknowledgment of the need for a higher power comes quite naturally and as it says in the New Testament, "He who seeks shall find." Our drives and instincts then take their rightful place and the test is passed.

On the day to day practical level accepting our lives as though they were pre-planned, living in the context of ultra-responsibility becomes puzzle solving. We literally become more in control of our life by having the scales of ignorance lifted from our eyes, enabling us to see with increasing clarity the meaning of our life's drama.   To ignore our ultra-responsibility is to be like the child who comes home from school without his homework assignment and lacking that, the child cannot work the problem, let alone find the solution.

PROPER USE OF THE WILL

In this book references are made to various men and women who throughout history have at least one thing in common; they have attempted to raise the level of consciousness in themselves and in their fellow man. Now, I suspect the motives of these individuals varied and I know the means by which they tried to effect this consciousness-raising varied as well.

You need only mention the dialectical methods of Socrates and Plato, the poetry of Blake, the preaching of Jesus, the fasting of Gandhi, the prose of Tolstoy, the oratory of Martin Luther King and the personal demonstration of Buckminister Fuller to point out a variety of methods. To arrive at their various goals and motivation is a bit tougher. For some, it appears they just wanted to get people thinking; others were more interested in motivating people to action and still others may have been more interested in motivating people

309

into action resulting in some sort of spiritual peace. Whatever the motivation, all wanted to raise the awareness, to bring more light, more knowledge and more truth into the world. The underlying motive, I believe, in each case was to encourage some insight, some knowledge, and some vision, and that, if shared and accepted, would make the world a better place. In many instances the people mentioned in our book were concerned about the world they lived in and they were concerned because, more than anything else, they felt that most citizens of this world were selling themselves short. Like the prodigal son mentioned in the New Testament, they felt that the citizens of this world had been settling for pig slop when they could be eating the fatted calf. To use another Biblical simile, they also felt that like Esau, most people in society had forfeited their true birthright for a bowl of porridge.

Once again, just what the fatted calf or birthright might symbolize is different for different people. In some cases it means more stuff and in others, it means more freedom, it means more hope and it means more love; but in almost every case it is a yearning for more dignity. (Definition of dignity - elevation of character; intrinsic worth; excellence.) Note: Both Biblical stories referred to above have to do with one's birthright.

I am not a scholar in the area of comparative religions but it seems to me the story of redemption in religion, is almost always the story of restoring or reclaiming ones birthright. To experience the atonement is to experience the restoration of one's right to be called a Son or Daughter of God, to have ones character elevated, to realize ones intrinsic worth, to experience excellence and to be restored to dignity. That is the story of redemption. But, it does not stop there because redemption does not mean we experience superior humanity, it means we experience our divinity, and we no longer have to search for the qualities of God because we realize these qualities within our very own nature – THE IMAGO DEI. These qualities include love, peace, serenity, oneness and timelessness.

Once we experience redemption, we become aware that we had sold out - that we had relinquished our birthright. We now know we had settled for porridge and pig slop when all the time we were meant to be partaking of the fatted calf. We have experienced the contrast.

Now we know the difference between being a child of the world and a child of God. We know the difference because we are now "a new creation." 2 Cor: 5:17

The Apostle Paul, in the context of the above-mentioned passage, says because we are a new creation, because we have a new awareness, a new consciousness, we should "no longer" look at ourselves or anyone else from a human point of view. That sounds like radical stuff! If we aren't to look at ourselves from a human point of view, what point of view are we to look from?

Before we answer the question lets look at another interesting point in this particular message from the Apostle Paul. We have previously talked about the importance of making a choice when it comes to spiritual growth. It appears that this is just what Paul had done; he had made a significant decision, a choice. He said in the past he had looked at people from a human point of view, he said he even looked at Christ from this perspective. One gets the feeling that Paul for a time found himself being pulled back and forth, looking at things from a human point of view and also from his new vantage-point as a new creation. But, he says "no longer," no longer will he be pulled to and fro. He had become aware that a choice between these two must be made and he was ready and willing to make this decision. He said, "**From now on!**" he was only going to look at life from this new perspective.

In the Big Book, *ALCOHOLICS ANONYMOUS,* page 85, Bill Wilson (the co-founder of AA) writes about the proper use of the human will. The implication is that the only proper use of our will is to align it with the will of God. It appears to me that Paul is determined to do just that. He has grown weary of his own lack of resolve. He has decided to be a victim no longer. He has made the decision to claim his "birthright" once and for all.*

---

* We don't know exactly when this was written but we do know it was not early in his ministry. He had already visited Corinth in person. He then went to Asia where he apparently wrote the first letter to Corinth. At the end of that letter he says he will visit them again after he passes through Macedonia. Now, as he begins this second letter he lets them know that he went through hell while he was in Asia and explains to them why he did not stop in Corinth and spend the winter with them. He obviously had been

Personally, I feel I have gone through a similar transformation and I have watched hundreds of my fellows, both men and women, young and old, go through it. One of the situations that makes this transformation so difficult is the one I just described, the one that Paul evidently went through. The process of making a definitive decision to look at life from just one perspective, through *A NEW PAIR OF GLASSES*** and through those glasses alone.

While one may not agree with everything Tolstoy says in his book, *THE KINGDOM OF GOD IS WITHIN YOU,* I do not think one can easily disagree with the point, that if you discover the truth within, you should not ignore it and you should commit yourself to it completely. You should no longer listen to the old voices but listen to the voice within. You should no longer act in accordance to the voices of human institutions, but in accordance with the voice of integrity, the voice of the Kingdom.

The *COURSE IN MIRACLES* tells us that as we live our life we have only one choice, the choice between fear and love and it encourages us to "see only love." Other ways of saying "see only love" is to say "see only unity, see only oneness, see only peace, see only God." The more I get to know the voice within, the Kingdom within, the clearer it becomes. It is not a human voice or a human perspective. Contact with this Kingdom presents me with a choice.

---

through a lot. He says that at one point while in Asia, he "despaired of life itself." In the chapter preceding this statement Paul is much more positive. He says, "We are afflicted in every way, but not crushed, perplexed but not driven to despair, persecuted but not forsaken, struck down but not destroyed." II Cor: 4 Vs 8,9

This (and other verses) tells me that Paul is saying he has been through a lot, that he has learned a lot and that he has grown a lot. He also says life in the last few years has taught him a whole bunch, and one thing stands out and that one thing is to quit looking at life from a "human point of view." The implication is that when you look at the world from a human point of view you can easily become a victim and "despair of life itself." However, when one looks at life from the higher mind, you may be "crushed and perplexed but not driven to despair."

**A book written by Chuck Chamberlain a beloved departed member of the A.A. fellowship

This choice is between a life filled with old ideas, old illusions, old impressions, dependency on human institutions, and my old habits versus a life that is freed from all of this by seeing only love. This is not the way of man; this is the way of the Divine. This is not life seen from a human point of view, but life seen from a higher consciousness. This is life viewed from the "Kingdom within."

I have not reached any kind of perfection in my relationship to this consciousness. I am not sure I know anybody who has, but I have tasted enough perfection to know the commitment to it pays an unbelievable dividend. (Unbelievable only from the human point of view, not unbelievable from the new perspective.)

Let's look once again at Kae's poem, which expresses her motivation to continually pursue this greater consciousness, and her desire to use her will in the proper way and toward the proper goal.

YOU LEAD - I'LL FOLLOW

When my ego wants to take command
I have to stop and think - too easy to
topple - to reach the brink - to become
self-involved selfishly and then suffer
because - nature doesn't allow the ego
much ground without a painful turn around.

So - just remain innocent and wait for
the call and life evolves from the soul
satisfying and stable and full of surprise
and leads you on paths where you'd
never arrive with the ego in command.

So I try to identify my ego and keep
it in line by repeating with meaning
addressed to my soul, "You lead -
I'll follow," and then I feel wholesomely whole.

313

At this point, let's review what man knows about this consciousness. What did Paul mean when he said he was no longer going to see from a human point of view? In chapter 14, "What Is A Meta For?" we wrote in some detail about our two operating systems. In Romans, Chapter 8 verses 14 and 15, Paul gives us a brief but apt description of the two systems. He says, "For all who are led by the spirit of God are sons of God. For you did not receive a spirit of slavery leading to fear again, but you received a spirit of adoption as sons." Once again we see a reference to birthright, restoration and the idea that we are not so much sons of earth but children of a Higher Realm.

Another reason for selecting this passage is that Paul used two words that I believe capture the essence of the human and/or ego-system. Those two words are slavery and fear. "You did not receive the spirit of slavery to fall back into fear." The ego system is a fear-based system that perpetuates our slavery. Once again I refer you to Tolstoy's *THE KINGDOM OF GOD IS WITHIN YOU* using the Russian Church and its Czarist government (both of which claimed to be Christian), to illustrate how far short they had fallen from their supposed intentions. Tolstoy shows in graphic terms how the institutions of government and the church ignored what he felt to be a pivotal aspect of Jesus' teaching, "non-resistance of evil by force." Because that teaching had been ignored, all (in Russia) ended up living in fear and both consciously and unconsciously subservient to an inhuman and unjust system. As we know this condition became so intolerable that it resulted in the peasant revolt of 1917.

Although technology has changed life a great deal in the past one hundred years, much of what Tolstoy described exists today, even in our own country. To illustrate: In a recent twelve-step meeting, which I regularly attend, the topic was fear. A young mother expressed fear that her children were going to be taken from her. A military man stationed at the nearby Air Force Base expressed fear that he was going to be shipped to the Near East. A black man expressed his fear concerning police harassment. A businessman, who was having financial problems, told how he was afraid the IRS was going to force him into bankruptcy. A woman was being sued because her dog was annoying the neighbors. She was afraid because she felt that she was going to lose her dog or maybe something worse. Two people shared acronyms for F.E.A.R. while letting the others know how they identified with them. The acronyms were; False Evidence Appearing Real and F__k Everything And Run. One young woman told about how paralyzed she became when fear took over and another explained how, when overcome with fear, she would start to isolate and avoid people as well as her responsibilities.

There are two sides to this situation. One is the institutionalized use of force, harassment, imprisonment, even torture and death to create fear in us and to make us obedient (slaves). Tolstoy says all of these are contrary to Christ's admonition to "resist not evil" and "to turn the other check." The other side to this situation is that people are getting the government they want and deserve. They are, for the most part, ego-oriented, self-centered, fear-based people who have participated in the development of these institutions either by passive cooperation or action. They have helped develop these institutions to grow, partly in order to help them get what they want or to protect what they already have. That is the crux of fear. FEAR AT ITS BASE IS THE FEAR OF NOT GETTING WHAT WE WANT OR OF LOSING WHAT WE ALREADY HAVE.

Should we in the United States be surprised that a great amount of fear pervades our society and violence is one of its results? I think not. If we look back at our history we will see that the very foundation of our country was built on two pillars. The first pillar consisted of high ideals of justice, equality and freedom. We see this demonstrated by those pilgrims who landed at Plymouth, Massachusetts; the religious colony led by Roger Williams in Rhode Island, the Quakers in Pennsylvania and New York and in the statement we call The Declaration of Independence. The second pillar was force, violence, separation, discrimination and abuse. This is noted by the fact of slavery and the discrimination apparent in the Indian Wars and the once popular cry, "that the only good Indian is a dead Indian" and the pattern of war that continues in our history.

These two pillars have been a part of our history and exist to this day. They are pervasive in the institution of our society and even the church. Few would contest that the church has and teaches high ideals but what about the practice of these ideals? We have noted previously that Christian Churches have used intimidation and force, even death to make people comply with its beliefs.

You may feel that the Crusades and the Inquisition are ancient history. You may also recognize some of these practices today in other forms and other places. Two instances, in which I was personally involved, serve to illustrate the existence of this dichotomy even in the church of today. Both incidents happened in the 1960s when I was a Lutheran clergyman and when civil rights were at the forefront of our Nation's business. The first: One Sunday, while studying in Chicago, I was asked to fill in as Pastor at a congregation near the University of Chicago. This area was going through transition and already quite a few black people lived in the neighborhood. When I went to the church prior to the service a gentleman who was obviously one of the pillars of the congregation met me. In the course of our conversation, I asked him how the church was responding to the change in the neighborhood. "Oh," he said, "we haven't had a bit of a problem yet. As you probably know, this church has a German background and although we haven't had German speaking services for years, some of our members still speak German. So our Pastor told us when 'those' (Black) people come to one of our services, just greet them in German and hand them a German hymn book and they won't want to come in." He added, "So far it has worked real good."

The second incident happened in a church that I was serving in South Dakota. Again, a pillar of the church (my own congregation) in a discussion about civil rights, told me in all sincerity that he believed that if we established reservations for the Negro just as we had for the Indians -the problem would be solved. I can hear some saying, "These are old examples, things have changed since then." I hope so. However, this morning's newspaper (Friday, August 31, 2001) included two front-page articles on racism, one local and one international. The headline of the local article reads, "College official resigns in wake of racial slur." At one point this man served as President of the College. The subtitle of the other article says, referring to a conference on racism, "On eve of gathering, U.N. conference is threatening to dissolve into acrimony."

We could add to the list above, the mind of a racist, the mind of a bigot, the mind of the spiritual self-righteous and so on. Each of us, if honest, could find a way to characterize our ego-mind. Such a characterization can be helpful because as my Sponsor tells me, "You don't have a problem until you are aware of the problem."

Towards the end of the twelve-step meeting mentioned above some other ideas came to the fore. One young man with a couple of years of good recovery shared that, early on, his Sponsor said "forget those other acronyms of FEAR and stick to Face Everything And Recover." (Sounds like the lesson of the buffalo; face into the storm.) He and others began to share some of what that means. Here is the essence of what was said:

"When I first came here I didn't really understand when you said 'just live one day at a time.' But I am beginning to understand, because I am developing a sense of now, and strangely enough it doesn't seem to have anything to do with time. I think that it must be one of those qualities of God that some of you have mentioned.*"

"I also have found this power within myself. I found it through the process of uncovering, discovering and discarding. I find that prayer and meditation and self-honesty are indispensable in this process."

"Through this program I am finding a faith and a love which is enabling me to overcome my fears."

"Our institutions may be screwed up but at this point, I can't worry about reforming institutions. I have to save my own ass."

"I have found that fear knocks at the door and faith answers and that faith knocks at the door and love answers."

---

* *A COURSE IN MIRACLES* says" the closest thing in this life to eternity is now"

"Through a conscious contact with a Higher Power which I have found deep down within my own being, I no longer live in fear most of the time."

"As others of you have mentioned, I too have a conscious contact with a higher power and as this grows, I find that I am in possession of the qualities of God, qualities that have already been mentioned in this meeting, qualities like love and peace and life. I mention life because I am living a life I never before imagined possible."

Several newer members mentioned how difficult it was to believe in a loving God after being brought up in homes or educated in parochial schools or in churches where God was used as a threat in the face of bad behavior. They said it was difficult to erase the childhood memories of Nuns, preachers and parents who told them of a God who was going to punish them if they were not good.

These are some conclusions that I have drawn from the above meeting and thousands like it.

1. There is a definite difference between the message of society and the message of twelve-step programs.

2. That difference is one of the major reasons why people need to go to the meetings often and continue for a lifetime. I know one participant who says each time he talks, "I have come today to be reminded of what I have forgotten since my last meeting." It is easy to forget because most of society including the church, TV, movies, magazines, neighbors, Government and schools are giving us a different message. For example: Force, anger and violence must be met with force, anger and violence in order to control or suppress it. The need to control or suppress is an outgrowth of fear.

3. That, if the churches are teaching a message of a loving God who can be found deep down in the midst our own being, it is a message that is not getting through to an awful lot of people.

4. That fear-based living is the human point of view of which Paul speaks and Love-based living is the new consciousness to which he points. He calls this new Love-based consciousness "Christ" consciousness. In Gal 2, verse 20 he says, "It is no longer I who lives but Christ who lives in me." Through this new consciousness he no

longer needed to look at things from a human point of view. He no longer needed to see himself as a slave to anyone or anything or to fear anyone or anything. With this new God Consciousness he could be in the world but not of it.

5.   That which Paul called Christ is a very real Higher Consciousness, but I believe it can and has been referred to by other names. As an example, Mahatma Gandhi became the prime example of the kind of Christianity Tolstoy talked about, and yet Gandhi never became a Christian. He assimilated this Higher Consciousness into his own faith.

As we noted above, the term "Christ consciousness" might well be an appropriate description for this kind of higher consciousness from which Paul was determined to see life. Others, as you might have imagined, have suggested "Buddha Consciousness" God Consciousness and Cosmic Consciousness which all refer to the same fear-free, freedom-based spiritual awareness. This is an Awareness that virtually everyone can experience with greater clarity simply by choosing to use their human will, to align themselves with this Higher Reality or Higher Will.

LESSON: A spiritual transformation changes our life, both its context and its perspective.

> "When you are full of your SELF
> the true essence of being,
> then all is true bliss
> and time has no meaning."
> By Kae

Chapter 36

THE SWORD OF DAMOCLES
Or Pain can be your Friend

In the twelve-step programs there is a saying: "This program is not for those who need it but for those who want it." It goes back to another old saying: "You can lead a horse to water but you can't make him drink." I suppose, when a horse gets thirsty enough he will eventually drink. Likewise, when we see that the pain in our life is of our own doing, we may see the need for another way. In Chapter 21 we referenced the story of the Prodigal Son. We saw the Prodigal Son become willing through pain to accept another way. The pain of his sojourn brought him to his knees. In this way, pain is our friend.

There is a spiritual axiom (truth) that says: "If we are disturbed, no matter what the cause, there is something wrong with us." This takes us back to the idea of ultra-responsibility. If we choose to ignore our responsibility, we can also ignore the spiritual axiom. On the other hand, if we choose to be responsible, we have to face the spiritual axiom head on. If we are disturbed, if we are experiencing psychic pain, then there is something wrong with us. A person living in a home where there is an alcoholic or addict can be tricked into thinking the problem is the other person. "If only they didn't drink or use, I would be all right." Don't fall for this, it is just another trick of the ego! Many in this predicament have found in Al-Anon (the organization that helps the families of alcoholics) the same recovery that their sick family member has found in another twelve-step program. Your pain is also your friend if you will just look at yourself rather than the other person.

Simply put, this means pain is a sign that we should transfer from one operating system to another. Sooner or later, operating on the ego-system will cause us pain and lots of it. When we reach this point, we have a choice, to delay switching over to the other system or to cover up the pain. Covering up the pain, as we have already indicated, usually means **more** - more alcohol, more work, more food, more drugs, more sex, more golf, more church activity, more feeling sorry for ourselves, or more feeling like a martyr. If a person is lucky this pattern will go bankrupt before it kills her or him. Going bankrupt means the pain of continuing the cover-up is worse then the pain we are covering up. When people realize this, "they will come to their senses" and decide to do something about the true cause of the pain rather than continue the cover up. This often means getting into counseling, treatment, a twelve-step program or another spiritual program (which includes meditation) that leads us to our TRUE ESSENCE.

If you are truly addicted or obsessed with your idol (whatever it may be) my recommendation is a twelve-step program because over the long haul, that is where you are going to end up anyway. Treatment can be effective, but it is costly and the benefits are often short-term. The kinds of problems we have mentioned demand, in most cases, a long-term support system. This is what twelve-step programs provide. Besides, you already have the most important ingredient needed to be successful in a twelve-step program; you have pain! If you can get that idea through your head, you are well on your way to recovery and a new life. Many come into a twelve-step program saying, "I am just sick and tired of being sick and tired."

You may ask, "What is recovery?" In a discussion about working the twelve steps in *The Big Book, ALCOHOLICS ANONYMOUS* it says, "If we are painstaking about this phase of our development, we will be amazed before we are halfway through. We are going to know a new freedom and a new happiness. We will not regret the

322

past nor wish to shut the door on it. We will comprehend serenity and will know peace."

These are the promises that can be realized by anyone who will acknowledge their pain, claim it as their own and forget about blaming others. Using our pain does not mean suffering for suffering's sake or being a martyr. It means recognizing that psychic pain is always a sign of resisting the call of our TRUE SELF. Our TRUE SELF wants to come forth and our ego is resisting and that results in an internal battle. The result of this internal battle is conflict and pain. The twelve steps are designed to help one put his/her will on the side of the TRUE SELF and thus to win the battle. As many twelve steppers put it, "Let go and let God." As Kae says when she experiences a disturbance, "You lead, I'll follow." This is the proper use of our will!

It is common among twelve steppers to refer to the word ego, as an acronym - ease God out. Based on my experience, this is not a totally accurate characterization of the ego. Easing God out may be one of the ways in which the ego appears to work, but the ego has at its disposal all the tools once attributed to the devil. The devil, in much of medieval literature, is shown to be a fierce combatant, wily to be sure, but fierce in his attempt to keep God out (not ease God out); to keep God from obtaining even a foothold in the soul of man. The devil knows that even a foothold spells his eventual doom.

In the little classic *SCREW TAPE LETTERS*, C.S. Lewis has Screwtape, a figure high in the devil's hierarchy, writing to one field agent, Wormwood, concerning his "patient." At first, Screwtape councils Wormwood on the procedures helpful in keeping the patient from any real contact with the enemy (God); then however, when the patient becomes a Christian, Screwtape is disappointed, but by no means does he feel that the battle is lost. He councils Wormwood "there is no need to despair, hundreds of these adult converts have been reclaimed after a brief sojourn in the Enemy's camp and are now with us. All the habits of the patient, both mental and bodily are still in our favor." The remainder of the letters center much of their council on just how to take best advantage of these mental and bodily habits. The following are all quotes from Screwtape's letters to Wormwood.

"One of our greatest allies is the church itself."

"There is nothing like suspense and anxiety for barricading a human's mind against the enemy."

"I do not think you will have much difficulty in keeping the patient in the dark."

"Once you have made the World an end and faith a means you have almost won your man, and it makes very little difference what kind of worldly end he is pursuing."

"Fun is closely related to Joy - It can sometimes be used, of course, to divert humans from something else which the Enemy would like them to be feeling or doing."

My own story seems to give credence to the idea that the ego (devil, if you prefer) doesn't mind at all if we talk about God, worship God, believe in God or even preach God as long as you don't discover God. Now, the ego knows that the TRUE SELF (God) is found deep down inside. So, all the ego has to do is keep us from looking there. The ego's game is purely one of deception and distraction.

Idols, which are frequently mentioned in the Old Testament, are in essence everything that is not God and that's what the ego uses to distract us with, everything! The ego uses everything to distract us - money, pleasure, fame, sex, religion, people, places and things. The ego uses all of these to answer the call of our discontent. Some lines from one of Kae's poems expresses this thought:

I am looking for my SELF
Peering out and searching wide
My ego joins the exterior search
Teeming with egotistical pride.
What clatter and chatter the ego can make
While the outside route urging me to take.

324

I believe that discontent is the one word that best describes most of us. I believe it was discontent that Thoreau was talking about when he said, "Most men lead lives of quiet desperation." Now the truth is there is only one reason we are discontent and that is our egos have sold us a bill of goods. Our egos have sold us on a phony world. To some degree, each of us realizes this, but what do we do about it? It's the only world we know.

Some say, "Is that all there is?" Others say, "Stop the world, I want to get off." My experience tells me that with the ego as my leader, it is my captor and only by putting the ego in its proper place can I be set free. When the false is abandoned, the real will be apparent. Only when I step from darkness can I see the light. When I find myself asking "is that all there is," when I get to the point that I am sick of the world and I want to get off, I find that I can because I begin to see the world I'm sick of is one of my own making.

When you realize it is a world of your own making, you can stop and you can get off. When you're sick and tired of being sick and tired, you can stop being sick and tired. It may take some time to get the job done but once you are on the path you will begin to see the light at the end of the tunnel. Now, sometimes you might feel that the light at the end of the tunnel is an oncoming train. This feeling can also assist you in your journey. I call that oncoming train feeling "The sword of Damocles." Much of the time today I live with a sense of peace and well being. At times however, I find that sense of well being overshadowed by an anxiety, a feeling of impending doom. It is this feeling that I started calling the sword of Damocles. I have shared this with Kae and my closest friends. On occasion, they will notice that I am distracted or out of sorts. When asked if I'm o k, I will just say, "Oh you know, the sword of Damocles." When I first started using this term it just referred to what at earlier times, I called "that damnable feeling." Recently, I got an insight into this that was a surprise. I went back and reviewed the story of Damocles.

. I knew that the story was from Greek Mythology and that Damocles was forced to sit under a sword held up by a single hair. What I didn't remember was why? That was the surprise. It was done in order to teach him the perils of leadership and it has become a term synonymous with the feeling of impending doom.

It didn't take me long to put two and two together. I experience this damnable feeling of impending doom when my ego has taken over the lead one more time. Today I recognize the sword of Damocles as my friend and I do whatever is needed to get back in touch with the Now and my TRUE SELF and get out from under the sword that is held only by a hair. Today I know that this pain, this damnable feeling, the sword of Damocles is my friend.

Finally, if a discipline like meditation and other techniques that lead to SELF-discovery are as important as we have implied, then truly, pain is our friend. Pain is our friend that reminds us to return to our program for SELF-discovery. This is nature's way! When our gums get sore we start flossing again. When we get overweight and can't get around without getting out of breath, we cut down on our eating. If we are filled with dis-ease, fear, dread, anger and anxiety we are reminded that nature wants us to be whole. Nature wants us to come AWAKE. Discipline is the key to our recovery and listening to nature (pain) is often the key to our discipline.

LESSON: Psychic pain can be the ally that helps motivate us to accept the discipline necessary to move us beyond the ogre at the gate. (The discipline is whatever it takes for you as an individual. However, we think it should always include some form of meditation.)

SUMMARY

PRACTICAL SPIRITUALITY

Each chapter in this section ended with a short lesson. Many of these lessons had something to do with surrender or a means to surrender. Surrender to what? The answer is, "Surrender to the mystery." Several times we have used the quote from Dr. Albert Einstein, "There is a mystery about it all." Practical spirituality is about acknowledging the mystery. Acknowledging the mystery in one way keeps us right-sized (humble). It also helps us to see that we are not isolated individuals but are a part of the whole. We are a part of something wonderfully mysterious! This mystery manifests itself in the tiniest cell of our body as well as the most distant galaxy in the universe billions of light years away. This takes us back to the concept of DEEP ECOLOGY mentioned in the Introduction.

It is good for us to remember that our minds by nature try to make sense out of all this and to solve the mystery. This attempt is not spiritual and it is not practical. Only by staying in touch with the mystery can we experience the practical nature of what we call spirituality. Living out of touch with the mystery, pretending we have solved the mystery, is not reality. Our minds are finite and in the final analysis there is no way that we can grasp the infinite. It is just too much for us! Albert Einstein understood this. If he could yield to this reality, so can we.

This does not mean that we shouldn't pursue science and understanding, but as we do, we should have a sense of humor about it. When and if we develop this sense of humor, we don't take ourselves so seriously. We don't give sway to the little general (ego). It is only with a sense of humility that we can recognize that this mystery is not just something out-there, but rather something of which we are a part. The mystery is with us, in us, and beyond us. In the mystery we live and move and have our being. When we see this we will recognize theology, religious creeds and words like "God" are humankind's attempt to grasp and understand the mystery in a way not dissimilar to science and its attempt to understand the unknown.

What then is the answer? The answer is "embrace the mystery." Yes, we must not only embrace it; we must surrender to it. This is the meaning of "let go, and let God". This is the meaning of the phrase in Twelve-step groups; "We are powerless." It is in embracing the mystery that we learn the importance of meditation because it is through meditation that we get in touch with the mystery. And when we do this, we find that the mystery, the unknown, is not hostile but friendly. The mystery is a force for good in the universe. When we meditate we find that the mystery has our interest at its core.

Most of us who meditate on a regular basis over a period of time learn the lesson of those who have meditated before us. We learn the lesson of the perennial philosophy - the mystery is friendly, the mystery is LOVE. This is practical because getting in touch with the mystery has carryover. It carries over to our relationship with the Planet. It carries over to our relationships with those who inhabit the Planet. It carries over in our daily activities.

In the final analysis the question for you boils down to this: Do you want to be directed by the mystery, which is friendly and has your interest at heart, or by the world around you and your finite monkey-mind?

Note: The Appendix contains a wealth of information including web-sites that can help you find meditation centers, twelve-step groups and other Spiritual resources. We have also listed WEBSITES relating to

many of the people mentioned in this book. For your convenience the
first page of the Appendix is a table of contents.

A VISION

SECTION V

Chapter 37

A VISION FOR THE FUTURE

Institutions Working Together to Support the Symphony

Even though I have been critical of the institutional church, I know that for many, church membership is a positive experience. I do not want to minimize this experience nor do I want to detract from the positive contribution that institutional religion has had and continues to have on society. I am critical because I believe that the church must learn from its history and do better. In the portion of the Big Book, *ALCOHOLICS ANONYMOUS* (previously quoted in the chapter "How Do You Start Your Day,") it says:

"If we belong to a religious denomination which requires a definite morning devotion, we attend to that also. If not members of religious bodies, we sometimes select and memorize a few set prayers that emphasize the principles we have been discussing. There are many helpful books also. Suggestions about these may be obtained from one's priest, minister, or rabbi. Be quick to see where religious people are right. Make use of what they offer."

I believe that the twelve-step programs are a present day manifestation of the "perennial philosophy," and therefore are indebted to many individuals that have been involved in religion institutions. In addition, it is a well-known fact that the founders of A.A. were greatly aided by a number of clergymen in the development of the program in its infancy. However, in the years that have followed, the relationship between religious institutions and the twelve-step programs at best present a mixed picture.

While many churches, temples and synagogues support and even rent their facilities to twelve-step programs, others resist the movement and a few are defiant. I must add quickly that many in twelve-step programs have returned to their churches, temples and synagogues and found new meaning and purpose in their worship. However, this too has, in some cases, had a negative side. Some who have returned to their religious institution have been weaned away, both actively and passively, from their twelve-step programs with tragic consequences.

Note to Clergy: If your conscience and convictions will allow you to do so, encourage members in recovery to remain active in their recovery programs as well as your religious activities. The following stories attempt to point out an area in which, I believe, both the churches and the twelve-step programs experience some weakness. It is also an area in which the churches may be of maximum benefit to recovering people as well as the general public.

I WAS GIVEN A CHOICE

After practicing Transcendental Meditation for about five and one-half years, I frequently started to experience a sense of the ABSOLUTE in the midst of my everyday life. In other words, I experienced the transcendent apart from meditation itself. These five and one-half years are best characterized by the word vicissitudes. For it was a period of continuous change, up and down mood swings and alternating conditions. My life either seemed to be going very smoothly or very badly. My psychological existence resembled being attached to a pogo stick. The contrast seemed, at times, to be almost unbelievable. This period of my life was covered in some detail in the Chapter entitled "The Road of Trials."

At one point I consulted a Psychiatrist and was prescribed Lithium, a natural salt-type drug that has been successfully used by many people suffering from manic-depression. I was told that I was not manic-depressive but seemed to be having some manic-depressive-like symptoms. Twice before in previous years, I had sought out counseling for what seemed to be a marriage problem. My marriage often seemed to be the focal point of both the good periods as well as the bad. Kae and I marveled many times at what a good relationship we had and how terrific it was that two people could find such happiness together. At the same time we were absolutely confounded when, in spite of our obvious love for each other, everything seemed to fall apart.

Another area of frustration for both Kae and me had been the vocational one. In the eight years away from the ministry I had thirteen different employers. Out of those thirteen, six either went bankrupt or ceased business in the State of Washington. Twice I had to quit work because of a back problem and on five occasions I had tried selling insurance, real estate and investments and, in spite of what appeared to be some aptitude for sales, I was not able to make a living as a salesman.

Besides the medical problems already mentioned, at times I had very little energy and suffered frequently from abdominal and back pain. On two different occasions I had cancerous growths removed from my eyelids. In those times when everything seemed to be going smoothly it did not mean that problems were nonexistent. On the contrary, as I look back on it now, it just seems that there were periods when I was living above the problems (thanks to my twelve-step programs and meditation) and periods when I was not.

With this brief background let me tell you about a curious incident that happened in April, 1979. I was three months into a new job selling investments. I started out fairly strong but my back, injured the previous year while managing a donut shop, started rebelling because of the large amount of time I spent driving the car. It seemed likely that my back might require surgery. The second growth on my eyelid was just diagnosed as cancer and my relationship with Kae seemed to be strained.

I found myself in a mood of resignation, not despair or even depression, but resigned. In this mood, I went to a businessman, a born again Christian who belonged to the church I was attending and told him my story. I went to him because I had this recurring feeling that maybe he could help.

Larry listened to my story attentively. When I was through he told me that I was indeed fortunate, because he and another born-again Christian, along with a local Clergyman were going out to pray for a sick lady. He then added, if I liked they would come back by his office and pray for me. He informed me that they had been doing this quite a lot recently and that they had witnessed some miraculous healings but certainly not in every instance. I told him I was entirely ready for God to do anything He could for me, that I had lost all confidence in being able to get the job done by myself. I also indicated that I believed in God, prayed often but recently hadn't seen any significant results from my prayers.

At any rate, we made a date to meet again in his office later in the afternoon. The date was kept and the young Clergyman proceeded to lead the meeting. I repeated my story to him and included a run down of my alcoholism, divorce, resignation from the ministry, etc. He then explained to me about the anointing of and the gifts of the Holy Spirit. Among these gifts, he talked about the gift of tongues. He felt I should seek these.

I told him I was quite willing to have any and every gift that God wanted me to have. I also told him that I daily sought God's will and the power to carry that out. He said he was glad to hear that and that they would pray right there for my healing and for the anointing of the Holy Spirit. He then said, "before I do this let me make sure you don't belong to any sects or practice anything which might be contrary to the work of Christ." He cited several organizations including Transcendental Meditation. I responded by telling him that I did practice Transcendental Meditation and that I found it to be beneficial in my recovery from alcoholism and asthma. He said that I must quit the practice and renounce it before he could continue with their desire to pray for God's anointing on my behalf.

336

At this point I told the three of them that I could not do that because, besides the other benefits I had mentioned, meditation played a significant role in restoring me to a conscious relationship with the Christ and that I was closer to Him now than ever before. As I said this, my heart seemed to gently, but firmly, jump up and down in my chest. I didn't let on that anything had happened and I wasn't sure at the time that I should put any significance on it. But I did seem to be assured that for now I had said the right thing. However, I told them I would start praying about this matter.

During the next three days I spent considerable time in prayer, Bible readings and contemplation. On the third day I decided I would go to a TM residence course before I made any decision to quit the practice of TM. The residence course was about ten days away but each day seemed to get brighter and brighter as the time for the course approached.

The course itself was beautiful. These courses combine extra meditation time with tapes by Maharishi Mahesh Yogi, which help to better understand the value of the T.M. technique. One tape showed Maharishi responding to a questioner, telling him how beautiful it was that people followed Jesus. I talked with other Christians attending the course and they felt that their practice of TM had deepened their appreciation for Jesus and his message.

Not long after the course, I read a newspaper article by Rabbi Levine, a very well known and respected Rabbi in Seattle. The Rabbi made it clear that TM had been very beneficial to his spiritual life but in no way could he see that TM was in itself religious. I knew that Maharishi was neither a Jew nor a Christian but indeed, a religious man. I concluded that TM is neutral in regard to religion but the practice of TM, over a period of time, refines the nervous system and opens up areas of the mind and heart that allows for a greater appreciation of spiritual dimensions. As I have said before, it enables one to have eyes that see and ears that hear, a condition that Jesus pleaded for. I was forced to make a choice. Today I know, led by the inner MYSTERY, that we have been talking about, I chose LOVE rather than "tongues."

"If I speak in the tongues of men and of angels, but have not love, I am a noisy gong or a clanging cymbal. And if I have prophetic powers, and understand all mysteries and all knowledge, and if I have all faith, so as to remove mountains, but have not love, I am nothing. If I give away all I have, and if I deliver my body to be burned, but have not love, I gain nothing." (I Corinthians 13, 1-3)

ANTHONY DE MELLO S.J.

One book I find very inspirational and have on my "recommend you read" list is *AWARENESS* by Anthony de Mello, an Indian-born Jesuit Priest. de Mello was a popular author of spiritual materials and for eighteen years was widely known for his retreats and workshops, which he delivered in both English and Spanish before his untimely death in 1987. A Spirituality Center at Fordham University was established in his name.

The emphasis of the book is on meditation and becoming aware of one's TRUE SELF. The following is a quote taken from the de Mello Spirituality Center Web Site.

> *"AWARENESS* - Often recommended as the first book
> to read in order to appreciate de Mello. The book is a
> verbatim record of a four day conference given by Tony
> de Mello the year prior to his death. Letters have been
> written, telephone calls have been made from all over the
> world attesting to the power this book had on the life of
> one reading it. A typical comment, "I have read this book
> fifteen times. My mind is still blown. Every time I read
> it, I discover something new that applies to my life."

In my own search for Centers that I could recommend to people to learn techniques practiced within their own religious preference, I hoped to be able to recommend the de Mello Center to Roman Catholics. This hope was dashed when I read this headline to a short article. "Vatican condemns work of Jesuit author." (See Appendix VII– DE MELLO for the entire article) In spite of this news, I continue to feel that Anthony de Mello is a symbol of the kind of

338

church needed as we begin this new Millennium. The following in part describes such a Church.

****

I believe the preceding examples reveal an aspect of religious institutions at the beginning of a new Copernican revolution. As we discussed earlier, when science started to find evidence that the earth was not even the center of the solar system, let alone the center of the universe, religious institutions dug in their heels and called it blasphemy. The institutional authorities did all they could to silence these pagans and heretics and scuttle their message.

As we enter this new millennium we are on the doorstep of a new discovery and a new revolution. The ramifications of this discovery will be far greater than that of Copernicus. This new discovery is new only to science. The new discovery is "PURE CONSCIOUSNESS." We have noted that this is not new to man's experience. None other than St Augustine (354-430) seems to have expressed this very notion in his writings *CONFESSIONS* (See: Appendix V –MEDITATION). I predict that some time in this new millennium it will become a very big deal. PURE CONSCIOUSNESS will become the basis for man's new understanding of himself that Csikszentmihalyi claims we will need to survive. Already it is increasingly seen as the "center post" in the lives of many men and women.

Just as all scientists were not ready to accept the Copernicus theory, so, today most scientists and academics are suspicious of this new field of study called "Consciousness." This suspicion, however, will not keep science from progressing in this arena. I believe that, in the end, science will not only verify that there is such a phenomenon as pure consciousness but it will discover and rediscover techniques that will enable man to experience these higher states of consciousness. I believe science will discover that certain diets are beneficial to maintaining such a consciousness. They may find that certain nutrients are absolutely required for such a state. If so, these nutrients will be made available in pills, powders and food supplements. They may find that some kind of gene therapy or gene manipulation will be beneficial. There will also be continued experiments with drugs in this area. I say "continued" because experimenting with mind-altering drugs such as LSD is and has already become a part of these studies in its frontier stages.

As more and more verifications of this state or phenomenon become known and the techniques, diets, etc. are refined, they will become a part of our educational system. At some point I believe that the attainment of higher states of consciousness will be one of the major goals of education (See: AppendixVIII – "FIVE STEPS OF EDUCATION). Naturally, consciousness in these institutions will be approached in a secular way.

Now science and education and even governments will do their thing. It is not to these that I am addressing my pleas. It is to the institutions of religion. For, as you have seen in these pages, higher states of consciousness, even the understanding of pure consciousness have been a part of man's religious traditions from the earliest days of man's history. As a result I believe that religious institutions should not drag their feet nor dig in their heels when they hear about progress in this area - rather, they should become a part of the process for they have in their histories the pioneers of this study. They have the knowledge, the techniques, even some of the dietary information.

To be sure, progress is going to be made in this area by science but church institutions should not be behind the curve in this matter but ahead of the curve. In my opinion, Anthony de Mello was not a heretic but an example of someone ahead of the curve. Consciousness studies and meditation techniques should not be a threat to the Church. In fact, I believe this can and probably will become an arena in which the institutions of the church can regain their rightful influence in society.

Based on the above I appeal to everyone who should ever read these pages to recognize these facts and help reestablish the traditions of SILENCE seeking and meditation in our religious institutions. If this is not done, who will help humankind to understand the true and deeper meaning of these experiences? I remind you of the words of French philosopher, Henri Bergson: "The vital force (E'lan Vital) is consciousness and is of God if not God himself."

If religious institutions cannot take the long view and project themselves into the science of the future and if they cannot set aside their parochial differences in order to interpret for mankind the larger picture, then they will default on their purpose. However, I am optimistic! I believe that somehow by the grace of the Creator, these institutions will catch the vision and become aware of the relationship of PURE CONSCIOUSNESS to the KINGDOM OF GOD. My greatest hope is that sometime in this new millennium the majority of religious institutions will become aware of their common purpose and in so doing will share a new oneness. I further feel that this new appreciation for their common purpose may also give rise to a new respect and appreciation for our differences.

In the midst of this, I can see a healthy rebirth of ceremony and tradition within the various bodies of belief - a rebirth that celebrates both the diversity of our histories and practices, as well as the march toward the common goal where the E'lan Vital gently (sometimes not so gently) leads us. My hat is off to all those who are already involved in this process.

Throughout this book I have made an effort to point out the huge difference between concept and metaphor. It is for the most part concepts (teachings and dogma) that divide the various institutions of religion. Concepts are one of the things that can cut people off from their own spirit (SELF) as well as from our brothers and sisters throughout the world. Concepts can be the "ogre at the gate." As an example, I watched a man struggle to find a God who would give him peace. He was stuck in his mind with the teachings of his youth and try as he might; he couldn't get out of them. One day, after years of this struggle, he announced to his friends that he had had a spiritual experience, that he had found peace. He said, "I have found that the twelve inches between the head and the heart are the most important journey in life and the longest distance known to man." I believe that the institutions of the Church need to be reminded of the truth in this statement. We also need to realize that when a person completes this twelve-inch journey, no matter what concepts, metaphors or techniques were used to get there, the destination is the same - DIVINE LOVE!

Chapter 38

WHEN?

During the first days of the Coalition's war with Iraq (2003) my longtime good friend Don Tastad was sending me feedback by e-mail as he read a pre-publication manuscript of this Book. In one e-mail he said that the war was interfering with his reading time. I, too, had been watching live television showing huge bombs falling on Baghdad and reports of atrocities by the regime in Iraq on their own citizens. The reports also told of an American soldier who had intentionally killed two of his own officers and wounded several others.

A few days later, with the war still raging, my friend finished the book and included in his final comments were the words, "When? I've just been watching CNN (television news station). The solution to the world's problems hasn't occurred yet! When indeed will this New World that you talk about come into being? Certainly, not yet!"

Whenever someone talks idealistically about a new day or a New World the logical question is, "When?" When will this new day or New World come into being? The response generally has been answered on two levels: one on the level of the individual and the other on the level of society. For those who believe that higher levels of consciousness are available to virtually all people, the answer to

"When?" is <u>NOW</u>! NOW is <u>not</u> about <u>time</u>. NOW transcends time but as Mahatma Gandhi implied, we can begin to experience something of the new world on the personal level as soon as we are willing to begin the disciplines that make it possible. The answer to "When?" on the level of society is more complicated. <u>It is about time</u> and, in order to keep it in perspective, we must take the "long view."

"When?" is one of the questions that Plato seemed to be addressing in his book, *THE REPUBLIC.* When will society rise above human pettiness, inhumanity and conflict to order to fulfill the promises of freedom and democracy? Plato's answer was that this would be possible when the leadership becomes enlightened. In his book Plato outlines the kind of discipline (education) that future leaders must experience and endure, for them to achieve such a state of enlightenment.

"When?" is one of the questions that the people of Palestine were asking of Jesus. They said, "When will the Kingdom of God be restored?" Jesus' answer was, "The Kingdom of God is near you." In effect he was saying that it is here, you only need to recognize it.

"When?" is one of the questions that both Teilhard de Chardin and Sri Aurobindo attempted to answer. Both implied that humankind must continue to evolve before this New World can come into being. It is my belief that they were talking about social evolution as well as physical evolution. As already discussed in this Book, it may well be that we have already arrived at the state of physical evolution where this New World is a possibility. However, it is certainly obvious that our social evolution has far to go!

Near the end of his book, *THE KINGDOM OF GOD IS WITHIN YOU,* Leo Tolstoy talks about the New World. In order to illustrate what it will take to get to this New World, he used the illustration of Columbus taking off into the unknown and persevering until he arrived at the New World. He also addressed the question "When?" Over one hundred years ago he used a simple scientific observation of salt crystallizing in water to answer the question "when?" (as described by Tolstoy in the quotation below) Today perhaps nuclear science gives us the answer to this question. The term "critical mass," has almost become a cliché in our day. However, the term originated during the Manhattan Project (in 1942) that marked the beginning of nuclear fission, the nuclear age and the atomic bomb. The term is a reference to the amount of fissionable material necessary to sustain a chain reaction. The amount was found to be surprisingly small. Some in our age have applied the term "critical mass" in an attempt to answer the question "When?" They say that because all minds are joined, when a certain percentage of minds reach higher states of consciousness, it is probable that a chain reaction will be set off and soon all of society will become enlightened.

"When?" Leo Tolstoy said it this way in 1893:

"Men need only understand this, they need only cease to trouble themselves about the general external conditions in which they are not free, and devote one-hundredth part of the energy they waste on those material things to that in which they are free, to the recognition and realization of the truth which is before them, and to the liberation of themselves and others from deception and hypocrisy, and, without effort or conflict, there would be an end at once of the false organization of life which makes men miserable, and threatens them with worse calamities in the future. And the kingdom of God would be realized, or at least that first stage of it for which men are ready now by the degree of development of their conscience."

"Just as a single shock may be sufficient, when a liquid is saturated with some salt, to precipitate it at once in crystals, a slight effort may be perhaps all that is needed now that the truth already revealed to men may gain a mastery over hundreds, thousands, millions of men, that a public opinion consistent with conscience may be established, and through this change of public opinion the whole order of life may be transformed. And it depends upon us to make this effort." (*THE KINGDOM OF GOD IS WITHIN YOU,* page 356-357)

EPILOGUE

On September 10, 2001 this Book, except for a few minor corrections, was finished. It was our intent within the next few days to print forty copies for distribution to relatives, friends and acquaintances. On September 11, 2001, after viewing on live TV the second plane hitting the World Trade Center and within minutes seeing both towers crumble to the ground, I started reviewing the ideas in this Book and the relevance for the world in which we live. Before the day was over I said, "I won't change a thing, I'll just add an exclamation mark! By that, I literally meant, an exclamation mark!!

As I said before, it takes time for me to assimilate things, to make them my own, to be assured that they are not just of ego but from somewhere deeper. Nature gave me that time. A few days after the September 11th terrorist attack I had a serious kidney infection with blockage. This resulted in two different hospitalizations. Following my recovery we had a series of houseguests. By this time I had, of course, watched a lot of TV news and spent time discussing the events with my friends. Subsequently my idea about the "Explanation Mark" changed and I thought a chapter relating the events of September 11th to this Book might be in order. It didn't take me long to realize that it was still too soon. On November 11, 2001 (exactly two months after the attack on America) I sat down and wrote the following:

EXCLAMATION MARK

We have capitalized many words in this Book to indicate from the human point of view the various facets of the experience of SELF. In the following, we use the word CONSCIOUSNESS. I believe the experience of PURE CONSCIOUSNESS is the most comprehensive experience of this REALITY. I suggest that this piece should be read frequently as a means of moving you towards the awareness of THAT (PURE CONSCIOUSNESS). Some have experienced a settling effect by frequently reading this piece.

Several times I have referred to Bergson's reference to consciousness, "if not God, it is of God." We have also said that the solution to our human dilemma is simple, not easy. It is simple because all we need do is become conscious of CONSCIOUSNESS. But, this is not easy. Why? Because we think we are conscious! But we are not conscious of CONSCIOUSNESS, we are conscious of thoughts, feelings, sights, smells, tastes and what we hear. We think that this consciousness is being awake, but truly being awake is being conscious of CONSCIOUSNESS. CONSCIOUSNESS is SELF and being awake is being conscious of this SELF. We are conscious but not of SELF, but of self. Being conscious only of our self is being asleep. Some traditions call it being ignorant. This is valid, because we are ignorant of CONSCIOUSNESS (SELF).

In this Book we have suggested methods for uncovering SELF - uncovering (chipping away the layers) all those things that come between us and wakefulness: first, by becoming aware of what all those things are and secondly, by becoming willing to let them go. We also have suggested methods such as meditation and service to others which enable us to discover that which is hidden, PURE CONSCIOUSNESS. What we have called ego (the little general) is self-consciousness but it is not CONSCIOUSNESS of SELF. Self-consciousness is contact with the world through the ego while consciousness of CONSCIOUSNESS is awareness of who we really are!

APPENDIX

CONTENTS

APPENDIX I

TRANSITION I
THE PERENNIAL PHILOSOPHY

Note to the reader: As you begin reading this material, I feel I need to warn at least some readers about the nature of this piece. It is a piece of 6000 words that covers the last 50,000 years of man's history. It emphasizes the last 2500 years of that history. It uses terminology and refers to many people with whom you may not be familiar. The point of the article is to highlight some of the material from my study. In this three-year study I proved to my own satisfaction that there has been a continual strain of human experience that can rightfully be called the "Perennial Philosophy." The Perennial Philosophy is the notion that humankind is capable of having a direct contact with that that is usually referred to as God. As Leo Tolstoy discovered, the kingdom of God is within you. My study also brought to light that there are forces opposed to us getting in touch with this internal value.

You need not get caught up in all the details and even if you find yourself getting a bit lost, I urge you to continue. I feel that reading through this material will have value. Even though it is just an overview and a brief one at that, it is designed to give you some confidence that this is the TRUTH that we are missing. Direct contact with that which can rightly be called God is that which is missing in our world. (As you can see from the words above, this material, which originally was a transition between Part II and Part III has presented some problems for some readers; consequently we have moved it along with Transition II to the Appendix.)

This section is intended to be a bridge between the first two sections and the third section (The Vision Quest Hero). In it I will share with you some highlights from an aborted attempt to prove the existence of the UNIFIED FIELD. I set out to do what Albert Einstein spent much of his life trying to do and could not accomplish.

(This last sentence I hope you realize, was written with tongue in cheek.) Nevertheless I did recently spend more than three years looking into history, philosophy, psychology, science, anthropology, music, poetry and mathematics. My hope was that I could show in a graphic way that they all fit together and what makes them fit together is the idea that all truth is the manifestation of the UNIFIED FIELD.

What I discovered is that I <u>could</u> do this. I could make everything fit. What I also discovered (which was to be expected) is that making it fit depends on who you study in each of these fields. For instance: in psychology you have to choose Jung not Freud; regarding evolution, Bergson not Darwin; in philosophy, Plato not Aristotle; in poetry, Blake or Whitman not Kerouac; in theology/religion, de Chardin not Jerry Falwell. When all was said and done, I had to admit to myself that the only thing that made all these disparate thinkers unite was my own consciousness. How then can I communicate this to you unless your consciousness is one with mine. At this point I found comfort in the words of Albert Einstein who said, "Problems cannot be solved at the same level of consciousness that created them." With that comfort I share these notes with you.

I acknowledge but make no apologies, for using material here that has already been used or will be used again later. I believe if something is good or true or beautiful, it bears repeating.

****

One of the most important concepts to come out of my study is the knowledge that mankind's history can be understood as a search for truth. It can be understood in other ways as well; as a struggle for survival, for power, for territory, for food or for wealth. But, the honest struggle for ideals and ideas is a search for truth. *A COURSE IN MIRACLES* says, "All is love or a search for love." Could something akin to love be the truth for which we are all searching?

One of the first things that I did when I started this study was to review (several times) Joseph Campbell's, *TRANSFORMATION OF MYTH THROUGH TIME.* This is a fourteen-hour video tape series that begins with a look at the earliest artifacts of man. These artifacts give scholars clues as to the customs and beliefs of early man. The

351

series continues through history up to the present, looking at the beliefs, religions and customs of mankind. One thing that stood out in all of this was the fact that man has always been seeking to make sense out of his life, to find meaning and purpose. In fact, Campbell says that the principle function of myth has always been "to put us and keep us in harmony with the universe."

Man's concept of his universe, as we well know, has changed and evolved over the last 50,000 years. When our perception of the universe changes, truth in a sense changes and myths have to go through change and adaptation as well. But Campbell believed his studies proved that while the outside conception of man's universe changed, there was a truth that did not change. He says this was apparent in the very first signs of myth that we found in grave artifacts.

Campbell shows us in various myths throughout time, the persistence of the belief that there is both a relative changing world and an ABSOLUTE or unchanging realm. He tells us that the sun which frequently shows up in mythology often represents this unchanging realm and that the moon represents the ever changing - two truths, two realms, one ABSOLUTE and one relative. He also indicates that throughout history, cutting across continents, race and custom, man has always related the changing world to that which is essentially exterior and the unchanging to something deep down within his own interior - that man lives, moves and has his being in the midst of two values, one seen, relative and changing, and the other hidden, ABSOLUTE and non-changing. As we continue our discussion keep in mind that we are talking about these two values.

In ancient Greece Socrates, Plato, and Aristotle, 2,300 years ago, dealt with these concepts and tried to arrive at some understanding of "truth." Aristotle and Plato, although in agreement on many things, parted company over this particular issue. I am not going into detail, and I am not going to try to prove my position, but it is my opinion that Plato's notion of "truth" was superior, precisely because it gives greater credence to the concept of two realms and the ancient ideas of ABSOLUTE and relative, interior and exterior. In so doing he gave emphasis to the interior and the ABSOLUTE.

It is also my belief that had the Roman Catholic Church based its theology on the philosophy of Plato and the neo-platonists, rather than Aristotle, institutional Christianity might have stayed more in touch with the idea that the Kingdom of God is a value to be experienced within one's own being. If neo-platonists like Plotinus who wrote the following had been given their due the Church might then have developed principles which would have allowed it to be more flexible in applying its message to a changing perception of the universe. In other words, when one experiences the ABSOLUTE within, it provides a stability, which enables one to be more open to change without.

"When we see God (says Plotinus) we see him not by reason, but by something that is higher than reason. It is impossible however to say about him who sees that he sees, because he does not behold and discern two different things (the seer and the thing seen). He changes completely, ceases to be himself, preserves nothing of his I. Immersed in God, he constitutes one whole with Him; like the centre of a circle, which coincides with the centre of another circle." (Plotinus 205-270)

There is some evidence that Thomas Aquinas, a canonized Saint of the Roman Catholic Church, realized this fact in the last days of his life. For centuries now St. Thomas has been considered the prince of theologians having written a number of books that became central in the preparation of new priests. Oddly, in the last years of his life, St. Thomas entered into silence. He didn't talk and he didn't write. Shortly before he died he came out of silence and all but denounced what he had written. It seems reasonable to conclude that in his years of silence he got in touch with the divinity within in a way that he had never done before. If this is true, he no doubt found himself more comfortable with the philosophy of Plato and the neo-platonists, for their philosophy reflects this inner knowing. All of St. Thomas' writings were based on the philosophy and science of Aristotle, which reflected a static universe.

It is interesting also that Mahatma Gandhi, who grew up in the midst of the Hindu tradition (a tradition which at it's best, nurtures ones awareness of that ABSOLUTE value of life) said, "It is because we have at the present moment everybody claiming the right of conscience without going through any discipline whatsoever that there is so much untruth delivered to a bewildered world." (*WORDS OF GANDHI,* page 13) I am sure, because his life was a demonstration of such things as prayer, meditation, the practice of silence and sacrifice, that he was saying that the first step to truth is to become acquainted with the truth which is within. We know from the mystics of all religions that this truth is essentially experiential and nonverbal, that it is a knowing that finds no adequate expression in the relative, and that there is a gap between the two realms, a gap that poets and artists have tried to fill and almost to a person would admit that they have done so imperfectly. But there is an interesting relationship between the nonverbal "language" of the ABSOLUTE realm and the high ideals and principles which have presented themselves from time to time in the history of mankind. The relationship is twofold: One, such high ideals have come from those in touch with that inner realm and secondly they take root in and are recognized by those who are likewise in touch with their inner Being. Thus we have Gandhi, a Hindu man in touch with this inner realm recognizing the great and powerful principles contained in Jesus' Sermon on the Mount.

Listen to these words of Gandhi, "The truth is God and God is truth." "A man with a grain of faith in God never loses hope, because he ever believes in the ultimate triumph of truth." Gandhi, although imperfect, was considered by many to be the embodiment of truth, the combination of inner knowledge and high ideals. He says, "Faith is a function of the heart. It must be enforced by reason. The two are not antagonistic as some think. The more intense one's faith is, the more it whets one's reason. When faith becomes blind, it dies." It seems to me that Albert Einstein was saying essentially the same thing when he said "science without religion is lame and religion without science is blind." I would paraphrase this as follows: investigation and knowledge of the relative world without knowledge of the ABSOLUTE world is destructive, and knowledge of the ABSOLUTE, which does not investigate and apply these truths to the relative world, is impractical.

This is a good time to once again remind ourselves of Bergson's point that the mode of expression natural to reason (a function of the mind) is the concept and that the mode natural to the intuition (a function of the spirit) is metaphor. In other words the language of the mind is concepts and the language of the spirit is the metaphor. As I write, I am struck by just how correct Protestants are in their insistence on the "authority of the word" and at the same time, I am equally struck by how wrong they are when they apply the same authority to all words just because they are in the Bible. They rob the spirit of its role by insisting on a literal interpretation rather than to appreciate the metaphor through which the spirit can speak. It seems to me that Jesus' thoughts about putting new wine in old wine-skins (a metaphor) may have some relevance here. Could it be that wine represents the ABSOLUTE which is ever new. And wine-skins represents the ever changing, which must always be taken into consideration. If you read the New Testament looking for both wine and old wine-skins, I think you will find that some words have more authority than others. I also think Paul's words apply here when he says "His spirit bears witness to our spirit." These words bring us back to Gandhi's statement about discipline. If we have not nurtured and become aware of the ABSOLUTE realm within (the spirit), we do not recognize and are not wholly committed to the great principles. The great principles have difficulty witnessing to and resonating with our inner essence and vice versa. I heard someone say, "the twentieth century has been the bloodiest in the history of man because our technology has outstripped our morality." I believe this means we have become more familiar with and more knowledgeable about the changing realm of existence while ignoring the ABSOLUTE realm found within. In this state we can be familiar with the great principles, but we are not able to distinguish them from other interesting and even laudable thoughts and ideas.

We have discussed briefly the search for truth, where truth is found, how truth is heard and in the case of Gandhi (and those like him), how truth is lived. Now I would like to discuss facing the truth. This is not easy for many of us, but I believe it to be essential both to the individual and society. In order to get right into this I am going to use an example that many do not even want to talk about, let alone face. Some even deny that this event ever happened. I am talking about the holocaust, the murder of six million Jews during World War II. Other examples could be used - the murder of Stalin's political enemies, the massacres in Cambodia, etc. But we will use the example best known to us, the holocaust.

What happened? What went wrong? I confess at the outset I am not an authority on this issue. I have been to a Holocaust Museum. I have seen the movie, "Schindler's List." I have talked with survivors and I know that something went wrong! You don't take millions of people from their homes without the general population knowing something was going on! You don't put six million people in ovens to burn without the general public knowing something about it! We do have documented stories of Catholics and Protestants like Schlindler who tried to do something but most would agree, not enough happened! Why didn't people want to face the truth, then and now? Why did the Churches for the most part remain quiet?

One word, FEAR, probably accounts for the majority of the non-action. The truth is that in the face of fear, the good becomes the enemy of the best. I don't know who first said this and I don't know when I first heard it but it is a principle that should be brought to the foreground. In this case there is little doubt that the good was the enemy of the best and it allowed six million people to die.

Some no-doubt said, "I don't want to put my family in jeopardy. I don't want to lose my job. I love my country and I have to accept that it knows what it is doing. I don't want to be thrown in jail myself." All of these are good reasons for not saying or doing anything. If I had been there I might have been one of those who did nothing for a good reason. But does doing nothing for a good reason make it right? I use this very vivid illustration from recent history in order to focus our attention on the fact that ideals have a hierarchy of values and indeed the good can be the enemy of the best. The point then is, that the hierarchy of our values can only be determined by one who is in touch with the realm within and only one who is in touch with this realm will have the necessary courage of his/her convictions.

****

Some years ago I spent a week of summer camp with ten teenagers. My goal with these young people was to get them to think about their philosophy of life. I started by asking them to share their philosophy of life with the group. Most of them said that they had really never thought about it. Of course they had, but they had never thought of it in those terms.

We then started dealing with some of the more specific philosophical questions. Like - What is the purpose of life? What is the meaning of life? How does one find meaning? How does the school we attend help us find meaning and purpose? How does it help us develop a philosophy of life? How does the church help? Is our philosophy of life based on reason and logic or on faith; does it evolve out of our inner experience? Are the principles by which we live and make choices something known to us only as teachings or do they resonate within the interior of our consciousness? If you have answers to these questions, are they your answers or just the answers that have been passed on to you by your parents and teachers? Are they really your answers?

As the week progressed the discussions became more lively and virtually all of the teens were involved. Quiet times as well seemed to be used by several for active contemplation. Towards the end of the week we discussed two ideas: Socrates' "know thyself" and Jesus' "Know the truth and the truth will make you free." One young man in particular started putting the two together. He suggested that perhaps the truth that sets us free is the truth about ourselves and all we have to do is know it. This, as you might guess, led to an all new discussion and the week ended on a very high note.

I am sure that those of you schooled in classical philosophy can see that although we did not use the language of the great philosophers, these young people did deal with many of the great philosophical questions and entered into some of the classical debates. The boy who put Jesus and Socrates together did what many of those great philosophers were not able to do. The questions that arise out of putting the two together are: What is the truth about ourselves that will set us free? and What does it mean to know it?

****

Why did Socrates say "know thyself?" Frankly it's not what most of us think! It has little or nothing to do with the theories and therapies of modern psychology. Socrates was born in 470 B.C. in Athens, a time and place that was rich with genius. It was a time that produced great literature and great architecture. Socrates was born into a rich tradition that concerned itself with the health of the soul. This tradition went back over a hundred years to the tiny island of Samos in the Aegean Sea. Samos was the birthplace of Pythagoras, the man we all know from our high school geometry classes. (the square of the hypotenuse, etc.) Pythagoras' interest in mathematics was primarily for spiritual reasons. He believed that the purpose of life was to establish a relationship with God. Because he saw the relationship between mathematics and the physical world he had the conviction that the study of mathematics was a purifier of the soul. The followers of Pythagoras saw in mathematics and science a mode of life that was 'pure,' it was a pursuit of truth and such a pursuit was a pursuit of a relationship with God. The pursuit of science and mathematics led them to philosophic formulations, the most significant being the <u>concept</u> of form. Form, to them, meant limit and these <u>concepts</u> were applied to two other fields in which they made significant contributions, namely music and medicine. The central idea they saw in both of these fields was harmony. Harmony meant taking into account proportions and limits. The Pythagoreans looked upon the body as a musical instrument and felt that health was a matter of the body being in tune. (This idea will be used as a theme in section four of the book entitled, "Practical Spirituality.") Disease was a matter of imbalance and being out of tune. It is evident that Pythagoras influenced both Socrates' and Plato's thinking.

As I said Socrates and Plato were born in a time that was rich and flourishing with culture and ideas that has great influence in their lives. In fact, the growing awareness of differing cultures and races with different ideas about life was one of the ingredients that stimulated Socrates' pursuit of truth. The growing question that philosophers were addressing at that time was whether it was possible for the human mind to discover any universal truths that applied to all men. Could there, for instance, be a universal concept of "goodness" if people were incapable of knowing any universal truth? A group of philosophers known as the Sophists were generally skeptical. Socrates was not. The foundation on which he placed his optimism was not in the facts of the outside world where the Sophists were looking but within the interior life of man. Socrates said that within the interior of man is the seat of knowing and that knowing can lead to doing. He saw this interior seat of knowing as the psyche (soul) which is to "know and influence our daily conduct." Socrates believed that behind the world of facts was an order that could be discovered only by becoming acquainted with the soul. Thus the phrase, "Know thyself." For, according to Socrates, to know oneself was to know ones soul and to know ones soul was to know beauty, truth, goodness. He also believed that the fruit of this kind of knowing would be right conduct.

This kind of truth or knowledge that we have been talking about, that deals with the inner experience, is called SUBJECTIVE TRUTH and is at least in part, according to Baruch Spinoza, intuitive. Spinoza (1632-1677) was a Jewish philosopher of Spanish-Portuguese decent. He had Rabbinical schooling and was later banned from the synagogue on charges of atheism and free thought. He was seen to be teaching a form of Pantheism (all is God). Pantheism in Judaism as well as in most Christian institutions is considered heretical. Spinoza spoke of three levels of knowing. The first he called imagination, those ideas derived from the senses which he said were specific but vague and inadequate. The second he called reason and this is the area of concept (science and mathematics). He said that this was adequate and true. In the third level intuition is viewed in terms of both the first level, imagination, and the second level, reason. In the first level, intuition relating to imagination would be seen as specific but in the second level, reason is seen in its context or in terms of the whole. Now if this eludes you, you are not alone! It is my belief that as a philosopher Spinoza, also a Mystic, is trying his hardest to describe the mystical (interior experience) with concepts rather than metaphors. Was he successful? You can be the judge!

Be it as it may, Spinoza actually helps our discussion in the following ways: first, he broadens the concept of subjectivity to include intuition and the mystical. In his thoughts about imagination and reason, he introduces us to the difference between appearances and <u>empirical</u> <u>knowledge</u>. Often we say something is true based on appearances. It appears that the sun rises in the morning and sets in the evening. It appears that this piece of wood is solid and unchanging. But <u>reason</u>, based on science and mathematics, tells us another story. Empirical knowledge or knowledge based on facts after investigation, especially scientific investigation, is the stuff out of which the so called "Age of Reason" was born and with it a near worship of the scientific method. The names are many and they include Conte, who was the father of logical positivism which says facts should be studied in relationship to things with no attempt to study their inner essence and Descarte, famous for his "I think, therefore I am." Descarte was a mathematician as well as a philosopher and felt that truth like mathematics must be clear and distinct.

Another idea about truth, which we covered earlier, was put forth by William James, the psychologist. This idea does not pertain to our present discussion but because of its importance in latter discussions about practical spirituality, it needs to be mentioned again. James did not want to get involved in philosophic discussions about truth. He just boiled it down to one idea, "if it works, it's true." The philosophy that developed around this idea is known as pragmatism.

****

Several years ago I strolled through a discount book store waiting for a book title to catch my eye. Sure enough, one did, a book entitled *SACRED UNITY* authored by Gregory Bateson. I had never heard of Bateson but after reading the table of contents and the fly-leaf, I bought the book. I soon found that it was not a light read and I set it aside. During the years since then, over and over again, I have been enticed by the title and have taken the book from the shelf and given it a further try. Finally I was determined to find out why this book kept reappearing in my consciousness.

Bateson is introduced in his book as: "Anthropologist, Biologist, Philosopher, student of behavior and experience in virtually every arena of human life. Gregory Bateson (1904-1980) was one of the most far reaching thinkers of the twentieth century." With interest, I also learned that his first wife was the famous Anthropologist, Margaret Mead and he had joined her in research in both New Guinea and the Island of Bali.

As I dug into the book, I realized that Bateson had arrived at an understanding of modern man's problems that was not unlike my own understanding. However, Bateson had arrived at this position by what appears to me to be a totally different route. If I understand him correctly, he arrived at his position by changing his thinking. That, in turn, altered his perceptions. In other words, he <u>thought</u> his way into a new way of living and perceiving. I, on the other hand, have found myself <u>living</u> my way into a new way of perceiving and thinking. This is not the first time I have been aware of this difference.

It appears to me that Plato, like Bateson, arrived at a similar level of consciousness by changing his thinking. This change in thinking and the resulting transformation of his perceptions happened during his tutelage with Socrates. It appears that Plato was so impressed with what happened to him during this period, that he set up an academy so that others might experience a similar transformation. The purpose of Plato's academies, as can be seen in *THE REPUBLIC*, is to teach a philosophy that enables one to get in touch with one's inner being (a way of thinking that puts one in touch with the ABSOLUTE).

Bateson seemed to recognize that one can arrive at this value from differing directions. He at one point reminded his listeners that he was not a Buddhist but a scientist. According to Bateson, "If we have wrong ideas of how our abstractions are built - if, in a word we have poor epistemological habits* - we shall be in trouble - and we are." The trouble, according to Bateson, is in seeing ourselves <u>separate from</u>, instead of a <u>part of</u> (perception).

The articles in Bateson's book seemed to be largely written for academics and the message, for the most part, continued to elude me. I returned to the introduction and reread the following quote:

---

* Epistemology – science or rules for gaining knowledge

361

Now I a fourfold vision see,
And a fourfold vision is given to me
'Tis fourfold in my supreme delight
And threefold in soft Beulah's night
And twofold Always. May God us keep
From Single vision & Newton's sleep!

—William Blake, Letter to Thomas Butts,
22 November 1802

The "cure" Bateson (and Blake) are saying is to awake from "Newton's sleep" and to establish an "ecology of the mind" that will allow us to recognize our "sacred unity." But, how? "What I want to say, quite simply, is that what goes on inside is much the same as what goes on outside. And I say this not from anything like a Buddhist position, but from the position of an ordinary working stiff engaged in occidental science." (This reference to Buddhists I believe is a recognition that some Buddhists do experience the unity of life.)

Another quote in the introduction is the following from R.C. Collingwood's *SPECULUM MENTIS:*

"For we now recognize the nature of our disease. What is wrong with us is precisely the detachment of these forms of experience—art, religion, and the rest—from one another; and our cure can only be their reunion in a complete and undivided life. Our task is to seek for that life, to build up the conception of an activity which is at once art, and religion, and science, and the rest." (Note - do these words remind you of Einstein's words from his "My Credo?")

These quotes gave me clues as to what Bateson was about and they so intrigued me that I felt obliged to go back and find out more about both Blake and Collingwood. It seemed obvious from the quotes themselves, that Bateson must be trying to suggest a cure for something he recognized as a deep problem in modern man.

When I put the two writings in juxtaposition I was able to define Newton's sleep (the Newtonian clockwork, mechanical-like universe, the age of rationalism and the age of enlightenment that followed), as that which had forced us into a kind of sterile, spiritless environment of the mind - a mind set, that forces us to see things as separate and detached with boundaries and divisions. We can contrast this picture with the native American culture, prior to its contamination by European influence, in which they saw a spirit-filled or energized environment that was not divided into parts or separate from themselves.

When I got into Blake I knew I was on to something. William Blake saw imagination as the Divine Being in every person and felt that anything that held down or restricted that Divine imagination was destructive. He attempted to expose religious, scientific, philosophical and political fiction that had been accepted as truth. His works admonish all forms of tyranny; kings, priests, parents, nurses, schoolmasters, lawmakers, merchants. He was skeptical of any system that limited human imagination. He was hard on religion, which he said could not be codified (conceptualized). "Man," he said, "had made God in his image. That had constituted a fallen vision. The God within and not the God above is the creative energy that can redeem humankind from its erroneous dichotomies."

Robin George Collingwood (1889-1943), as I suspected, expresses some of the same concerns. *SPECULUM MENTIS* was published in 1924 to provide the reader with an answer to the question: "How can I achieve happiness?" The answer was to develop a unified human experience that resulted from a knowledge of human experience and its interrelationships. (see quote on the preceding page)

I was beginning to feel that I understood Bateson and what he meant by "ecology of the mind" and "creative unity." He is saying that what we are is what we see. If we are divided and spiritless within, then that is what we see in our environment. If we don't see the fragile relationships in our environment, then we quite naturally and thoughtlessly destroy them. If we don't see the unity within, then we can't see the unity without.

****

363

Above we made reference to the Native American culture. The revival among Native Americans of their ancient traditions seems to me to be based on the recognition of nature's unity. This oneness with nature, the universe and the tribe are evident in the mythological stories handed down through the generations usually by the elders to the young. These stories often have as their central character what Frank B. Linderman calls an undergod. He is the creator of the earth, but as an agent of the Great Spirit.

Among the tribes of the Northwest plains this creator is called Napi or Old Man. Napi is both hero and trickster. The stories of Napi are a source of teaching great truths as well as great entertainment. For Old Man is both a comical character and hero. As singer/song writer Jack Gladstone writes, "Napi is an archetype found commonly in tribal societies the world over - part hero, part antihero (so human an animal) you never know what Napi is gonna do next—." Napi seems to possess all of the qualities of man's inner essence talked about by the various philosophers mentioned previously in this transition. Qualities like imagination, intuition, mystery and, in addition, humor and playfulness are a part of Napi's makeup.

Gladstone, a member of the Blackfeet Tribe, learned the stories of his people at his grandmother's knee. He has, in recent years, turned these legends into song. One of these songs is entitled, "When Napi Became a Wolf." One aspect of these legends is that although Napi is Creator, he is always learning from that which he has created. In the first verse that follows, Wolf Chief speaks to Napi. Notice the significance given to the concept of choice.

> "As we all grow old, it's
> through choice we grow wise
> Napi listen close if you can
> Through this transformation
> you may realize
> The love that binds our wolf clan."

In the next verse Napi is transformed into a wolf and through the eyes and ears of a wolf he sees and hears the sacred in every living thing:

And then by choice Napi fell
under his medicine spell
He woke behind eyes of
different sheen
His new ears heard the world
and each moment unfurled
The sacred in every living thing
When Napi Became a Wolf.

And thus the lessons are taught and handed down from generation to generation. Kae and I heard Gladstone in concert in Glacier National Park. After the concert, I spoke to Gladstone briefly and purchased one of his recordings. (See web-page Appendix III for website.)

Sometime later while reading Joseph Campbell once again I realized that Gladstone himself was the embodiment of the type of Hero that Campbell says takes the same form in every culture. Campbell refers to this myth as "the vision quest" and it was the subject matter of his first book, *THE HERO WITH A THOUSAND FACES.* In these myths the Hero is called to go on a quest, to find a boon, a vision. In these myths, like Napi becoming a wolf, the Hero is asked to go into another world. There he faces great danger and in the midst of this peril he discovers what was missing in his consciousness. Armed with this new wholeness, the hero goes back to his own world and shares his discoveries.

Gladstone learned these myths as a child at his Grandmother's knee. His gratitude to his Grandmother is expressed in every concert by singing a song that he wrote in tribute to her. As a boy he learned to play the guitar and was an outstanding athlete. He attended the University of Washington where, I suspect, he learned about the archetypes of Jungian psychology as he refers to them in his concerts. Gladstone also played football for the Washington Huskies and was on the 1978 Rose Bowl championship team.

During these years he experienced a growing interest in his native culture. Following his graduation, he returned to Montana where he started to study his heritage in earnest. This study reunited him with the stories that his Grandmother taught him and he realized that this was a message that was needed by both the Indian and the broader culture of our day. In the last fifteen years Gladstone has given hundreds of concerts at college campuses, high schools, grade schools, powwows and festivals. In my mind, he is a modern "Vision Quest Hero." Like Gregory Bateson, William Blake, R.C. Collingwood, Socrates, Plato and St. Thomas Aquinas (on his deathbed), Gladstone urges us to discover the source of our unity, The Hero within.

APPENDIX II

TRANSITION II
SPIRITUAL PSYCHOLOGY

If you were to sit in on a nurse's report in a modern hospital you might be surprised to hear the patients reviewed in the following manner. (Typically nurses have a report session at the shift change.) "The gallbladder in 201a is having some discomfort, otherwise he is doing fine. The kidney infection in 201b continues with elevated temperature and will be evaluated by a Specialist today. The femur fracture in 202b is still in a lot of pain and continues on Demerol. 202a is a new patient with possible carcinoma of the cervix and is being evaluated. 301a remains comatose and the family continues to be a pain." The name of the patient may or may not be used but ultimately the patients have been reduced to a disease, a room and bed number - a depersonalization that can't possibly help in the healing process.

In 1963 and 1964 I was involved in an attempt by a major Chicago area hospital to treat the "whole person." The approach was called "Human Ecology" and it tried to look at the patient as a person rather than a disease. It further tried to recognize that a physical crisis might also cause or exacerbate other problems - social, family, economic, spiritual and/or psychological. In other words, the goal was to counteract the depersonalization that takes place in a hospital and to see the person in their entirety - their wholeness.

The Staff included nine specially trained clergymen. I was one of them. The special training included working on the floor as an orderly (carrying bedpans giving baths etc), scrubbing in on surgeries, assisting in the birth rooms and spending time in the psyche ward. In addition, each of us was assigned to a Doctor for a week. During that week we were the Doctor's shadow. If he or she got called out at three o'clock in the morning we got up and went with him or her. If he went into surgery, we did too. If the Doctor saw patients in the office we were there usually introduced as the Doctor's assistant. All of this was to help us not only see the patient differently but also the Doctors, Nurses and not least of all, ourselves differently. I remind you, seeing things differently is one of the themes of this book.

Following this training, we were expected to be emissaries throughout the hospital for the concept of "Human Ecology." Our main responsibility was to the patient. We were the people on the staff that always had time to talk to the patient. In fact, our job was to encourage the patient to talk - to let us know how they were feeling. Visits usually started with small talk. During this we observed the patients - were they anxious?, did they seem apprehensive or frightened? If so, we encouraged them to talk about it. We asked questions about family, jobs, religion, etc. If we learned anything we thought would be helpful to their Doctor or nursing staff, we would ask the patient's permission to share this information with the staff. Sometimes we suggested to the staff that a social worker or a psychiatrist should be considered as a part of the treatment team. We always tried to find out if the patient belonged to a religious faith. If they did have a religious affiliation, we would ask the patient if we could call their priest, rabbi or pastor and let them know that they were in the hospital. We were always assessing which patient needed or wanted to see us again.

We were also encouraging (in a subtle way) the hospital staff and Doctors to live up to the concept of "Human Ecology;" to treat the whole person and to always keep in mind the patient was a human being and not a disease.

Now, over thirty-five years later, I still look back at this period as one of the best experiences of my life. I also look at the effort at "Human Ecology" to be admirable. In a limited way, it was an effective countermeasure to the depersonalization that seems almost inevitable in a modern hospital setting. However in spite of the fact that this concept was developed and backed by a number of very fine, very bright and dedicated individuals, this program has almost entirely gone by the wayside. The hospital still thrives but any serious effort to practice human ecology, as it was originally designed, no longer exists. I believe the concept was flawed from the very beginning because it was based on a limited understanding of the nature of man.

As I reflect on that period of my life I now know that even though I enjoyed the entire adventure I was never completely comfortable with or understood my role. As Chaplains we dressed in a white hospital jacket and a clerical collar. This garb was meant to represent a different kind of chaplain. As a group we were probably a little more liberal than our counterparts in the parish ministry. We knew our role was to minister to people from all religions and not to proselytize. We received a training that was outstanding but we were not all that different. We still represented a God who resides in heaven. We were still dealing with belief systems.

One thing we were asked to do in order to improve our effectiveness with patients was to prepare "verbatims." A verbatim was a word for word recollection of our session with a patient. We would have verbatim sessions several times a week - this was a time when our group would gather together. We often invited psychiatrists, psychologists and/or a social worker to sit in with us. Together we would spend an hour or two going over someone's verbatim line by line. The verbatim would be picked apart and analyzed from every direction possible. The hope was that this exercise would improve our people skills as well as help us to further define the concept of "human ecology."

How different my verbatims would be today. The following is a fictional representation of a verbatim that I would like to submit today. While fictional, it is based on a number of similar patient contacts that I had while serving as Chaplain.

VERBATIM

Chaplain Rich   November 1, 1999

The patient is a white married female, thirty-nine years old and a mother of three teenage children - Robby - thirteen, Sarah - fifteen, Dell - sixteen. She is an inactive Roman Catholic. She does not want her Priest notified. The patient (Mary) was admitted to the hospital with breast cancer and has undergone a radical mastectomy. She was told that they were hopeful that they got all the cancer but they are not

369

certain and she is now undergoing further treatment. This verbatim represents the third session with Mary. The first was a routine initial visit. In the second session Mary showed a willingness to talk about her family and job but not her illness. As we ended the second session, she said, "Chaplain, please come back."

Verbatim - third session

Chaplain - "Hello Mary."
Mary - "Hello Chaplain."
Chaplain - "How are you feeling today Mary?"
Mary - "Physically, I'm feeling better."
Chaplain - "You're feeling better physically but otherwise your kinda down?"
Mary - "I guess that's it."
Chaplain - "Do you want to talk about it?"
Mary - "Kind of—(long pause) I'm frightened."
Chaplain - "Mary, I'm sure you are. No one goes through what you have been through without experiencing fear. Let's talk about it."
Mary - "I have tried to figure out why I don't want to leave the hospital. I thought it might be Doug. (pause)
Chaplain - "Your husband?"
Mary - "Yes."
Chaplain - "You're concerned that the mastectomy might change your relationship?"
Mary - "I've had some thoughts about that but I don't think that's it. Doug has been up here every day. He holds my hand and assures me that he loves me and that everything is going to be OK."
Chaplain - "If I hear you correctly, you seem to be saying you have some concerns in this area but it is something the two of you will be able to work out."
Mary - "Yes, I really do."
Chaplain - "If that's not your biggest source of fear, what do you think it is?"

Mary -   (long pause) (starts to sob) "I don't want to leave the kids."

Chaplain -   "You're concerned that you're going to die?"

Mary -   (sobs) "Yes."

Chaplain -   (hands Mary some tissues) "And the thought that most haunts you about dying is leaving the children?"

Mary -   "Yes."

Chaplain -   "Mary, I have reviewed your chart and talked to your Doctor and I can tell you that they are not hiding anything from you. Your Doctor is what I would call 'guardedly optimistic.' I'm not telling you anything new. Just assuring you that you know everything there is to know."

Mary -   "Thanks, I needed to hear that Chaplain."

Chaplain -   "Mary, the next months are not going to be easy and one of the most difficult things about next month will be the not knowing."

Mary -   "Yes Chaplain, that's what's hard - the not knowing."

Chaplain -   "Mary, the resource to get through this, no matter which way it goes, is in you."

Mary -   "I'm not sure I know what you're talking about."

Chaplain -   "I'm talking about that which is the basis of every major religion and many philosophies of life. I'm talking about remembering who we really are. Most of us don't know who we really are but it is in times of crisis that we often remember. Mary, may I ask you a question?"

Mary -   "Certainly - at least I guess I'm certain." (laughs)

Chaplain -   "It won't hurt. The question is this - Have you ever felt that you are more than you think or realize?"

Mary -   (pause) "Yes,—yes, I have had that feeling."

Chaplain -   "Mary, that something more is what I call the Hero within." Or in your case I guess it would be proper to say Heroine

Mary -   "Do you mean God?"

Chaplain -   "You can call it God if that feels O.K. to you. Some people are not comfortable with the word God. I call it the Hero within, I'm not sure it matters what we call it. What does matter is that we connect with it."

Mary -   "I think I'd like that but I don't know if I can."
Chaplain - "You have already begun. When I asked you if you had ever felt that there was something more to you than what you had been able to realize. You remembered - that is the beginning. Let me leave you with this little story that I read in the book CHICKEN SOUP FOR THE SOUL. It's a nice story that says something about the whole idea of remembering."

"The story is about a little three year old girl with a new baby brother. Standing beside the baby's crib and looking at him, she was heard to say, 'Baby, tell me about God. I am starting to forget.' Mary I believe there is something of truth in this story - something we all need to remember."

With this we said our goodbyes and I let her know that all she needed to do to reach me was to have her nurse call the Chaplain's office.

If, on subsequent visits, Mary had resonated with the idea of remembering, I would have underscored this with information like the following:
"New scientific findings are beginning to support beliefs of cultures thousands of years old, showing that our individual psyches are, in the last analysis, a manifestation of cosmic consciousness and intelligence that flows through all of existence. We never completely lose contact with this cosmic consciousness because we are never fully separated from it. This is a concept found independently in mystical traditions throughout the world; Aldous Huxley called it the 'perennial philosophy.'" *THE HOLOTROPIC MIND* by Stanislav Grof, M.D.

At some point, if Mary seemed receptive and if her stay in the hospital permitted, I would have either introduced or given her some literature on the "The World Community for Christian Meditation." (See Appendix III WEBSITES)

****

Martin Buber (1878-1965) is one of the most important representatives of the human spirit in the twentieth century. As a young man he went through a period of uncreative intellectual pursuit and spiritual confusion. This all changed when he experienced a sudden conversion after recalling some words of the founder of Hasidism, known as the Baal-Shem-Tov. Buber related the following experience in his book, *HASIDISM AND MODERN MAN.*

> "It was then that, overpowered in an instant I
> experienced the Hasidic soul - - - - Man's being
> created in the image of God I grasped as deed,
> as being, as becoming, as task - - - - -At the same
> time I became aware of the summons to proclaim
> it to the world."

As a result of this experience he entered into a period of isolation that lasted five years. During this time he turned to study and contemplation. He emerged from his study with the belief that he had discovered an important truth - a truth that needed to be heard by the world not just by the Jewish community.

The literature in which Martin Buber immersed himself was that which emanated from European Jewish communities of the eighteenth and nineteenth centuries. (Mostly in Poland and the Ukraine) This literature, the legends of Hasidism, revealed to him what he considered to be a very unique community of people - a community that he said was born out of a crisis of faith. This crisis of faith was the result of a "lie" and teachings based on this "lie." The lie that was being taught to many of the Jews of this period was that the Torah had been fulfilled and that the messianic period had arrived. Two different individuals taught this lie, each proclaiming that he was the messiah. When it became apparent that these individuals were not what they proclaimed to be, these communities experienced wholesale, self-doubt and discouragement. In the midst of this confusion they sought some kind of direction. Many turned from Judaism to the worship of Allah, others to Jesus, and those who remained, Buber says, were poisoned. The poison consisted of false teaching, false belief, false leadership and the disillusionment that resulted.

Most of us can relate to this poison, at least on some level, if we will recall the times we have been duped by some clever person. I remember buying a rather expensive vacuum cleaner from a fast-talking salesman when I was still in the Seminary. I was having trouble finding enough money to buy the books that I needed for my studies. What I did not need was a new expensive vacuum cleaner. Our apartment consisted of one room with a small area rug.

Some years later, I bought a recreational lot. Again, a smooth talking salesman appealed to my ego desires and I bought something that I couldn't afford and had no need for. In both cases I ended up feeling duped, stupid and full of anger. I had been poisoned and for a long time whenever someone would try to sell me something I closed my mind and if they persisted, I would become angry. Like the early Hasidic Jewish communities, I had been poisoned. Someone had convinced me of a lie - the lie in my case was that I needed these things. I didn't need them at all.

In Germany, in the late 1930's and early 1940's, a man convinced many people that they were superior to others, that they and they alone had the potential to build a super race. Hitler was a master salesman and Germany and its people are still working to rid their nation of the hurt and destruction that this lie caused. They had been poisoned and the poison has lingered as guilt, and embarrassment. They had been duped and sold a lie and in many ways have tried to hide from these facts.

It was into such a situation that a Rabbi (known as Baal-Shem-Tov) came to provide an antidote to the poison. As it turns out it was an antidote so effective that the scholar (Buber) respected by Christians and Jews alike, spent much of his life trying to bring to the attention of the twentieth century this community of Jews. In the following paragraphs I will try to give you some insight into the antidote Buber discovered in the teachings of the Baal-Shem-Tov.

It seems clear that the antidote had its foundation in the Kabbala. (Jewish mysticism) but Buber says that it went beyond the Kabbala, it was the Kabbala and more. The body of literature referred to as the

Kabbala is sometimes seen in Gnostic terms; in other words, its truth is for the few, for those in the "know." The Hasidic community, according to Buber, is exemplary because it lived a form of mysticism that was for all, not just for a few. It was a community of families living daily lives conscious of God's Shekina (God's inner presence). Buber says, "The Shekina embraces both the 'good' and the 'evil' but the 'evil' not as an independent substance, rather as the 'throne of the good.'"

It is in this context that the community learned to live with the fantasy, the lie, the evil urge.

In Buber's words, "Who is a hero? He who masters his urges. He compels the evil urge to teach him and he learns from it and every man recognizes and grasps the quality with which he must serve God by that for which he longs. Again, Hasidism has established the fact that one can give the direction less force that breaks out in the desire, the direction of truth, that one can make the blind force see."

Buber says, "That the essence of the Hasidic message consists in founding a renewed relationship to reality." In some belief systems the goal is to effect a relationship with God by denying, as much as humanly possible, the world of the senses.

Hasidism is quite the opposite! It embraces the world as that which contains the divinity, the divine spark. Much as a shell contains the nut so does the material world contain the spark of the divine. Hasidism teaches that man is the one who is responsible for liberating the divine spark from both himself and the world around him.

The encrustation of the divine and that which results from that condition is what Buber calls reality; and, that living in reality (not the lie) is redemptive. Here reality is being contrasted with fantasy and mood making. In modern churches an effort is often made to appeal to the emotions to set the stage with music, preaching and other effects. Mood making may have some benefit but it is not reality. Reality is getting in touch with the spark enclosed in the shell. (To use the language of Hasidism)

The Baal-Shem-Tov taught the community that this was done in the context of the reality of daily life – a daily life that consisted of sickness, death, heartache, prayer, meditation, involvement with family, community and work. Gershon Scholem says in his *MAJOR TRENDS IN JEWISH MYSTICISM* that "the major development in Jewish mysticism to be found in Hasidism lies in the fact that all of the secrets of the divine realm are presented as a mystical psychology. It is through a descent into one's own self that a person penetrates the spheres separating man from God.—For the Hasidic master, it is his duty to endure or survive the tensions of the world's contradictions and in that way alone redeem the opposites."

This concept of reality-based redemption reminds me of two experiences in my own life. The first was the introduction to the T.M. technique. I was told this technique was to be used twice a day for 20-30 minutes in conjunction with my daily life. It was explained that my daily life was a part of the process. The following illustration was used to clarify the relationship between daily living and meditation.

In India, when people dye their cloth, they dip it in the dye, then hang it in the sun to dry. The sun not only dries the cloth but also fades the dye. The cloth is then placed in the dye and again hung in the sun to dry and fade. Each time this process is completed, a little more of the dye remains in the cloth. Likewise in each meditation one experiences something of the ABSOLUTE value of life and upon returning to daily life that value fades, but with continued repetition more and more of the ABSOLUTE value of life becomes permanently set and more and more a part of one's daily life. It is in this process of daily reality that one becomes conscious of the divine spark within. As time goes on the meditator recognizes the divine in the other person and finally one's unity with all.

The other experience is that of twelve-step programs. A person who comes into a twelve-step program for their first meeting is a person who has not been living in reality. They have been living with the illusion and fantasy that their drug of choice, be it alcohol, narcotics, food, sex, gambling or another person, place or thing, can make their life meaningful or happy. They have been living a lie and the lie has finally led them to some type of bankruptcy - financial, legal, emotional, physical or spiritual. In Hasidic terms they have come face to face with their "evil urge" and must accept its reality or allow it to destroy them. The process that follows is reality based. With the support of the group the individual is reintroduced to reality one day at a time. The reality is that you can't continue to do what you have been doing without destroying yourself and possibly others. The reality is that you need help. The reality is that you need help from a higher power. The reality is that this power exists. Reality is the nut, both the shell and the seed (spark).

The newcomer to a twelve-step program is often told that the program is pragmatic. "It works" - that it works by living the principles one day at a time. Like the Hasidism of eighteenth and nineteenth century Europe, twelve-step programs are pragmatic, they work. They are reality-based and although most twelve-step people do not think in these terms, it is practical mysticism (conscious contact with a higher power). Like Hasidism, twelve-step programs encourage daily prayer, meditation and a life of daily service. The promise is that in time one can become God conscious and life itself will be "happy, joyous and free;" however, not above or apart from the vicissitudes of daily life. The goal is progress not perfection. I believe that most people who have been around a twelve-step program for any length of time would understand Buber's words when he says: "We must transform the element that wants to take possession of us into the substance of true life." In such a transformation, self becomes SELF, love becomes LOVE and god becomes GOD.

APPENDIX III

WEBSITES AND LINKS

When I first started thinking "I am going to write a book" there was no such thing as a personal computer and certainly, no internet. Over the years of spiritual growth and discovery for both Kae and I, there has been a revolution in technology that has had an impact not only on us but also upon society as a whole and millions of individuals. Today, we (Kae and I) not only have a computer; we use the internet daily and have our own website. We doubt that we could have completed this book if it were not for the computer. We also know, that it is a better book because of access to research information over the internet.

Along the way we not only set up the family website but also decided to use it as a further resource for our readers. Instead of listing website in the text of the book we decided to put these links in our website (including links to many of the individuals mentioned in the book) thereby allowing them to be updated and expanded as needed.

We think that some readers may even find portions of our family oriented website interesting. However, we do have one note of caution. If you are able to pierce Rich's anonymity with this material, his name should not be used on radio, television or press.

A portion of the proceeds of this book will always be set aside to maintain our website – a further resource for the readers of this book. Visit us at:

genericgod.com[*]

Upon reaching "genericgod.com" website, go to Link Index to find specific link such as Aldus Huxley, Joseph Campbell, Meditation, etc.

---

[*] We have applied to the office of Patent and Trademark to register "genericgod™ as a trademark.

APPENDIX IV

IN WITH AND UNDER

Following the Protestant Reformation three basic interpretations of the words of Jesus, "this is my body, this is my blood," existed. These words became the heart of the Mass, or as it is called in Protestantism, the Communion. The three interpretations are called Transubstantiation, Con-substantiation and Symbolic.

Transubstantiation was and remains the view of the Roman Catholic Church. The belief is that when these words are spoken in the Mass the bread and wine mystically turn into the body and blood of Christ.

Con-substantiation is the view that Martin Luther set forth which says that the elements do not turn into the body and blood during Mass (Communion) but the mystical Christ becomes a part of the elements. Luther said that Christ is there "in, with and under the bread and wine."

Symbolic, the view of some reformers, said that Luther did not go far enough into his reinterpretation of the Catholic view. Those reformers felt that it should be recognized that Jesus was using the bread and the wine as symbols of his body and blood and that the use of the bread and wine in Communion was to symbolize Jesus' death and resurrection.

Having studied the perennial philosophy, the writings of Joseph Campbell and Eastern thought, I have come to what I consider a fourth view. Campbell, in his works, refers a number of times saying something to the effect, "It is all there" meaning that Jesus was using language that was similar to that used in other cultures. In ceremonies other cultures (both past and present) have used the common elements (fruit of the earth) such as wine and bread to recognize the Divine in all things.

The Kabbalah of Judaism (teachings some claim go back to the time of Moses) talks of the Divine spark, which is in all things. In Eastern thought the material world is seen as a manifestation of the

379

Divine. Therefore, I suggest a fourth view, which I would call the Sacrament of Life. This Sacrament of Life combines both the view of Luther and the reformers that followed him. The bread and the wine are symbolic of all of life and there in the midst of all things material, is the Cosmic Christ, the Divine. He is IN, WITH and UNDER it all and the bread and wine are symbols of it all. Thus, the rite of communion is a symbol of life's sacramental nature. When we attend such a service we celebrate the Sacrament of Life.

In this regard we recall the plaque over Carl Jung's door which said, "Bidden or not bidden, God is present." At its best then, communion is something we become aware of and this awareness allows us to regard life as Holy and thus we celebrate the Sacrament of Life. In her book on Mother Teresa Kathryn Spink says the following:

"Christ, the bread of life, the Word made flesh, silently present in the Eucharist, 'to satisfy our hunger for love' –Mother Teresa had been granted a sacramental vision of God fully present in the world, her own understanding of which would become more comprehensive with time. Somehow she must communicate to her young Sisters something of the depth and richness she already knew. If she was concerned with small practical considerations such as how the Sisters cut their hair, she never lost sight of the deeper vision. Ultimately what she sought to develop in them was 'the constant awareness of the Divine Presence everywhere and in Sisters with whom we live, and in the poorest of the poor.' She wanted them to live in union with God and with one another. Silence was at the root of that union, for God was the 'friend of silence.'"

"We need silence to be alone with God, to speak to him, to listen to him, to ponder his words deep in our hearts. We need to be alone with God in silence to be renewed and transformed. Silence gives us a new outlook on life. In it we are filled with the energy of God himself that makes us do all things with joy." (Direct quotation from Mother Teresa) **MOTHER TERESA** by Kathryn Spink, page 74

APPENDIX V

MEDITATION

As I sit to write the final article for this book it is the middle of January, 2004. In the past year both *TIME* and *NEWSWEEK* magazines have had cover articles dealing with meditation in a positive way. I have also noticed a number of positive syndicated articles in my local newspaper. In these articles medical doctors, social scientists and researchers in the areas of psychology, brain chemistry and consciousness are singing the praises of meditation.

My own experience in the past two years has been, at best, mixed. I have been involved with three different programs, each with separate backgrounds and somewhat different philosophies that promote meditation in my home city. They are all struggling to survive. However, the benefits to individuals who are active in these programs are unmistakable!

Several non-meditators who have read this book have urged me to include some material that would help them to start a meditation practice. At first I was very reluctant, feeling that most people need a support group in order to sustain a meditative practice on a regular basis. My experience of working within the context of support groups over the past two years has changed my attitude about this. Maybe the support group that is needed is not a specific meditation program as such, but rather a 12 Step Program, church or even a medical community which encourages prayer and meditation as a part of ones daily routine – a daily routine that fosters health, serenity and joy. In addition, I am excited about the following material that seemingly has been given to me as a gift to share with you!

PURE CONSCIOUSNESS

Kae discovered the following excerpt by Saint Augustine (ENTERING INTO THE JOY) in the book, THE ESSENTIAL

MYSTICS, edited by Andrew Harvey. I want to pay my respects to Mr. Harvey and thank him for this fine contribution to the history of mysticism. I have used this book on a number of occasions in order to quote the Mystics of the past. I feel this quote by Saint Augustine is the best description of PURE CONSCIOUSNESS I have ever read. As such it is also a beautiful description of the intended goal of spiritual meditation.

ENTERING INTO THE JOY

Imagine if all the tumult of the body were to quiet down,
along with all our busy thoughts about earth, sea, and air;

if the very world should stop, and the mind cease thinking
about itself, go beyond itself, and be quite still;

if all the fantasies that appear in dreams and imagination
should cease, and there be no speech, no sign:

Imagine if all things that are perishable grew still—
For if we listen they are saying, "We did not make ourselves;
He made us who abides forever"—imagine, then, that they
should say this and fall silent, listening to the very voice
of him who made them and not to that of his creation;

So that we should hear not his word through the tongues
of men, nor the voice of angels, nor the clouds' thunder,
nor any symbol, but the very Self which in these things
we love, and go beyond ourselves to attain a flash of that
eternal wisdom which abides above all things:

And imagine if that moment were to go on and on,
leaving behind all other sights and sounds but this one
vision which ravishes and absorbs and fixes the beholder
in joy; so that the rest of eternal life were like that
moment of illumination which leaves us breathless:

Would this not be what is bidden in scripture, Enter thou
into the joy of the Lord?[*] Saint Augustine

SAINT AUGUSTINE

Saint Augustine will be our Guru or Master, as we pursue our path
into meditation; not because he was a Christian, not because he was
appointed Bishop of the City of Hippo in North Africa in 396, not
because he was a great and influential writer, but because he was a
man with whom most of us can identify. Many of us can identify
with this man because he walked the road of the Vision Quest Hero.
"For Saint Augustine the discovery of God through Truth, Beauty and
Goodness marks an inward path." (*DICTIONARY OF PHILOSOPHY
AND RELIGION* BY W.L. Reese) In his youth he was carried away
by the pleasures of life. He was a worry to his parents and selfish in
his pursuits. In fact, he was so like many of us that one Twelve-Step
Program bears his name. (The Augustine Fellowship – SEX AND
LOVE ADDICTS ANONYMOUS was started in Boston, MA in
1976.)

Saint Augustine's youthful pursuits led to a kind of bankruptcy
and ultimately to a transformation. In the end he was able to say
something that all of us need to learn. The words are, "Our hearts are
restless until they rest in Him."

TECHNIQUE OR PRACTICE

Our premise is that meditation is a technique that enables one to
get in conscious contact with PURE CONSCIOUSNESS – "to enter
into the joy of the Lord." Our guru, Saint Augustine, was a religious
man and he interpreted his experience as a religious experience. One
need not begin with the premise that PURE CONSCIOUSNESS is

---

[*] The phrase, "enter into the joy of the Lord," is found twice in Matt 25. It
was used by Jesus in the context of the parable of talents.

religious or even spiritual. However, I believe that it is very helpful to begin with the premise that PURE CONSCIOUSNESS - IS!

1. Find a quiet place where you can sit comfortably. (This can be on the floor or in a straight back chair – spine should be straight. One should practice at least once a day - twice a day is even better – start with five minutes per session and work up slowly to at least 20 minutes per session.
2. Read – Saint Augustine on Pure Consciousness – This is for the unconscious mind – close your eyes – relax your body.
3. Contemplate for a few moments on the words, "Entering into the Joy of the Lord" (as you do this continue to relax the body)
4. After a moment become aware of your breath – and as you do, start gently (mentally) saying to yourself while inhaling, "Joy in" and while exhaling, "fear out." Continue in this manner throughout the duration of your meditation. (If possible, breathe through the nose.)
5. When you have completed the time allotted, before opening your eyes, take a minute or two to become aware of your environment. Stretch a little. This time helps us to keep from taking stress into our non-meditative state. (Into our activities).

SOME SUBTLETIES OF THE PRACTICE: Our overall attitude towards the procedure should be, "Easy does it." We take a never minding attitude toward outside noise, thoughts, feelings, restlessness and so on. If we feel like scratching our nose, we do so. There are no distractions. They are all a part of the process. Just let them be. If the feeling of joy or bliss seems to take you away from awareness of your breathing or the mantra, let it happen. When you are once again aware of distractions, easily come back to awareness of the breath and the mental saying of "Joy in, fear out." If the mantra fades away or becomes more subtle, that is good. When you become aware of this and other thoughts, just gently reintroduce the mantra. The key to progress in meditation is regularity.

APPENDIX VI

POEM BY PAMELA POLLARD

I FORGET

I'm not my body in full sight,
I'm not my busy brain,
I AM a being, full of Light,
But I forget – again!

Where am I then,
Where do I dwell?
Where is the core of me?
Invisible, but fit and well,
I have a soul – that's ME!

But where am I?
I still don't know.
What is it makes me, ME?
The part that can direct the flow
Of thought and action, free.

Each man contains a Light Divine,
A light we cannot see,
It's part of Life, both yours and mine,
And is in every 'me.'

It has been called by many names
Throughout our history,
But few have learned,
Much to our shame
That God is within me.

My body merely is a tool,
For use on earth this round,
A vehicle to use at 'school'
Until I earn my crown.

(*BEYOND THOUGHT,* Pamela Pollard, page 24-25)

APPENDIX VII

DE MELLO

Vatican condemns
Work of Jesuit author

VATICAN CITY – The Vatican denounced writings by a popular Jesuit author Saturday, warning of "dangers" contained in his works.

A Vatican commission said several works by Anthony de Mello, an Indian-born Jesuit priest, contradict Orthodox Roman Catholic doctrine. De Mello, who died in 1987, wrote Books characterized by some as New Age. They have been best sellers in many parts of the world. "Already in certain passages in these early works and to a greater degree in his later publications, one notices a progressive distancing from the essential contents of the Christian faith," the Congregation for the Doctrine of Faith said Saturday. Among the works were "One Minute Wisdom," "Wellsprings: A Book of Spiritual Exercises" and "Walking On Water." Officials at the Jesuit headquarters in Rome were unavailable for comment.

APPENDIX VIII

FIVE STEPS OF EDUCATION

1. Information – Often we think information is education, but it is only one aspect of education.

2. Concepts – Concepts are the basis for all research. You need to conceive in order to create.

3. Attitude – An integral aspect of education is cultivating the right attitude. Proper attitude at the right time and place determines your actions and behavior.

4. Imagination – Imagination is essential for creativity for the arts. But if you get stuck in imagination, you may become psychotic.

5. Freedom – Freedom is your very nature. Only with freedom do joy, generosity and other human values blossom. Without freedom, attitudes become stifling, concepts become a burden, information is of no value and imagination becomes stagnant.

(Knowledge sheet – 256, June 7, 2000 – Author – Sri Sri Ravi Shankar, founder of the Art of Living Foundation)

APPENDIX IX

THE TWELVE STEPS

<u>Step One</u>
    "We admitted we were powerless over alcohol—that our lives had become unmanageable."

<u>Step Two</u>
    "Came to believe that a Power greater than ourselves could restore us to sanity."

<u>Step Three</u>
    "Made a decision to turn our will and out lives over to the care of God as <u>we understood Him</u>."

<u>Step Four</u>
    "Made a searching and fearless moral inventory of ourselves."

<u>Step Five</u>
    "Admitted to God, to ourselves, and to another human being the exact nature of our wrongs."

<u>Step Six</u>
    "Were entirely ready to have God remove all these defects of character."

<u>Step Seven</u>
    "Humbly asked Him to remove our shortcomings."

Step Eight
"Made a list of all persons we had harmed, and became willing to make amends to them all."

Step Nine
"Made direct amends to such people wherever possible, except when to do so would injure them or others."

Step Ten
"Continued to take personal inventory and when we were wrong promptly admitted it."

Step Eleven
"Sought through prayer and meditation to improve our conscious contact with God <u>as we understood Him</u>, praying only for knowledge of His will for us and the power to carry that out."

Step Twelve
"Having had a spiritual awakening as the result of these steps, we tried to carry this message to alcoholics, and to practice these principles in all our affairs."

APPENDIX X

ALCOHOLISM - QUACK, QUACK!

Our dear friend, Monica Harris has written and published a delightful children's book called *ANIMAL THERAPY*. Recently I had an opportunity to do some animal therapy of my own. I was asked to talk to a young man who had gotten himself in serious trouble with the law. The problems were all as a result of drinking alcohol. I took the young man to breakfast. We sat in a back corner of the café where we could not easily be overheard.

He knew that I was in the process of writing a book but he had little idea of the subject matter. After a few minutes of small talk I asked him if he knew why I had invited him to have breakfast with me. He said, "You want to talk to me about the trouble I'm in." I said, "right on." In order to break the ice and add some humor I added, "I also want to talk about some animals." "Why animals?" he asked. I replied that in times like these we learn a lot from the animals. I added that before the white man came to this country the American Indians continually learned lessons from the animals that they observed. For instance, they recognized that the buffalo always faced and slowly walked directly into the many storms that blew through the plains. I asked the young man (who we will call Dane) why he thought they did this and what the Indians learned from this action. Dane was silent for about thirty seconds and then he said, "They walk into the storm because they can get through it faster." He paused for a moment and then added, "If the Indians were travelling they probably learned that it helped to follow the buffalo." I replied, "Right! – Now do you have any storms in your life?" He got a grin on his face and he said, "You know I'm in a big one now."

I then entered into a short soliloquy about the importance of facing our problems and not running away from them. I told him, like the buffalo he was going to get through this ordeal with less difficulty and perhaps even faster if he faced it head on.

391

Then I looked Dane square in the eye and seriously said, "The most important issue you have to face in the next five years (he was going to be on probation for five years) is whether or not you are a duck." He sat us straight up in his chair and said, "A duck?!" I replied, "Yes, a duck." I then asked him how many times he had been in trouble with the law in the last three years. He responded, "five times." I asked him how many of those times had something to do with alcohol and he replied, "All five." I then said, "I don't know if you are an alcoholic or not and it doesn't really matter what I think. However, I am going to say again the most important thing for you to determine in the next few years is whether or not you are a duck." I added, "I'm sure you realize that I am using the term duck as a synonym for alcoholic. In A.A. we often say, "if it looks like a duck, waddles like a duck and quacks like a duck, it's a duck." He looked down and didn't say a word.

We sat in silence. Finally I said, "A.A. had nothing against drinking. In fact, the Big Book, *ALCOHOLICS ANONYMOUS* says, 'if you can drink like a gentleman our hats are off to you.'" (Dane had been told by the judge he had to attend two A.A. meetings a week for the next two years and during those two years any drinking of alcohol would be a violation of his probation.) I wanted him to know that it was the Judge, not A.A. that was asking him not to drink. I said, "A.A. is for "ducks" who have a desire to quit drinking, not for people that are sent there by a Judge. "I am quite sure the Judge has sent you to A.A. to give you the opportunity to find out whether or not you are an alcoholic. Believe me, if you go there with an open mind and with the attitude that the Judge is trying to help you, you will be much better off."

I then shocked Dane a little bit when I said, "Dane, I don't know whether you are an alcoholic but I do know that you are either a duck or a horse's ass. You are either an alcoholic or really dumb." He said, just a little miffed but still with a grin on his face, "What do you mean?" I responded, "If you picked a fight with Mike Tyson (heavy weight boxer) and he knocked you down, if you were lucky, you would probably have the choice of getting up and trying again or walking away. If you got up and tried again I'd say you were a little stupid. But you just told me that you got up and tried to beat alcohol at least five times in the last two years. I don't know which one you are but your history tells me you are either a duck or a horse's ass. If you have the ability to drink like a gentleman and you don't do it, you are a horse's ass. If you can't control your drinking, you are a duck." With compassion, I leaned across the table and quietly said, "Dane, if you are a duck you are not dumb, not bad, not weak-willed; you have a progressive disease[*] called alcoholism. Progressive means that over any considerable time your control over alcohol will become less and less. Like many diseases such as cancer, alcoholism is a progressive disease. That means it gets worse and worse over time."

I continued, "Dane, if you can drink like a gentleman my hat is off to you. If you can drink like a gentleman but keep getting your butt kicked by Tyson (alcohol) then you are a horse's ass. If you <u>can't</u> drink like a gentleman you are a duck. A.A. is for ducks who want to treat their disease. It's here to help you be a buffalo and face the tough storm. Dane, believe me, in the next few months you will be making the most important decision you have ever made. If it turns out that you are a duck, your life depends on this decision."

---

[*] I recently talked to a Medical Doctor friend who has specialized in the treatment of alcoholics for many years. He told me that current scientific studies in the field of alcoholism make it absolutely clear that alcoholism is a physical disease. He said it is complicated disease with a genetic component, a mental obsession and a psychological/spiritual aspect. Our discussion included research into a very addictive pain killer called THIQ. Interesting articles about THIQ and it's relationship to alcoholism can be found on the internet using a search engine.

APPENDIX XI

GENERIC GOD

During the week following September 11, 2001 I spent several days in the hospital with a kidney infection, blockage and stones. As fate would have it one of my nurses was a middle-aged man who was studying for his Doctor's degree in History. When I told him that I was retired he asked, "What do you do with all your free time?" I told him that I had just finished writing a book. This seemed to arouse his curiosity and he started asking me questions about the book. He asked, What's the subject?" I replied, "Spiritual psychology or practical spirituality." Then he said, "Do you have a name for the book?" I responded that over the years I had worked with several names. He wanted to know what they were so I told him.

The next day when he returned for his shift he told me that he had been thinking about my book and he thought the best name was "Generic God." He also said that he wanted to buy one of the books when it was published. I suggested that if he were willing to give me some feedback I would be pleased to give him one of the pre-publication copies.

When his shift ended he handed me a piece of paper with his name and address on it so that I could mail him a copy of the book. Then he turned around and as he left the room he said, "I'd call it "Generic God." Some days after I returned home from the hospital I was sifting through my old files and I stumbled onto the following piece. After reading it I felt that my friend from the hospital had a valid point!

GENERIC GOD

On that summer day in 1973 when I left my family, my friends and my job, I also left my church and my belief system. Looking back, there is no doubt that I was a very sick puppy on that day, but I truly believe that two things motivated me. First, the knowledge that something was wrong with me and I was hurting and pulling down everything and everybody I cared about. I felt that if I got out of the picture they would have a chance to survive and maybe I would too. Secondly, I intuitively knew that if I were going to survive, I would have to start by building on the new-found integrity that I was experiencing within.

I had the desire to start building anew but I had not reached the bottom yet - that took another eight years. During those eight years I found and used my tools, but I really didn't do much building because, as I see it today, I really hadn't made the choice between the "two systems." I really hadn't decided to turn my life over to the new authority. I gave it some trial runs and they worked rather well but my ego didn't like being out of the driver's seat.

Trying to use our two systems (ego and the ABSOLUTE) at the same time is as difficult as trying to run one of those Seattle City buses on diesel and electricity at the same time. It is very unproductive and very uncomfortable. Marianne Williamson, author and a spokesman for *A COURSE IN MIRACLES,* says that having one foot in each of these two worlds is the most uncomfortable place we can be. As I indicated in "My Story" I had the feeling I was on the right track but I just could not put it together. It took a series of relapses to awaken me and set me straight. These relapses were usually emotional in nature but in the end, they resulted in a return to drinking.

It was only when I found myself sinking into the gutter one more time that I finally made the choice, and finally understood that a complete surrender of the ego system was going to be necessary. That surrender included a surrender of my old ideas and my old belief system. Let's remember that I had invested a lot in my belief system. In a real sense, I had staked my life on it. I'm not just talking religious beliefs here like the concept of salvation; I'm talking my career, my future and my retirement. But it had all let me down, for some reason it didn't work. Believe me, I tried every way I knew to make it work, but in the end, it didn't.

With this as my legacy as far as faith was concerned and after eight years trying to get it all back together, and then in the throes of an alcoholic relapse, I finally surrendered to the authority within. At that point it was only an inkling of a higher power and the memory of that experience which had taken place eight years earlier. But it was there with that memory and that inkling that I started to build a new life. The first plank of my new life was, "You can't put your faith in a belief system. At best you can only trust what the belief system may be pointing to." The second plank was, "In as much as I have turned my life and will over to the authority that I have found within, I will then have to wait for it to reveal itself further before I can come up with any more planks." In other words, I had to trust in the integrity of what I was experiencing and I couldn't turn it into a teaching or doctrine or concept. I had to let it BE.

During the past fifteen years I have added another plank to my new life or if you will, my new belief system. It is: "Relying on the power and authority within works." Pure and simple, "it" works! I put quotes around the word "it" because people ask me, "What is this "it" you are talking about?" I tell them I'm not sure, but I think it might be what other people call God, it might even be what other people call Christ. I don't know for sure, but "it" has revealed some things to me and as best I can, I will share "it" with you.

As I have indicated throughout this book, I have come to know the authority within as my SELF. You may ask, "Why isn't that a plank in your belief system?" The answer is that what I experience as my SELF is totally unexplainable. It is something beyond human vocabulary and human comprehension. I can't put it into words but my experience of my SELF does remind me of some of the things I used to say about God when I was preaching from the pulpit. Should I put in a new plank in my belief system that says my SELF is God? I don't know, but I have given that a lot of thought. My best answer to this date is captured in the words of Henry Bergson, who said of consciousness: "if not God, it is of God."

I haven't put in another plank in my system because when I experience my SELF I am also experiencing the unseen reality which is beyond my self, an expanded SELF that is somehow connected with each of you and with all of nature. I can't put another plank in my system based on this awareness because there are no words adequate to describe the experience of this awareness.

That's where I am. But because I want to communicate with you about this stuff, I feel like I need to give "IT" a name. I've given this a lot of thought, years of thought, and what I have come up with is the name, Generic God. This name works for me, because it is my belief that you have within you the ability to experience your true SELF and that when you do, it won't be long until you will sense that your SELF is God or connected to God and this God stands apart or at least transcends your belief system.

Now, let's explore the word "generic." Funk and Wagnall defines it as, "having a wide general application and applicable to every member of a class." The class that applies in this particular case is Homo Sapiens. Generic God then would be a God with a wide general application and applicable to every member of the Human Race.

Now, let's look at the term, generic, as popularly used in the retail industry. A generic product is one that is not sold under a brand name. It is sold under its generic name. If it is wheat cereal, it is sold as "wheat cereal," and not "Wheaties" or any other brand name. If it is laundry soap it is sold and packaged as "laundry soap" and has no brand name such as "Tide." The generic product could well be the same product as the name brand; it is even possible that it could be a superior product. The real difference however, is found in three things: the packaging, the promotion and the cost. The cost is determined largely by the demand and the demand is determined in part by the success of promotion, which includes its packaging. As we all know, God also has some brand names, names that are promoted, sometimes very aggressively. Various denominations and religions package these names: Names like Jesus, Allah, Jehovah and Vishnu.

My experience tells me that the same God deep in the psyche of every human being is the one being packaged. The one being packaged is Generic God. The problem with promotion and packaging is that it can get carried away. When I was in sales, I was told over and over again "don't sell the steak, sell the sizzle." What that meant was; don't sell the product, sell what it will do for you. I believe that this kind of philosophy has crept into religion. That is why we are being sold salvation. Salvation is the sizzle, not the steak.

But I found out that the power within me; the power I call Generic God is more than any concept of heaven or salvation. Generic God needs no promotion, no packaging. Generic God is not Substitute God. Generic God is real God and each of us already has an ample portion deep within.

I honestly believe both society and the individuals in it are suffering because religions are selling the sizzle and not the steak. They are selling the box, not the product. They have lost sight of the product. It is hidden beneath promotion, the doctrine, the rituals the socializing and their collective ego.

Consider the following in the light of the above:

I assume the experience of "realized expanded SELF" is common to all who enjoy higher states of consciousness. I also believe that most if not all people have access to these higher states. Furthermore, these higher states of consciousness are desirable and should be coveted by all. I believe that this is the correct way of understanding the message of Jesus and other spiritual leaders.

My more limited experience of such states tells me that speaking from the position of "the realized expanded SELF" it would not be at all difficult to say "I and the Father are one." Nor would it be unusual to say the words written in the Bhagavad-Gita, "I am that, thou art that, all that is, is that." When I first started experiencing some sense of the "expanded SELF" I returned to reading the Bible and found it to be all new. Today I see in the Bible the same message that I have been talking about throughout this book. When I read that Jesus said the Kingdom of God is like a "mustard seed" I think of the seed, I think of that inkling, that glimmer within, that seed that has grown in me and become my SELF. When He says the Kingdom of God is like a "pearl of great price" I say Amen! I wouldn't and couldn't trade this experience of knowing my SELF for anything. The Gospel of Thomas says, "The Kingdom of God is within you and it is outside you. When you know yourself, then you will be known, and you will understand that you are children of the living Father..." (*FIVE GOSPELS, Page 172*)

BIBLIOGRAPHY

The books below represent a partial bibliography. We have tried to give proper credit for ideas and content in the manuscript. The nature of the book's evolution over a thirty-year period virtually insures that some material was used from sources long forgotten and not given proper credit. If such is noticed, please let us know and we will correct this in future editions.

The starred books are those I would want with me if I were stranded alone on a deserted island.

*Anonymous – *A Course in Miracles.* Glen Ellen, CA., Foundation for Inner Peace, 1975

*Anonymous – *Alcoholics Anonymous.* New York City, Alcoholics Anonymous World Services, Inc., 1976

Anonymous – Dr. *Bob and the Good Oldtimers.* New York: Alcoholics Anonymous World Service, Inc., 1980.

Anonymous – *Twelve Steps and Twelve Traditions.* New York: Alcoholics Anonymous World Services, Inc., 1952.

Bach, Richard. *Illusions.* New York: Dell Publishing, 1977

*Bartlett, John, *Familiar Quotations.* Boston: Little, Brown and Company, 1882.

Bateson, Gregory. *A Sacred Unity.* New York: Harper Collins Publishers, 1991

Bateson, Gregory. *Steps to an Ecology of the Mind.* New York: Ballantine Books, 1972

Becket, Samuel. *Waiting for Godot*

Bloomfield, Herald, M.D. *TM,* New York: Delacorte Press, 1975.

Brenneman, Richard J. *Fuller's Earth; A Day with Bucky and the Kids*

Bucke, Maurice. *Cosmic Consciousness,* New York: E.P. Dutton and Company, Inc., 1901.

Bunyan, John. *Pilgrim's Progress,* Chicago: Moody Press, 1964.

*Campbell, Joseph. *The Hero With a Thousand Faces,* New York: Princeton University Press, 1949.

Campbell, Joseph with Toms, Michael. *An Open Life.* New York: Harper and Row, 1989.

Campbell, Joseph with Moyer, Bill. *The Power of Myth.* New York: Doubleday, 1988.

Canfield, Jack/Hansen, Mark. *Chicken Soup for the Soul,* Deerfield Beach, FL: Health

Coleman, Daniel. *The Meditative Mind.* New York: G.P. Putnam's Sons, 1988.

Capra, Fritjof. *The Web of Life.* New York: Doubleday, 1996

Castaneda, Carlos. *The Teachings of Don Juan: a Yaqui Way of Knowledge.* New York: Ballantine Books, 1968.

*C., Chuck. *A New Pair of Glasses.* Irvine, CA: New-Look Publishing Company, 1984.

Csikszentmihalyi, Mihaly. *The Evolving Self.* New York: Harper Collins, 1993

Csikszentmihalyi, Mihaly. *Flow.* New York: Harper Collins, 1990

Csikszentmihalyi, *Finding Flow.* NewYork: Harper Collins, 1997

Csikszentmihalyi, Mihaly. *Creativity.* New York: Harper Collins, 1996.

Damasio, Antonio R. *Descartes' Error*

*De Mello, Anthony. *Awareness.* London: Harper Collins, 1990.

De Waal, Esther. *The Celtic Way of Prayer*

Eddy, Mary Baker. *Science and Health with Key to the Scriptures*

Edwards, Denis. *Human Experience of God,* New York: Paulist Press

*Eiseley, Loren. *The Unexpected Universe,* New York: Harcourt, Brace & World, Inc. 1964

Eiseley, Loren. *All the Strange Hours,* New York: Charles Scribner's-Sons, 1975.

Exley, Helen, Editor. *Words of Joy,* New York: Exley, 1997

Freeman, Laurence. *Light Within,* New York: The Crossroad Publishing Company, 1986.

Finley, Guy. *The Secret of Letting Go, St.* Paul, MN: Llewellyn Publications, 1990.

Five Gospels

*Fox, Emmet. *The Sermon on the Mount,* New York: Harper Collins, 1932.

Gandhi. *Words of Gandhi*

Grof, Stanislav, M.D. *Holotropic Mind,* New York: Harper Collins, 1990

Gurdjieff, G.I. *The Psychology of Man's Possible Evolution*

Haeri, Shaykh Fadhlalla. *The Elements of Sufism,* New York: Barnes & Noble, 1990

Harris, Eugene. *I'm OK You're Ok*

Harris, Monica. *Animal Therapy*

*Harvey, Andrew (Editor). *The Essential Mystics,* New York, HarperCollins, 1996

Hawkings, Steven. *A Brief History of Time*

Hirschfield, Jerry, M.A. *My Ego My Higher Power and I,* Van Nuys, CA: High Productions, 1985.

Hirschfield, Jerry, M.A. *The Twelve Steps for Everyone Who Really Wants Them,* Minneapolis, MN: Compcare Publications, 1975.

Homer. *The Odyssey,* New York: The New American Library, 1937.

Howard, Vernon. *Psycho-Pictograph*

Howard, Vernon. *The Power of Your Super Mind,* Englewood Cliffs, New Jersey: Prentice Hall, 1975

Huxley, Aldus. *Island,* New York: Harper and Row, 1962.

Huxley, Aldus. *Brave New World*

Huxley, Aldus. *Perennial Philosophy*

Huxley, Aldus. *Man and Religion (*Big Sur Tapes, 1959)

James, William. *The Varieties of Religious Experiences*

Jung, Carl. *The Undiscovered Self,* New York: Mentor, 1957.

Jung, Carl *Sunchronicity*

Jung, Carl *Psychology and Alchemy Collected Works of C.G. Jung, Volume 12*

Kafka, Franz. *The Trial,* Toronto, Canada: Random House of Canada Limited, 1937

Khalsa, Dharma Singh M.D. *Meditation as Medicine.* New York: Fireside, 2001

Lair, Jess. *I ain't Much Baby- but I'm all I've Got,* New York: Doubleday & Company, Inc., 1972

Lewis, C.S. *Screw Tape Letters,* New York: The McMillan Company, 1962.

*Maharishi Mahesh Yogi (Translator and Commentator). *Bhagavad-Gita,* New York: Penguin Books Ltd, 1967.

Marcel, Gabriel. *Being and Having,* New York: Harper and Row, 1949.

Maslow, A. *Religions, Values, and Peak-experiences.* New York: Harper & Row, 1964.

Matt, Daniel C. *The Essential Kabbalah,* New York: HarperSanFrancisco, 1995.

Mother Teresa. *In the Heart of the World*

Ouspensky, P.D. *The Fourth Dimension*

Ouspensky, P.D. *The Psychology of Man's Possible Evolution,* New York: Random House, 1974

Ouspensky, P.D. *Tertium Organum,* New York: Alfred A. Knopf, 1959.

Peck, Scott. *The road Less Traveled*

Pollard, Pamela. *Beyond Thought*

Radin, Dean (Ph. D). *The Conscious Universe,* New York: HarperCollins, 1997.

Redfield, James. *The Celestine Prophecy*

*Reese, W.L. *Dictionary of Philosophy and Religion,* New Jersey: Humanities Press, 1980.

*Richo, David. *Wisdom's Way* (Quotations for Meditation for private distribution) Revised 2003

Rybicki, Richard. *The Importance of Being Human.* Royal Oak, Michigan: Arete' Press, 1980

Satchidananda. *The Yoga Sutras of Patanjali.* United States of America, Integral Yoga Publications, 1978.

Schachter-Shalome, Zalman, Rabbi. *From Age-ing to Sage-ing.* New York, Warner Books, 1995

Severy, Merle (Editor). *Great Religions of the World.* National Geographic Society, 1971

Singh, Tara. *Commentaries on a Course in Miracles.* San Francisco, CA: Harper San Francisco, 1986.

Spink, Kathryn. *Mother Teresa*

Stone, Irving. *The Agony and the Ecstasy*

*Teilhard de Chardin, Pierre. *Hymn of the Universe,* New York: Harper and Row, 1961.

*Teilhard de Chardin, Pierre. *The Phenomenon of Man,* New York: Harper and Row, 1959.

Tipler, Frank J. *Physics and Immortality*

*Tolstoy, Leo. *The Kingdom of God is Within You,* Lincoln: The University of Nebraska Press, 1894, (1984).

Venkatesananda, Swami. *The Concise Yoga Vasistha,* Albany, NY: State University of the New York Press, 1984.

Watts, Allan. *The Meaning of Happiness*

Wilbur, Ken. *The Eye of the Spirit,* Boston: Shambhala Publications, Inc., 1998.

Williamson, Marianne. *A Return to Love A Woman's Worth,* New York: Random House, 1993.

Wolf, Fred Alan. *Taking the Quantum Leap.* New York: Harper & Row, 1981

ABOUT THE AUTHOR

Rich Kae claims to have been working on this book for thirty years. He also claims that one thing and one thing alone has been his motivation. That one thing was the discovery of something within himself in the midst of his darkest hour. He calls this thing, "integrity."

His discovery of "integrity" (a truth) led him like J in Kafka's "The Trial" to obsessively work on "his case." Working on his case involved massive reading, life style experimentation, seminars, meditation and travel to foreign lands. It meant, as the title to his book states, uncovering and discovering and in the final analysis, it meant finding the treasure beneath his excavated psyche!

Printed in the United States
40458LVS00004B/67-144

9 781418 406745